SO LITTLE
DISILLUSION

*To my mother-in-law, Mrs. Joseph C. Shinkman,
who saved all her son's letters home
from London and Paris;*

*And to our sons Paul, Christopher and Bernard,
the joy of our forty-year marriage.*

SO LITTLE DISILLUSION

An American Correspondent in Paris and London

1924-1931

Edited by Elizabeth Benn Shinkman

The "Introductory Note", © 1959 Kay Boyle, is reprinted
with permission of Watkins-Loomis Agency, Inc.

"The Regained Generation" was published originally by
Michigan Alumnus Quarterly Review, Spring, 1960.

Library of Congress Cataloging in Publication Data

Shinkman, Paul, 1897-1975.
  So little disillusion

   1. Shinkman, Paul, 1897-   2. Foreign
correspondents -- United States -- Biography. 3. Foreign
correspondents -- Europe -- Biography. I. Shinkman,
Elizabeth Benn. II. Title.
PN4874.S476A37 1983   070.4'33'0924 [B] 83-16591
ISBN 0-914440-68-3

EPM Publications, Inc., 1003 Turkey Run Road, McLean, VA 22101
Printed in the United States of America

Book and jacket design by Tom Huestis

CONTENTS

Paul Shinkman, 1927

Down in a little Hampshire fishing village which crouches on the right bank of Avon, I was having dinner in the dreary second floor dining room of one of the town's best hotels. There were a few other mournful diners in the room, but I noticed a young bank clerk, and we presently started to chat.

His ideas interested me. He believes, for example, that he can learn more about people in five minutes from the teller's window than he can in five years through the newspapers!

The last was not said to disparage my own profession. We simply agreed that perhaps the kindliest fate that could overtake the world would be to have its newspapers and other media of indirect exchange rolled into a huge ball and ignited in an effort to signal Mars.

If people in different parts of the world, he said, could have a five-minute chat with each other once a year, they could undo practically all the damage done between them by the newspapers and professional peacemakers.

I told him that my five-minute chat with the English and the French had extended to four years, and that some day I should put it between covers.

Paul Shinkman
1928

*   *   *

PART II

PARIS EDITION

Shinkman family group, 1909. (Left to right) Olga, Paul, Bernard, and Maxine (Susie).

INTRODUCTION

Paul Shinkman's long and successful career as a newspaperman – from foreign correspondent to radio news commentator – began in a shed behind the family home on Gold Avenue in Grand Rapids, Michigan, at the turn of the century.

His older sister had converted the shed into a playhouse for her brothers, and here P. S. had his first experience as reporter, editor, production manager, sales representative, and sole proprietor of the *Child's Den Weekly*. The paper had four pages, measuring 4 x 5 inches, divided into columns, and was filled, in a childish hand, with news of the immediate neighborhood. At 1¢ a copy, it was much enjoyed by the faithful Gold Avenue subscribers.

Fifteen years later, P. S. and his friend Tom Dewey (the future Presidential candidate) were throwing themselves, heart and soul, into the all-absorbing task of getting out their college paper, the *Michigan Daily*, at the University of Michigan in Ann Arbor. So fascinating was the work that P. S. found himself falling behind in his studies, and in his senior year the Administration would not approve his nomination to the editorship. Nevertheless, he had had an invaluable experience that launched him directly into his career as a newspaperman.

During summer vacations, he had worked as a reporter on the *Grand Rapids Press*, but his first full-time professional job after graduating from college was with the Chicago City News Bureau.

His "beat" was the court of the famous Judge Landis, in the days of Al Capone's gangland, and his source material was the more sordid police reports. Much as he loved his work, there were times when his sensibilities were severely tried by the degradation he had to witness. On one occasion, in the routine course of his assignments, he was even sent to cover a hanging. He was given a chance to refuse, but he decided to face the ordeal as part of his training in his chosen career.

Covering crime stories around the clock, he paid no attention to his health. Regular meals never crossed his mind. He soon became seriously run-down, succumbing at the end of the winter to pleural pneumonia. With no antibiotics yet available, he battled his way back to health.

During six months of enforced recuperation, P.S. was introduced to Carl Van Vechten's best-selling novel *Peter Whiffle* which was probably responsible for steering more young Americans to Paris in the early 1920s than any book before or since. It took fire with P.S. The seed that Van Vechten had planted in his mind soon grew to an obsession, drawing him irresistibly to the Old World.

Once returned to work, he counted the weeks as they brought in the pay checks, until he could save enough money to realize his dream.

The opportunity finally arrived in the spring of 1924, when he received a prospectus for a "college boy" tour to Europe aboard the steerage class of the old *Saxonia*. It seemed to be an answer to prayer. The group rate was perfectly suited to an impecunious young journalist. After a summer of travel in France, England, Germany, Spain, and Italy, he was expected back in the States in the fall of 1924, but the romantic pull of Paris was so strong that he cashed in his return ticket and began to look for a job with one of the English-language newspapers that abounded in Paris at that time.

How this venture, undertaken on a shoestring (his budget was $400), became the foundation for a journalistic career that spanned fifty years and two continents, is told here in his own words – letters, diaries, and feature articles – by Paul Shinkman.

His accounts of early adventures, often concerned with minor financial crises (as when he and Bill Shirer ran for their lives from an irate sacristan in a little church in Rouen, who chased them looking for a *pourboire*) reflect the experiences of countless American expatriates. Living in France was cheap by American standards in the 1920s. The franc was worth about 4¢ – but even so, after a summer of travel, the money was gone, and with no job in the offing he reluctantly wrote to his father in Grand Rapids, asking for financial help to get home.

His father's remittance had barely arrived when he received a *pneumatique* (an underground telegraphic system peculiar to Paris) from Bernhard Ragner, asking him to come to work with the Paris edition of the *Chicago Tribune* the next day! Scarcely able to believe his good fortune, he quickly accepted the post and began working in September 1924. His first responsibility was to check the arrivals at the leading hotels each day. Headlines in the paper told of literally thousands of Americans pouring into France on every large liner, and it was important to track down celebrities, particularly those with a Chicago background. Throughout the fall, his interviews with these celebrities appeared at least once a week, and on December 15, 1924, his page-one story received a by-line for the first time.

His injunction to his family in one of his early letters to "hang on to my letters so that when I get home I shall have some tangible evidence that I really am here" was faithfully adhered to. In them he gives background accounts of how he obtained some of the interviews – notably with Fritz Kreisler and with Mary Garden – which are even more entertaining than the articles themselves.

By November, his column "Latin Quarter Notes" was appearing regularly; it continued for the next two years. On the side, he did a weekly column called "Paris Letter," or "Rambles in Paris," for the *Italian Mail,* an English-language paper published in Florence.

When P. S. first arrived in Paris in 1924, the young expatriate American writers were just coming to flower. James Joyce had stunned the literary world with *Ulysses* only two years before; Scott Fitzgerald's *The Great Gatsby* was still a year away; and Ernest Hemingway would not establish his reputation until two years later, with the publication of *The Sun Also Rises.*

P. S. enjoyed to the full the bohemian life his job required him to live and he soon became an habitué of the Café du Dôme. Here, and at the neighboring Rotonde and the Sélect – all three near the intersection of the Boulevards Montparnasse and Raspail – he picked up gossip for his "Latin Quarter Notes." He also kept busy covering shows put on by the innumerable artists in the area. Foujita, Hiler, Warshawsky, Brancusi, Norman Bel Geddes, Homer St. Gaudens, Roy van Auken Sheldon, and Bernhard Gutmann, are some of the names that appeared regularly in his column.

"The Cafés Dôme and Rotonde are favorites with the Americans," he wrote in an article for his home-town newspaper, the *Grand Rapids Press.* "The Dôme is frequented by the artists, students and literary folk, who gather on its terrace to discuss the latest gossip of the Quarter. The Rotonde, on the other hand, is the rendezvous of those tourists in search of atmosphere who at the same time like to season it with luxury. An expensive dinner, an 'almost' jazz orchestra, and a smooth dancing floor are offered by the Rotonde to those seekers after Bohemia, and they go home after several hours of this wild life of the Latin Quarter with 'something to write home about.' Perhaps on their way in they have glimpsed a few members of the 'horde of Montparnasse,' a group of painters who make the Rotonde their headquarters. Quaintly garbed ... their beards and flowing locks would cause a sensitive barber to faint. Now and then the 'horde' holds a grand reunion parade, led by Grawovsky, the cowboy of Montparnasse, who, although he has never seen America, has adopted the picturesque dress of our western cowboy, even to the spurs.

Meanwhile, from the opposite side of the street, the 'Dômers' look on, if at all, with indulgent smiles. While the two cafés are only a few yards apart, they might as well be separated by oceans. One may, upon occasion, drop into any of the tiny French bars in the Quarter, but never by any chance would one be found in the rival café."

The Dôme was at that time truly a "home away from home" for the Left Bank

American colony. As Wolfe Kaufman would much later recall, – "During its heyday, the Dôme was as good an address for Yanks in Paris as the American Express, and its bulletin board in the central hall (near the bar, natch) sported mail for many indigents who have since become famous."

The pay scale for reporters on the Paris edition of the *Chicago Tribune* was unbelievably low (starting around $60 a month). Such wages scarcely covered the basic necessities of food and shelter, and often the shelter bordered on the sordid and depressing. P. S. describes a barren room he shared in Paris with an English student on meager scholarship funds to study at the Sorbonne: "high ceiling, colorless bare walls, worn floor, and high French windows hung with ragged lace curtains. Two cots, two cabinets, three straight chairs, and two small tables placed together and covered with a faded blue cloth. Above, a tattered silk-shaded electric light. At one side, an unused French fireplace with a hectic row of books piled carelessly across the top.

We have been told the building was an old monastery of the seventeenth or eighteenth century. Yes, it is picturesque, it has atmosphere, but not entirely of the desired kind ... But it is a room in Paris ... And I am living in it ... sharing it with my fellow mortal from Oxford University, who seems happily blind to its shortcomings."

But P. S. spent very little time in his room, especially when he discovered Sylvia Beach's bookshop Shakespeare and Company, after which the emphasis in his "Latin Quarter Notes" began to swing more toward writers than artists.

His horizons also broadened when he added theatre criticism to his other work – this at a time when the Paris stage still maintained much of the glamorous aura created by Sarah Bernhardt, with whom he had become fascinated after seeing her on tour during his student days at the University of Michigan in Ann Arbor. There were Sacha Guitry, Yvonne Printemps, the Pitoëffs, Elvire Popesco, Isadora Duncan and her brother Raymond, and, of course, in the music halls, the sensational Josephine Baker, who was responsible for starting the rage in Paris for black entertainers that became known as *Le Tumulte Noir.*

But the show most certain to lift the spirits of even an impoverished reporter was *Chauve-Souris,* the perennial revue produced by the Russian director Nikita Balieff. From one season to the next, all of London, Paris, and New York waited impatiently for his newest production, and P. S. gives us a dramatic glimpse of the great man at work backstage.

P. S. had a great feeling for drama, and in his letters from Paris he not only dramatized the life of the Latin Quarter, but he also dramatized himself as the mythical "count," or "hero." He enlivened his letters with "skinny-ginger" drawings depicting the "count," always in moments of crisis! The very first sketch showed his dramatic arrival at the Place de l'Odéon, when he and his shipmate Franklin McCoy, finally reached Paris.

His life for the next three years – much of it rough sailing – typified the enthusiasm, the glamour, and the constant struggle against poverty of the young hopefuls in the art world. But his writing also conveys the sense that literary and artistic history was being made by the denizens of that small, magic area of Paris known as "The Quarter."

Elizabeth B. Shinkman
March 1981

*   *   *

AN INTRODUCTORY NOTE

By Kay Boyle

In the 1920s, the writers of America and Ireland were in the midst of a revolution a revolution against literary pretentiousness, against weary flowery rhetoric, against all out-worn conventions. But it should never be forgotten that it was a needed revolt, and because it was needed, a sense of discovery and adventure animated the life of the writer at that time. In those days in the twenties in Paris, inspired by Eugène Jolas, we wrote pamphlets of our own and distributed them along the streets and in the cafés. We signed manifestoes, not necessarily concerning political matters, but on any questions which seemed of burning importance to us, such as the revolution of the word. We followed, with no humility whatsoever, in the tradition of Pascal, Voltaire, Chateaubriand, Victor Hugo, Zola, so that the world would know exactly where we stood. We followed not only with arrogant pride in what we were – a portion of the contemporary conscience – but without pity for the compromiser or the poor in spirit of our time.

But just because the writers of the twenties were in revolt, it did not for a moment mean that they all agreed. The adherents of Joyce, for instance, were voluble and frequently violent on the subject of Miss Stein's lack of ear and eye; and the followers of Gertrude Stein expressed themselves with equal passion on the subject of Joyce's "heterodox technique and his wilful maiming of words." And we who were young in those far-off days trembled if, through some callousness in social perceptivity, Gertrude Stein and James Joyce were invited to the same function. I saw this happen twice, but there were many wine-drinking, champagne-drinking guests moving between them, so there was no need for them to speak to each other; and Joyce's eyes were bad, very bad, at that moment, so he was not expected to see who was seated across the room. But it was strange to know then, and even stranger now, that it was neither blindness nor the movement of strangers that lay between them, but – deep and impassable – their opposed concepts of a new syntax and vocabulary.

We brash American exiles proclaimed in Jolas' magazine *transition* that "Prudence is a rich, ugly old maid courted by Incapacity." And these words in which we believed so passionately were not our own. We borrowed them from William Blake, and we took from him as well: "The Road of Excess leads to the Palace of Wisdom," and "The Tigers of Wrath are wiser than the Horses of Instruction." It may seem strange that we, engaged as we were in the battle of the revolution of the word, should have taken for spokesman the poet of another century, and an Englishman at that. And yet it is not strange if one considers that James Joyce in *Ulysses* followed a way already prepared by Latin poetry, and if one reflects that Bloom, the wanderer in Ireland, was brother in spirit to the wanderer of the *Odyssey*; or that Sam Beckett's early prose works established his own *Inferno*, and *Purgatorio*, and *Paradiso*; or that Ezra Pound gave his canti the structure of the *Divine Comedy*. Joyce and Beckett were both Dante scholars, impassioned students of the work of that exile of another century. Although Dante did not choose exile, as the two Irishmen did, still he too was a wanderer, joining those – as he himself described it – "to whom the world is their native country, just as the sea is to the fish."

*   *   *

CHAPTER 1

FIRST IMPRESSIONS

*It has always been my dream to reach Paris
for the first time just before twilight.*

July 1, 1924. Who has not been told that only fools and Americans ride first class in Europe? As a matter of fact, Americans invariably travel second class – unless they are planning to squeeze the very maximum out of a dollar, as were McCoy* and I when we landed at Cherbourg. Then they line up with the students and peasants at the third class window.

We had reached Cherbourg rather late Tuesday night and decided it would be folly to take the beautiful ride to Paris in darkness. So we stopped at a hotel, and came away on the morning train. It has always been my dream to reach Paris for the first time just before twilight.

With but a few moments to spare, we dashed through the iron gates, showed our tickets to the man in uniform, and asked him which car we were to board for Paris. He languidly indicated the one before us. We gaily stepped up into one of the little compartments, finding no necessity to push along the occupants as I have since learned to do. The compartment was definitely empty. And such luxury! Pearl grey upholstery and water colors placed artistically on the walls.

Who can forget the ride through Normandy from Cherbourg to Paris? It was beautiful – gardens, varicolored houses of fairy tale architecture with their red-tiled roofs, steep gables, casements, and beloved geraniums.

As we sped through the sunny fields of Normandy, a thought struck us simultaneously ... perhaps this was first class! But we had been directed here by

---

Editor's Note: Paul Shinkman and Franklin McCoy (the latter a language major whose knowledge of French made him the natural spokesman for the two) had shared a cabin on the *Saxonia* for the group-rate college boy tour. Dr. McCoy was later to become head of the language department at Colby College, and the two men remained lifelong friends.

the attendant. We would not worry about it. Then the words *"I Classe"* caught my eye on the door of our compartment. So we *were* in the wrong car! I suggested that we look up the conductor at once and get the matter adjusted. As we deliberated, the Commander-in-Chief of the French Armies himself entered – or at least, so he appeared with his magnificent uniform, gold braid, and pompous demeanor.

"Billets, messieurs!" he said with authority. We produced our third class tickets. He consulted a little book and then named what appeared a frightful sum – the difference we were to pay! But we wished to ride third class, we faltered, and we had been directed to this car. A torrent of unintelligible French accompanied by forceful gestures of pounding the palm of one hand with the other was our answer. We indicated that we would retire to the third class section. "Not so easy!" I believe he must have said in French, although all we could understand was "Payez! Payez!"

We looked at each other in dismay, then dug deep into our pockets and silenced the old man, who retired considerably ruffled. The ride was worth it, but it was not pleasant to reflect that only fools and Americans travel first class. We obviously belonged to the latter category, and it looked as though we had qualified for the former as well!

We arrived at the great dismal Gare St. Lazare, and after some dickering with a taxi driver, got him to understand that we wanted to ride with the top down to the Hôtel de la Place de l'Odéon. What a ride that was! Past the Madeleine, across the Place de la Concorde between the Champs Elysées and the Tuileries, over the Seine, and down the Boulevard St. Germain and to the Place de l'Odéon.

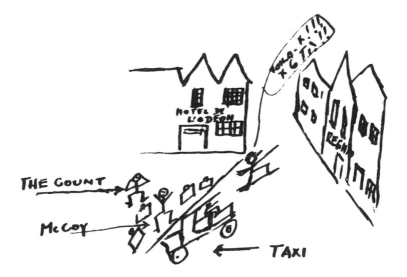

It was my duty to arrange hotel accommodations, while McCoy settled with the driver. Fearless, I plunged into the hotel (made famous by Carl Van Vechten in *Peter Whiffle*) and after peering around, spied a matronly little woman and requested "une chambre pour deux Américains." She excitedly rattled back a reply which, of course, I couldn't understand. After some gestures, it was clear that her hotel was filled. Meanwhile McCoy, surrounded by baggage, stood on the sidewalk while the taxi waited in case we needed to look further.

Suddenly, the old lady darted out the door and pointed wildly around the corner. I feared the place was on fire. Upon observing more closely, however, I saw she was pointing to a nice looking place marked Hôtel Regnard. "Très bien! Très bien!" she kept exclaiming. We got back into the taxi, rode to the Hôtel Regnard, and by the rarest good fortune, engaged a charming outside room on the third floor for 20 francs (about 55¢ per day) per person. Can you beat that?

We were delighted with our unexpected good luck. Think of looking across the square at the Odéon, where the divine Sarah Bernhardt made theatrical history! *

* * *

Editor's Note: For the next two weeks P. S. and Franklin McCoy settled down to enjoy Paris, before going their separate ways for further travel on the continent. Guidebooks in hand, they set out the first morning to see the principal sights, and, like so many inexperienced travelers, soon found themselves frustrated and completely exhausted. However, revived by the wine at an outdoor restaurant overlooking the Seine, they pushed on to Notre Dame, and further sightseeing.

Besides his letters home, P.S. wrote a series of sketches, recounting some amusing incidents experienced by the two greenhorns, covering a wide range of subjects, including the 1924 Olympic Games. Constantly watching expenses, they found the insistent request for tips thoroughly tiresome, but managed to make a game out of dodging the outstretched hands.

The two weeks, filled with sightseeing, opera-going, shopping, and enjoying French food and wine, flew rapidly past, but not before P.S. had fallen head over heels in love with Paris.

Paris is not always Elysium.
There are depressing days there as anywhere else…
Only they are less frequent
and of shorter duration.

Such a morning we had had. Crossing madly back and forth through the city in search of this or that treasure lauded in our guidebooks, only to find a disappointing mediocrity – or nothing at all.

Noon found us sipping an excellent wine at a little table before a restaurant overlooking the Seine. The towers of Notre Dame arose from the island a short way down the river. A delightful afternoon's prospect. Half an hour later found us wandering through the great dim cathedral. I was drowsy (the wine!), but recall inspecting scores of ancient religious vestments, some of them blood-stained. McCoy was ready for the ascent of the tower. I cowered at the prospects of several hundred steps. Besides, I would return for Mass Sunday, feeling much more energetic. We parted at the little tower entrance around to the left where a surly old shrew collected *pourboires.* I would wait below.

A stone balustrade a few steps from the street looked inviting, though not particularly soft. It was better than standing, and I stretched myself along the top, my back propped by the wall of the cathedral itself. Suddenly a frenzy of excitement on the sidewalk below me! I opened my eyes upon a young lady chattering indignantly at me in French. She pointed up at me with one hand, and with the other she angrily indicated an iron picket fence just below me. It seems she feared that I might roll from my resting place to become impaled on the fence below. By the time I rubbed my eyes and began to express my gratitude, she had disappeared.

*   *   *

On the Boulevard St. Michel there is a little tea room which takes its name from the famous street. A kindly old lady with beautiful grey hair sits behind a desk and smiles pleasantly when one enters and departs. When the visitor has finished eating, he carries his check up to the desk and pays the amount designated. Sometimes there is not even the formality of a check. One simply enumerates the items of his repast. These she writes on a piece of paper, then totals the prices and graciously accepts your three francs (15¢).

Our efforts at French seemed to interest our hostess. At each succeeding visit, our vocabularies were enriched by two or three new words. We would step confidently up to the desk and enumerate, "Deux chocolats, deux pains et beurre, et deux pâtisseries." On one such occasion, we were startled by a departure from the usual "Merci" and "Au revoir." The lady suddenly came hurrying around the end of the counter, and led us out upon the sidewalk. She pointed dramatically up at the inscription across the front of the awning. It read, "Restaurant de St. Michel – Pâtisserie." Some frenzied explanations from the long-suffering French lady made us realize to our chagrin that our lunch each day, by our own request, had consisted of chocolate, bread and butter, and two *bakeries!* We now smile each day as we step forward and say, "Deux chocolats, deux pains et beurres, et deux *gâteaux!*"

* * *

This morning we went shopping on the Boulevard St. Michel. My straw hat with its colored band has been very painful to me. It's so conspicuous and almost looks as though I wanted to flaunt my American nationality. So I bought a very smart light grey felt with a dark band. It's quite French but also good American style. How much? For once I enjoy answering the question – 25 francs, or $1.30. Parisian label and all!

* * *

The Luxembourg Gardens cast a peculiar spell. They are gay, but just a bit wistful, especially at twilight. My first visit was more in the nature of a second. I had already come under the spell of the place as described by Carl Van Vechten in his *Peter Whiffle.* Consequently, when I walked through the great iron gates the first time, I was prepared to be held for many hours.

A seat near the great fountain looked inviting. Several small boys were sailing boats, and the Senate Palace stood beautifully, but not too grandly, in the background. Old ladies walked slowly by, sometimes leading prancing children by the hand. Lovers arm in arm talked softly together, seeming to divine the path ahead by instinct. Young students with heavy beards and broad-brimmed black hats exchanged ideas with excited gestures. But over all hung such tranquility as is seldom encountered in such places. I began to dream of Peter Whiffle. Perhaps he had sat in this very chair.

An old crone (Van Vechten's word) suddenly appeared before me and coolly extended her hand. I was prepared for beggars and absently shook my head. She looked at me with some surprise and repeated the gesture more emphatically. "Mais non," I exclaimed impatiently, waving her aside.

This was too much. She burst forth in a flood of exclamations, excitedly pounding first the chair on which I was sitting, and then the palm of her hand. In some miraculous manner, I divined her meaning. It seems that park benches, as well as everything else in Europe, have their price, infinitesimal though it is.

It cost me 35 centimes to send her smilingly on her way.

* * *

Faust at the Opéra was a delightful prospect. Trusting to the Scot's instinct of McCoy, I had let him arrange for the seats. They were to be in the fourth gallery at the side.

The momentous evening arrived and we descended into the Métro in the Latin Quarter and emerged at the glittering Place de l'Opéra. The magnificent temple stood before us. An old woman (Europe seems full of them) rushed towards us. "Programme, libretto, score!" I accepted one of the programs and glanced at it to find that it was a mass of advertising with synopses consisting of a few paragraphs in French. I returned it to her and walked away with what I am sure were anathemas ringing in my ears.

An *ascenseur* whisked up to the top floor, where another old dame came flying towards us, seized the seat checks from McCoy, and led us triumphantly away to two closed doors. These she unlocked with great *éclat* and indicated two chairs in the loge. "Many thanks," murmured McCoy as he returned the checks to his pocket. The old shrew must have staggered. "Service!" she demanded with the immortal gesture and an impatient inflection in her voice.

There was no retrenching. The somewhat ruffled Scot handed her a coin, but we were not to be so easily rid of her. "Pour deux?" she shrilled, as though unable to believe her eyes. The sneer in her voice was too much for McCoy. He must have answered her with blazing eyes. She disappeared without further discussion. As for myself, I was busy gazing at the rows of crimson boxes and stalls, the tremendous crystal chandelier, the soft-colored evening gowns, and the white shirt fronts of the Rothschilds and Morgans on the tiers below.

*   *   *

Last night we went to the historic Comédie Française to see Molière's *L'Avare* and Hervieu's *L'Enigme.* Some of the finest acting I shall ever see.

Tonight, by way of variety, I went to see *Revue Printemps,* featuring Sacha Guitry, who has acquired some fame in America both as playwright and actor, and Yvonne Printemps, considered the *crème de le crème* of the music halls. The thing was very high class – and pre-supposed its audience's familiarity with the things and people satirized – Yvette Guilbert, Alexandre Dumas, Jacques Offenbach, the great Rachel, etc. The theatre, a little gem in red and cream, was built only last year, and is unmistakably of the *beau monde,* who were out in numbers.

*   *   *

Mount Olympus must have witnessed many magnificent spectacles but none more impressive than those which occurred on July 5, opening day of the 1924

Olympic Games. Contestants representing 45 countries lined up proudly behind their respective colors. The band struck up a stirring march, and the procession moved slowly around the great stadium. Wiry Japanese with bland smiles stood next to bearded Hindus, whose dark skins contrasted sharply with their white running suits. Blue-eyed Scandinavians marched behind sober-faced Arabians. Dark-eyed Frenchmen smiled at their friends in the stands, and the business-like Americans took things coolly.

When they had taken up formation in the center of the field there was a brief pause, then a few words spoken in French through the gigantic voice amplifier. A hush of expectancy and the whirring of winds overhead. Hundreds of doves of peace had been suddenly released and circled gracefully above the great amphitheatre as they flew happily homeward. A beautiful symbol. All of them disappeared save one, which seemed to grope blindly, unable to find itself. Possibly an unexpected portent in the great drama of national relations.

I went out a second time for the field events. I saw the Finnish wonder Nurmi break all Olympic records for the 1500 and 5000 meter runs. I got a tremendous thrill when the United States took first places in the pole vault and hammer throw, and the American flag was slowly raised in recognition while the band played the "Star Spangled Banner."

*   *   *

Every visitor to Europe must prepare himself for at least one shock. However accurate one's preconceived impressions of the Old World may have been, there is bound to be at least one completely overturned by reality. It may be the Opéra-Comique in Paris, which is not a theatre devoted to comic opera as many suppose, but a home of grand opera. It may be Christ Church at Oxford, not a church at all but a college.

My shock came on July 14. On that French Independence Day, I had vowed I would stand before the great Bastille in Paris and recall its dramatic fall and the birth of the Republic. As a special concession to a good friend whose birthday falls on that day, I announced that I would also think of him at the time and wish he were locked up inside the ancient fortress.

Shortly after luncheon, I walked around the corner of the Place de l'Odéon and boarded a bus marked "Bastille." I descended somewhat bewildered at the edge of a great open square. And where is the Bastille, I asked myself uncertainly. A single stone shaft marked the center of the square. I feverishly consulted my guidebook: "The Bastille was burned to the ground in 1789." It was a crushing blow, but I managed to drown my chagrin in a glass of grenadine on the sidewalk overlooking the Place de la Bastille.

*   *   *

Every American in Paris visits the Folies Bergère. The men, to see their worst expectations realized; the women, to click their tongues and say how shocking, when they secretly expected something equally risqué, if not more so.

Many of the scenes are not only in poor taste, but positively stupid. The entertainment at such moments is to be derived not from the stage but from the reactions of the Americans in the audience. Frankly shocked, yet not wishing to appear gauche on the one hand or vulgar on the other, they are in a pretty predicament. Why is the American so perpetually conscious of those about him? An Englishman in a dress suit would be unconcerned in F. W. Woolworth's!

It is an interesting audience – sailors on shore leave, American millionaires, college boys, beautifully gowned dowagers flashing with diamonds, Parisian *cocottes*. Between acts, they stroll leisurely about the adjoining cabaret. The Oriental dancers in the side-shows get busy, and the francs begin pouring in. A sumptuous Rolls-Royce stood at the entrance following the performance. Police surrounded it and held back the surging crowd. A young Hindu, apparently of royal blood, came out of the theatre, stepped into the car, and was whirled away amidst cheers and kisses thrown at him by the girls.

*　　*　　*

These past ten days simply defy description, at least from my pen. Paris has been all that I wanted it to be and more.

I will leave Paris on Wednesday for a week in London. After that my plans are pretty uncertain and will depend upon the exchequer.

However, Paris alone has been a wonderful experience and I won't feel badly if I can't have much more.*

*　　*　　*

**Editor's Note:* Shortly after writing this letter, P. S. left on a three-month tour of Europe. A chronicle of his summer travels is found in Chapter 4.

CHAPTER 2

LETTERS HOME FROM EUROPE
September 1924–April 1927

Introduction

Faithful as P.S. was with his letters home, his family was equally faithful in carrying out his injunction to save the letters. Today, they provide a wonderful insight into the life of a "Paris-struck" young reporter in the 1920s.

The letters tell, for example, of his first airplane flight over Paris, in a "beautiful, large passenger model, with seats for about sixteen," of watching Suzanne Lenglen play international tennis at St. Cloud, of an interview with the President of Mexico, of a Christmas gift from Sylvia Beach, a Latin Quarter brawl, and of continuous opera-going and play-going. But they are also full of small domestic details – sending home for more winter clothes since he could not afford to buy new ones, worrying about replacing his lost glasses, and always counting the cost of meals.

P.S. addressed most of these letters simply to "Dear Family," and sent them to his father and mother in Grand Rapids. His mother was then responsible for passing the letters to his two married brothers and older sister, and it was Mrs. Shinkman who ultimately saved the whole collection.

The only member of the family to whom he wrote individually on a regular basis was his beloved younger sister, "Sophomore Susie," a student at the University of Michigan, to whom he writes about the romantic night life in the Latin Quarter, an after-theatre supper in Les Halles, and his reactions to modern music and ballet. A letter written to her on the first anniversary of his sailing from New York gives a delightful picture of the crossing on the old *Saxonia,* with the refurbished steerage quarters full of college students.

27

With the aid of their own jazz band, the boys managed to break down the conventional shipboard barriers and were given the run of first class. One student is even known to have earned the price of his passage with bridge winnings in the first class lounge. P. S. seems to have attached himself to a French stage star who was on her way to fill engagements in London and Paris, though he assured his family that it was not a serious affair. In a later letter he comments, "This colorful, active life keeps me too busy to think about marriage. Besides, I couldn't afford it just yet."

As soon as he was established in his job with the Paris edition of the *Chicago Tribune,* he settled down to life in the Latin Quarter and made a wide circle of friends. His mother's distant cousin, a leading violinist with both the Lamoureux and the Opéra orchestras, provided him with some slight feeling of family stability, though the old gentleman ("Cousin Henri") seems to have been a little wary of his breezy young American relative!

The enchantment of life in Paris, dimmed only by occasional homesickness (mentioned often in his letters home, possibly to reassure his close-knit family that he was not being weaned away by the lures of Europe) never faded for him, in spite of the near-starvation wages paid to *Tribune* reporters at that time.

However, when it was possible to cover all expenses for a weekend trip to the cathedral towns of Rouen, Amiens, and Beauvais with $5, and when a party of three could "make it in style" to the theatre with drinks afterwards on $2, life could be enjoyed for a mere pittance. And enjoy it he did!

E. B. S.

*   *   *

My letters must sound like the ravings of a wild man,
and I'll bet you are trying to figure out how
I manage to get paid for anything I write.

Paris
September 15, 1924

Notice of your $150 remittance reached me Saturday morning, and this morning I had it converted into travelers' checks. I can't tell you how much I appreciate your taking care of this so promptly. I was down pretty low, and while I shouldn't have had to go without a bed and something to eat, it's not particularly pleasant to be hovering around the danger mark.

And now for the hardest part of my letter. You must give me your candid opinions. What would you think of my staying over here in Paris for the winter if

28

an opportunity presented itself? When I was in Florence, Italy, I met the editors of the *Italian Mail,* an excellent newspaper printed there in English. It is quite new but seems flourishing, and they were in need of a Paris correspondent. They were mighty fine to me, and after looking over a few little sketches I had written in Rome, offered me the job. Unfortunately the paper is but a weekly, and as they pay entirely at a column rate it would be practically impossible to make a living from that alone.

The editors of the *Mail* suggested that I also connect with one of the Paris papers. When I returned, I made a few calls following up some letters I had written stating my qualifications. I was quite flattered to get a reply from the Paris *Times,* but I haven't the slightest idea what kind of a proposition they will make.

September 20, 1924

It has been nearly two weeks since I got back from Switzerland, so you see I have been in Paris for almost a month altogether. I feel as though I know it pretty well and like it immensely. And as for expenses – you can live like a prince on just half of what it cost in America.

How's this for a 19¢ dinner – soup, roast beef with boiled beans, French fried potatoes, a huge basket of French bread, red wine, and Roquefort cheese.

For lunch this noon I had *boeuf sauté* (beef stew with onions), *pommes frites* (French fried potatoes), *pain* (bread) and for dessert a *mendiant. "Mendiant"* means beggar, and it is a little carton done up with blue ribbon and containing nuts, figs, and a bunch of dried grapes. The entire outlay was about 17¢ – tip 2½¢ (50 centimes). So you see, a chap has to be pretty poor to starve over here.

My room costs 66¢ a day and is ideally located in the student quarter. Wash basin in my room with hot and cold running water. French windows and all kinds of mirrors. (These French certainly like to look at themselves.)

I may be bounding across the waves on my way home when you get this. I am expecting to hear momentarily from the editor of the Paris *Times* as to whether or not he has any kind of a job for a rooky from America. But I really don't think there's a chance. While the paper is printed in English, a good knowledge of French is almost imperative, and that I haven't got. My personal opinion is that I'll be sailing merrily off towards the Statue of Liberty in about ten days.

September 24, 1924

I'm so excited I've been wandering around in a daze all afternoon. I've been offered a real job by the *Chicago Tribune* as a reporter on their Paris edition! I saw them this noon, and they offered me a job at 1200 francs a month (about $65), which would seem beggarly in America, but is really fairly good over here. It makes my head swim to think of the opportunity it gives me to make something of myself – if I have it in me.

You can rest assured that you would have nothing to worry about if I stayed over the winter. Paris is twice as safe a place to live as Chicago. You never seem to holdups and accidents over here; life moves along much more slowly.

As for the actual work, it's not the mad whirl of Chicago. I don't report until 11:00 in the morning, have an hour and a half for lunch if I want it, and leave around 7:00 at night. The only reason there happened to be this vacancy was that one of the reporters went to London and another was released.*

I can't help being a little puffed up, even though I am only on trial!

October 12, 1924

Dad's letter reached me a couple of days ago. I was glad to know that you think I should stay for a while longer, if I think the experience is what I need. With me it is not a question of "thinking." I *know* that for the kind of work I am best fitted for and want most to do, there is absolutely nothing that would be better preparation. After fumbling around trying to dope out a vocation ever since I left college, I believe that at last I am on the right track.

I know it's asking an awful lot, Mother, but do you suppose you could possibly send me my heavy overcoat and a couple of the heavy union suits that are packed in my trunk? It isn't cold yet, but I'd like to be prepared when winter comes. If you see my tuxedo and the black silk vest with my clothes, you might put them in the bundle. Practically any theatre or concert here at night is a tux affair, no matter where you sit. The other night, in one of the cheapest seats in the balcony, I don't believe I saw more than five men in business suits.

My work continues as fascinating as ever. It seems as though the sky's the limit as far as my experiences go.

*   *   *

* *Editor's Note:* The reporter in question had gone on a final drinking spree that cost him his job. P. S. was by then so low in funds that he had returned his rented typewriter and was printing job applications by hand. When he dropped a resume off at the *Tribune* office, the man in charge opened a desk drawer full to overflowing with applications. From sheer weariness, he put the latest addition on the top of the pile, instead of the bottom, where it belonged.

Maybe you'd like to hear about how your son burst in upon the President of Mexico. When I found out where he was stopping, I hopped out to the Hotel Majestic and was deferentially directed to Suite 10. Although a little surprised to find it on the first floor, I concluded it must be official headquarters and so let the footman knock. Not caring to wait for an answer, however, the latter coolly opened up, and before I knew what happened, I was inside with the door closed behind me!

I found myself standing in a large room entirely empty except for a table in the center around which four men sat eating lunch. The President! I tried to speak. They looked over at me in astonishment. For at least a half a minute there was not a movement on either side. (Now it is all perfectly clear to me – they thought, of course, I was an assassin!) Finally, one of them dared to come over to me and I managed to tell him what I wanted. He went over, talked with the President for a few moments (all I could hear was *manana)* and then came back and told me to return the next day. I don't believe I ever wanted quite so much to fall in a graceful swoon. It was awful, standing there staring at each other. However, I went back later and got a good story so it came out all right.

As for my birthday – I knew I would have to take desperate steps to keep it from being a horrible day. So I invited an American girl I have met here to have dinner with me. Her name is Helen Josephy, and she is a reporter on the *New York Herald,* our deadly rival.* She is a graduate of Smith, not too beautiful, but attractive, and has plenty of personality, and a lot of common sense. My clothes are just about shot, but I had my suit pressed, bought a new tie, shirt, and collar, and then we went out to make a killing. For dinner we hit the Ritz – about the swellest outfit in Paris, where the King and Queen of Greece, counts, dukes, and all the rest show up!

* *Editor's Note:* Helen Josephy went on to become one of the founding editors of *Mademoiselle* magazine, and was co-author, with Mary Margaret McBride, of a series of travel books, including *Paris is a Woman's Town,* and *London is a Man's Town.*

Dinner over about 10:30 p.m., we stepped into a taxi and whirled up to Montmartre for a taste of the so-called "high life." Stopped at a Russian cabaret, ordered champagne, and danced until about three. We had a great time. But it's got to last me for a year.

Don't think that I intend to indulge in any riotous living – but my birthday was a special occasion and I wanted to remember it.

Let me hear from you whenever you can, letting me know that everybody is all right. Being a Shinkman, I have to do just so much worrying, I guess. But you certainly don't need to worry about me. I'm taking first class care of myself.

Whenever you want me to come home, say the word and I'll come on the next boat.

November 16, 1924

Would it please you to know, Sis, that I thought of you in the great dim shadows of Notre Dame this morning? The place holds a mysterious spell over me, and I go there as often as I can. I can't get over it – the long vistas of grey gothic arches in perpetual twilight with a cluster of gleaming candles shining in the distance. High overhead, a soft rosy light streaming through the priceless jeweled windows. If there is any real proof of Christianity, it may be found in its art.

I probably owe my presence here as much to yourself as anybody else. It was at your "Housetop" just before dinner one night a couple of years ago that I picked up *Peter Whiffle* and read Van Vechten's words:

> "... more fields, more roads, more towns, and at last towards
> twilight, Paris. The drive through the streets that evening
> seemed like a dream and, even later, when the streets of Paris
> had become more familiar to me than those of any other city, I
> could occasionally recapture the mood of the first vision. For
> Paris in the May twilight is very soft and exquisite ..."

All those dreams have come true – with an almost uncanny reality.

Yesterday I received my first raise and am now drawing 1500 francs a month (about $80). In addition, I received a copy of the *Italian Mail* carrying my second article "Rambles in Paris." The pay is frightful, but the experience and prestige are worth something.

November 18, 1924

Luncheon is a ceremony with the French, who are never so happy as when they are eating. I have an hour and a half, which is really necessary, as the

32

cheapest little one-horse joint here serves up its meals with all the *éclat* of the Waldorf Astoria. Everything must be brought on in courses and ordered separately. The first morning, my friend and I nearly started a riot trying to get our ham and omelets served together (a queer people, these French).

And wine. A meal without wine is to them like lemonade without lemons. The first morning in Italy I had to drink about a quart of it before I could get breakfast. Can you imagine drinking wine for breakfast? Now I get a little bottle of good *vin blanc* with my meals for 70 centimes (about 4¢). But I can still drink water too. Nobody seems to care much for French beer.

November 23, 1924

You should have seen your dashing young son last Friday afternoon. I concluded it was about time I called on Mlle Liane D'Eve, the French actress, whom I met on the *Saxonia*. In private life she is the Comtesse de Millon. She had given me her Paris and London addresses and invited me to call some time. At about four o'clock, I donned my new pearl grey spats, blue suit, wing collar and polka dot bow tie, grey suede gloves, and, swinging a mean walking stick, taxied gaily to her apartment in the rue Juilliet Lamber! (Talk about your gay Parisian boulevardier! I'd have knocked down John Barrymore for a row of tin lizzies and I don't mean maybe!)

YOUR SMITTEN SON

← MLLE. D'EVE

Unfortunately the Countess was in London but I left my card (the way they do in the movies) and then returned to the *Trib* office where I threw a little shell shock among the gang.

Went to the famous Madeleine church Friday morning for a special celebration of the feast of Saint Cecelia. They sang a beautiful Mass composed a hundred years ago by Cherubini in honor of the anointing of King Charles X at Rheims. It was wonderfully beautiful – one hundred and fifty voices, a symphony orchestra, soloists from the Opéra, and the pipe organ. These are experiences that I enjoy! The Church was packed with French, English, and Americans, but I had a newspaper pass and managed to get a very good seat.

Wednesday night I'm going to the Opéra to hear a new opera *L'Heure Espagnole*. I have developed quite a fondness for modern music, and when one can get a seat for 18¢ there's not much excuse for not indulging the hobby! It's worth 18¢ just to walk down the grand marble staircase of the Opéra!

December 28, 1924

My first Christmas in Paris – away from home – is over. It was probably the least happy Christmas I have ever spent.

Christmas Eve I attended midnight Mass at a beautiful old church nearby and enjoyed it immensely. The music was beautiful, and I managed to keep in good spirits as long as they sang the old French carols. But when the organ and choir broke out in the "Adeste Fideles," my favorite Christmas hymn, it was almost too much. It made me think of our own family, singing Christmas hymns as we used to do on Christmas Eve back on Gold Avenue. I think it was one of the saddest moments since I have been away from home.

After Mass I took a stroll through the dim back streets of the Latin Quarter and then came home for some wine and cakes before I turned in.

On Christmas Day I slept late, did a little work for the *Trib* in the afternoon, and in the evening had a great time at the Christmas dinner and dance given at the U.S. Students' and Artists' Club.* The latter cheered me up a good bit, but frankly, I was relieved when Friday morning rolled around and Christmas was over!

Dick Forsyth sent me a beautiful leather cigarette case which he brought from Mexico. It has my initials hand tooled on it. It came the day before Christmas, and it was a scream getting the thing out of the customs office. When they located my package, the clerk said very deferentially in French, "If you please, sir!" Then, without waiting for an answer, he calmly seized a pair of scissors, snipped the string, and handed me the package to open up before the crowd and see what I had received for Christmas.

It was very amusing to watch people open their presents before an audience. One man got about a dozen gaily embroidered doilies from Germany! Another received something that looked like lavender crêpe de chine trimmed in old lace! A girl next to me received something that resembled a button hook! An older woman took out of her package what looked like a grandma's cap, then hastened to explain for the benefit of the crowd, that it was for somebody else.

As for the cash you sent me – thanks again! I have just about decided how to

---

* *Editor's Note:* The reason that P.S. slept late on Christmas morning was a simple one. His homesickness had reached the point on Christmas Eve that he felt the need to drink himself into oblivion. The wine and cakes were not the mild refreshments that he infers, but he was always careful in what he wrote his family to spare them worry.

spend it. I think I'll get three seats for *Rip* (delightful comic opera based on *Rip Van Winkle*) for New Year's Eve, and take Cecil Deighton and Helen Josephy. Afterwards we'll go to a café for a drink of wine to welcome in the New Year. We three would have a great time together and I could make it in style on $2.

February 25, 1925

Mr. Morrell of Buffalo is now in Paris on his way to England. Saturday night I took him and Cecil to an inexpensive little restaurant up in Montmartre. It's about fifty years old, and very few know about it. The food is excellent. A number of artists, including Monet, used to make it their rendezvous. Afterwards we went across the river to the Latin Quarter and had coffee at a student café filled with the most mixed group in the world – artists, writers, musicians, loafers, Sorbonne students, as well as people from practically every part of the World. I got hold of an old Polish artist I know and brought him over to our corner to talk about art and the fourth dimension. They seemed to enjoy it – we talked until two.

April 2, 1925

Dear Susie,

Last Saturday after work Ed Levitis stopped for me at the office. (I first met Ed, you'd probably be interested to know, in the top tier at the Opéra, when he came to me during intermission to congratulate me on my victory over one of the old crones in charge of seating, who had tried to force me to check my cane – for a fee, of course. He himself battled continually with the French over similar matters, and was happy to meet a like-minded compatriot!) We wound our way up to the very peak of Montmartre overlooking Paris, where there is a little square called Place du Tertre, which dates back several centuries and was the center of life for the old Parisian poets and artists.

We stopped at one of the little restaurants for dinner and found it crowded with young Frenchmen, all in exuberant spirits. Over in one corner there were a couple of chaps picking away at guitars. All around the room, with its low-hanging rafters, are grotesque paintings and cartoons, some of them really quite old.

The dinner was delicious, as dinners generally are in France. We sat and smoked and talked until nearly twelve and then left for a stroll through the narrow winding streets of the old artists' quarter. Streets lined with high stone walls and lighted with old iron gas lamps.

Quite by accident, we suddenly came across a little old stone house which was quite brightly lighted and with music going on inside. Ed inquired of a man passing and found it was Le Lapin Agile, one of the most famous of the old cabarets (*not* the kind of cabarets we have in the U.S., but the original kind, where artists get together to talk and sing).

We knocked at the door and were shown into a large room furnished with a few chairs scattered randomly about – low ceiling, heavy beams, at one end a crumbling stone grotto, and at the other a huge crucifix and life-size statues of a couple of saints. In the center sat the host in a French peasant costume, playing a guitar and singing Frenck folk songs. Once in a while, somebody asked for a glass of beer and he would step out and bring it in, much as one might do in his own home. The whole thing was very quiet, informal, and enjoyable. Nothing of the blazing Montmartre jazz band atmosphere.

Afterwards we walked slowly down the hill. It was early morning, and as we passed through the Jardin des Tuileries, you should have heard the birds singing and answering each other. Two of them on opposite sides of the park kept up a steady stream of dialogue back and forth. Then we dropped into a café where I scribbled a note to Helen Josephy, whom I had promised to see off to Italy at eight that morning.

Of course we had to see that she received it, so Ed had to walk around to her lodging with me and help me try to rouse the concierge. No luck. We had finally just about given up, when we decided to try once more. The great door suddenly swung open, and we entered the court. A window over at one side opened up, and a voice called out sleepily to ask what we wanted.

"Voulez-vous donnez cette lettre à Mlle Josephy, s'il vous plaît, Madame?" I asked in my best French. A long arm reached out (the owner was still in bed) and to my astonishment a deep voice replied, "Oui, oui, Monsieur." One of the few men concierges in Paris! However, I quickly covered my confusion with a generous *pourboire*.

By that time, the old women and *garçons* were beginning to appear on the streets in front of their houses, sweeping briskly away with crazy brooms and pouring huge pails of water around. The French make me think of little kids, the way they like to fool around with a pail of water.

Glad you like the "Latin Quarter Notes." Signed my full name to the column for the first time this morning – very fascinating work.

May 18. 1925

Inasmuch as France does not observe Mother's Day today, there were, of course, no special services. However, it's Jeanne d'Arc Day so I celebrated in honor of you, Mother, and Jeanne d'Arc at the same time!

Jeanne d'Arc is France's favorite saint, and they make quite an event of the day. This morning I attended solemn high Mass at the Notre Dame. The grey stone walls were decorated with the French tricolor and the sky-blue and white banners of Jeanne d'Arc. Three priests officiated, and the Cardinal Archbishop of Paris occupied his throne at one side in great state.

There must have been a hundred choirboys all in white. In the middle of the service there was suddenly a blare of trumpets and burst of drums in the rear of the church, and a band of boys in uniform came marching down the center aisle towards the altar. I believe they represented some Catholic anti-political organization. It was shock enough to see such a demonstration in old Notre Dame, but when several men followed, lugging huge baskets of *biscuits,* I nearly fell in a swoon!

They marched down to the sanctuary and in a little while returned, *passing out biscuits* to the people in the church! I took my cue from those around me and coolly helped myself to a biscuit when they reached me. Then everybody nonchalantly ate their biscuits while the services continued! I don't know yet whether they were serving light refreshments in celebration of the feast day. All I know is that I got mine.

NOTRE DAME

Lost my glasses a few weeks ago and was fuming and fretting about the inconvenience and expense of a new pair. I had to have them, however, and after taking all possible steps to locate the lost ones, I stopped in at an optometrist and had my eyes tested for a new pair. How much do you suppose the whole thing cost? (eye test, new glasses just like my old ones, and a case) Just 30 francs, or about $1.60! Can you beat that? I'm getting so I know how to really get something for my money. In fact, with the correspondingly low French salaries, one has to.

Had a peppy letter from Sophomore Susie a few days ago, telling me all the news. I'm really glad she has had her hair bobbed. It's come to stay. It's about the only thing you see here, and now is the time for her to try it out.

May 21, 1925

Saw Suzanne Lenglen, the famous tennis star, play the other afternoon at St. Cloud. They are having an international tennis tournament, and there are some wonderful players here. She didn't have to put all of her effort into the play but it was apparent that she is as at home on the courts as she is walking on the street. Perfectly confident, every minute. Shook hands with her afterwards and had a few words with her. She's about thirty and decidedly homely, I would say, and in true French fashion, she was made up like a chorus girl. Imagine rouging all up for a tennis match! I think she regards playing tennis before a crowd of people exactly the same as a theatrical performance. Of course the photographers were busy taking pictures all during the play.*

Yesterday afternoon I heard a symphony conducted by Koussevitsky, who has just returned from America. Did he get to Grand Rapids? He seems to be quite an exponent of the moderns. Yesterday they played a Prokofiev and a Roussel composition – both first auditions. The audience becomes quite excited here on such occasions and either applauds wildly or hisses and jeers. They did both yesterday following the Prokofiev number. I liked it myself very much – sounds like a boiler factory part of the time, but it certainly keeps you awake and leaves a definite impression.

Tomorrow night I am planning to hear Mary Garden sing *Tosca*. I know the publicity men, and they have invited me to any of the performances I care to attend. That's one of the joys of the newspaper business.

June 21, 1925

Dear Susie,

Just one year ago today, I steamed out of New York Harbor, headed for Europe and one of the greatest experiences I have ever had. What more appropriate way could I celebrate my first anniversary than by writing a letter to you?

I shan't forget the strange feeling of the ocean – an ocean actually whirling past as I sat somewhat dazedly in a deck chair. This was a culmination of a dream. The crossing was wonderful. A great spirit of friendship among the passengers, and the college men had free run of the first class. I made some great acquaintances.

Then came the mysterious night when we watched for the lights of the English coast out of the blackness. While we waited we hung over the bow of the ship and

---

* *Editor's Note:* This letter was one of several written on stationery headed "Café Brasserie du Dôme." The Dôme was used by the American colony not only for receiving mail, but also for sending it – the generous-sized sheets of free note paper being a boon to an impoverished reporter.

watched the porpoises as they glowed sulphurously in the water below.

Bishop's Rock was the first light to appear. I shall never forget the thrill as I realized that this was England! Next morning we were gliding in peaceful waters towards a row of hills. Flocks of seagulls circled about us, and it seemed to me they had come out to welcome the arrivals. From my little stateroom I remember gazing out through the porthole at placid green slopes sliding by. This was England.

As we paused in a sort of cove, with a flurry of excitement, a small steamboat drew up beside us and the representative of the Lord Mayor of Plymouth, a harmless looking, kindly old gentleman in frock coat and silk hat, came on board to give us a welcome. The boys played some jazz for him, cheered, and I took a snapshot.

That evening we reached Cherbourg and I decided to spend the night there so as to make the train trip to Paris next morning in the daylight.

Last week Helen, Lawrence, a friend of Helen's, and I went to Les Acacias, one of the swanky places to dance in the evening. At about 3:00 a.m. we left for Les Halles, the great markets of Paris where the produce is brought in from the provinces. The rows and rows of fresh carrots with their bright green tops were one of the most beautiful sights I have ever seen. The French have a positive knack for artistic decorations of that sort, and the stuff was laid out with an almost geometrical precision.

Afterwards we stopped at a little restaurant nearby and had some onion soup (a favorite dish of French farmers and laborers). It's delicious – made with a crust of cheese grating over the top. Home about five, and the girl from New York was sailing at 10:00 that morning from Cherbourg for America. She has been buying her trousseau in preparation for a big wedding.

August 30, 1925

The first day I got back from my vacation the city editor delighted me by assigning me to a grand luncheon which the chefs of Paris were giving in honor of the head chef of the Hotel Ambassador in New York, who is French and making a visit here. The affair was about the most staggering of its kind that has ever come off in Paris. With the cream of France's hotel directors and *chefs de cuisine* as guests, they simply went the limit and the result was such a feast as I shall probably never see again.

The most exquisite dishes served in perfect fashion. Three of Paris' master chefs were in charge, and the wines included a wonderful port with the iced cantaloupe to start off, a white wine with the next course, and then another red wine ("1914," the waiter whispers softly in your ear as he fills your glass), then champagne, then a fine cognac with the coffee and cigars! No, your son did not see double. Everything was very orderly. And besides, I had to write an account of the whole thing.

November 4, 1925

Glad you liked the perfume, Mother. I had such a cold when I bought it and smelled so many kinds in the swanky Coty shop in the Rue de la Paix, that I finally gave up and selected blindly. It didn't cost much and I hope you like the fragrance as well as you do the bottle! *Use it up,* I'll send some more. Coty is considered quite elite here, and their shop is a symphony in grey.

December 7, 1925

I'll ring off and go to lunch. My waiter, Ernest (pronounced Er-nest´), will be looking for me. I lunch cheaply although I must have more than I used to in America – generally a steak and potatoes (French fried), red wine, bread, Roquefort cheese, and coffee. It makes just the right luncheon for me and comes to just 5.25 francs, not including 50 centimes for Ernest. A franc is now less than 5¢, so you see it isn't expensive. I get a clean napkin on Monday (40 centimes) and have my own pigeon hole in which to keep it during the week. (Ah, these thrifty French!) And then, I have music with my luncheon. A very good little orchestra which plays all the popular operas, American musical comedy hits, and some very good French things.

December 22, 1925

Christmas is in the air, and as you can imagine, the French are all excitement. I plan to go to Midnight Mass at Notre Dame with several friends. Jay Allen and his wife (he writes for the *Tribune* also), Bob Sage and his wife (I knew Bob at Ann Arbor and he is now on the *Trib* too), Bill Smyser, his mother, two girlfriends, and myself, will comprise the party. Bill Smyser is a Harvard man who writes on the Paris theatre for the Boston *Transcript* and other American newspapers.

After Mass, we are all going to the Allens' apartment for something to eat and drink and a little dancing (the Smysers have a victrola). It should be great fun and will be after the true French fashion of celebrating Réveillon. Christmas afternoon I have been invited to several peoples' homes for a Christmas egg nog, and in the evening I am going to take Bob's wife (he has to work) to the Christmas dinner at my old hangout, the United States Students' and Artists' Club. They have a *real* dinner for only 10 francs. We'll spend the evening dancing. Everybody "dresses" for the occasion and has a great time.

Though I have been feeling a little blue the last couple of days, I will be home next Christmas. Two Christmases across the ocean away from everybody are about all I can stand. But, odds bodikens, Christmas will be much pleasanter than it was last year because I have more friends. So don't worry about me.

December 30, 1925

Dear Sue,

How can I thank you for the lovely book by Carl Van Doren – such a charming Christmas present! Of all the modern writers, he is undoubtedly the one I know least about and should know more about. You couldn't have made a more fortunate selection.

You might be interested to know that another book which I received was James Joyce's *Dubliners,* the gift of Sylvia Beach, who runs Shakespeare & Company, a little bookshop in the Quarter which is said to be one of the finest English-American shops on the Continent. She is a very good friend of the Joyce family and it was she who had much to do with the notorious *Ulysses,* still in rather bad repute, though it has caused a sensation and has just reached its seventh edition.

She autographed the book to me on the back page and says Joyce himself must have the front page. My friends Bob and Mave Sage gave me a copy of Joyce's *A Portrait of the Artist as a Young Man,* and with a copy of Christopher Morley stories on the way from the Sappington's, you see I am hovering on the brink of a literary *débauche!* What is your own opinion of Van Doren?

a Happy New Year

To Paul Shinkman

from Sylvia Beach

Paris 1926

Autographed copy of "The Dubliners", *given to Paul Shinkman by Sylvia Beach*

I was charmed with your last letter in which you described "dining at the dorm" and your first cigarette. As for the former, I considered it so good that I read that portion of the letter to a friend of mine over luncheon. His name is Eugène Jolas, and you will hear of him some day. He is something of a poet, having already published a book or two of poems, as well as numerous contributions to French and American literary reviews. He is a strange, rather fascinating character whose home is in Alsace-Lorraine, but who has spent much of his time in Paris. He sailed just a few days ago for this second visit to America. He was as amused at the letter as I was, which may flatter you.

Among my Christmas gifts, from my old friend the *Chicago Tribune,* came a bonus of a month's salary – 1500 francs! And what do you think I am giving myself for Christmas? A new suit and a pair of shoes. I have been running around looking like a rag bag for so long that I finally got reckless, stopped in at a tailor's, and ordered a suit to be ready Christmas Eve. It cost 500 francs ($20).

January 8, 1926

The day before New Year's, I took a very beautiful plant out to Cousin Henri's wife. It was a mass of bright red flowers with green leaves. I simply wanted them to know that I hadn't forgotten them and that I appreciated the number of times they had invited me for dinner. They were greatly pleased. As I came up the steps of their apartment building in the Rue d'Enghien, I could hear Cousin Henri's violin above. He is passionately fond of it and regards it almost as a child.

He is such a sweet, kindly old man. They complained about the rise in prices which has been going on all over France, and, he says, it's the musicians who suffer. People regard lessons as a luxury, and the first thing they economize on is music lessons.

He is not playing with the Lamoureux Symphony this year, having retired after thirty years. He also retired a few weeks ago from the great orchestra at the Opéra, where he played for years. I think it saddens him a little to realize that he must make way for younger men.

January 17, 1926

I simply must write at once and thank you for that wonderful letter that just came yesterday. I treasure my letters from home to such an extent that I carry them around for several hours, waiting for just the proper moment and surroundings to read them.

Consequently, I didn't read yesterday's letter until I had a little leisure and could drop into a cozy little café, select a seat in a quiet corner, enjoy my letter over some coffee, and perhaps a little glass of cognac or rum.

February 18, 1926

You will be interested to know that I have made my first airplane flight. It was wonderful, and if there is ever another war – me for the air service. I love it.

One of the largest airplane passenger services in the world has its hangar and field at Le Bourget, just outside of Paris. A week or so ago they invited a delegation from the American Legion here to come out and inspect their model equipment, which is said to be the finest in the world. The French lead everybody when it comes to aerial development, and Le Bourget is said to be the largest airport in the world.

I got in on the trip together with some other newspapermen and took about a half hour's flight with them over Le Bourget and northern Paris. The plane was a beautiful large passenger model with seats for about sixteen passengers, and you can leave it to another reporter and myself to grab off the two front seats – farther forward than even the pilot himself. There was nothing to worry about. They say that you are really safer in the air than on the streets of a big city these days.

Besides, if you fall you simply fall and it's all over with before you strike the ground. If a person must die, I should think it one of the most beautiful deaths possible. One simply flies off into space. The pilot told me we rose to an altitude of about 1500 feet and traveled from 40 to 50 miles per hour, although of course it didn't seem like anywhere near that.

Last night, I rushed to the fourth gallery at the Opéra to hear the company from the Royal Opera at the Hague sing Beethoven's *Fidelio*. It was fairly well done and I enjoyed the music very much – a most enjoyable evening for 30¢. The cost of living, however, is going up rapidly here and if I don't receive a raise in salary soon, I may come packing home even before spring, looking like a tramp.

Do try and keep up your French, Mother. You *are* going to come over eventually, and it will make the trip much more interesting.

March 20, 1926

Did you read of Jean Borotra, the French tennis champion who recently played in the States? One of my latest thrills came a week or so ago when he gave me a lift in his swanky sedan through the heart of the city. (I had been to interview him on his return to the U.S.) Can you just picture your charming son gliding through the streets beside one of the country's national heroes?

Ate my first snails fried in butter the other night – I like 'em.

April 26, 1926

Last Saturday afternoon a group of young American and British people chartered a small steamer on the Seine and took an afternoon cruise with luncheon served on board and dancing during the afternoon. I was along, and we had a wonderful time. One of my friends, Count Lansky (yessir, a real Russian Count) was managing the affair. He was educated in England, but like all the upper Russian classes was chased out of his country by the Bolsheviks, and is now living with his parents in Paris.

He is working for the *Tribune,* and a very nice chap. Canon Stimpson and his wife were along to chaperone the party. We went up the river quite a ways and got back to Paris in time for dinner. I'm fairly aching for a chance to take you and Dad on some of these charming little trips.

If things shape themselves in such a way that you can consider making definite plans for getting over this spring or summer, let me know *at once.*

June 17, 1926

Hardly been able to touch earth the last few days since receiving Dad's letter of June 3 announcing your definite sailing date.

Everything is awaiting your triumphant arrival and conquest of the French capital, my Lord and Lady.*

Editor's Note: The visit was a great success, and at the end of the summer P. S. returned with his parents to the States for a long vacation in Grand Rapids. But the lure of the Latin Quarter had not lost its hold on him, and by Thanksgiving he was once again in Paris, writing ecstatically about the welcome he received on all sides, and of his joy at being back in the beloved city.

November 27, 1926

Am I really back in Paris?

Four days have passed and I am still in a dream. I never realized what a hold these people and places had taken on me!

Of course, it's a most fortunate state of affairs because it's helped me fight off the inevitable homesickness. At any rate, I am infinitely happier now for having been home and in the family circle again. Everybody tells me that I have never looked better.

The trip back was most enjoyable, and I made some interesting acquaintances – a very fine old Swiss gentleman, an English chap, John Baker, who was returning from five months in the States against his will, and an American girl, who turned out to be one of the most charming creatures I have met. But the twinkling lights of the coast of France looked wonderful to me when we sighted land again.

We were obliged to land at the horrible hour of five o'clock in the morning. The tender came out for us in pitch darkness, and it was anything but a pleasant sensation to crawl from one boat to another in the cold black morning air. I was repaid, however. As I walked cautiously up the gangplank to the dock, I noticed a little group in the dim light. And there, smiling sheepishly, stood good old Ed. It quite bowled me over. I never dreamed of being met at Boulogne.

Well, that started things off on the right way. The welcomes have completely taken my breath away. They were delighted to see me at the hotel again, and M. Bardet himself came out to greet me when my taxi drove up. They gave me a rousing welcome at the *Tribune*, and I never knew how many of the boys I was acquainted with. When I took my laundry to the little shop around the corner Thursday, my old laundress and her ninety-year-old mother were so excited they did not know what to do. Then they had to drag out Kiki, their beloved cat, to give me a welcome also.

February 22, 1927

I think I told you in my last letter that your charming son is now city editor of the *Chicago Tribune* here. That, of course, means new responsibilities with the result that I have been kept pretty busy. My predecessor was very capable in many ways but things were in none too good shape. He was a poet (Eugène Jolas), and you can imagine what that meant. This, together with the changing around of our editorial offices, has mixed things up.

The new work is most interesting, and apparently I am making out all right so far, but I'm doing no boasting. It is quite different from the work I have been doing although it was not entirely new to me since, you remember, I acted as assistant to the city editor last year. The pay is still small, but I shall manage to make out nicely. Moreover, my friends tell me the prestige should be worth something.

I received a wonderful letter from Sis yesterday. She writes brilliantly and is not at all backward about telling me that the photograph I sent her (the side view) flatters me outrageously. After seeing such a miracle performed, she says, she has lost all her own terror for photographers!

The photographer, Ordione, himself neither liked the side view nor the front view, and preferred a semi-front view with a silly little smirk on my face that made me crazy.

April 7, 1927

The other night I went to a boxing bout with our assistant sporting editor, Roger Thibaud. It was very interesting and included an exhibition by Charles Ledoux, the French champion featherweight. The exhibition was refereed by Georges Carpentier, who, you may remember, met Dempsey for the world's championship.

As we were sitting on a café terrasse having drinks afterward, a man and a woman came by, gaily pounding each other, he with fists, she with her umbrella. Without my glasses on I couldn't make them out very well but assumed that they were having a friendly little tiff. Roger said they were actually fighting, however, and before we knew what had happened, she had been knocked flat on her back in the gutter.

I was stunned to see a man actually attack a woman physically, but Roger was on his feet in a second flying down a side street after the man, along with three or four other Frenchmen. I didn't mix in. However, the fellow dodged into a building and escaped, and meanwhile the girl, appparently a rather low type herself, had disappeared.

We had no sooner resumed our seats than there was a crash in the street directly in front of the café, and a car swerved around in a complete semi-circle. I looked up just in time to see a man flying through the air. The car had crashed into the curb, but by the time the police had arrived the man had picked himself up, apparently unscratched, and hurried away. I was certain he had been killed or very seriously hurt. I imagine he had been careless in getting in front of the machine, and realized that he had no complaint to make.

Was so cheered by your last letter, Mother. I don't know what I'd do without them. Yes, I do know – I'd simply come home.

*   *   *

CHAPTER 3

LATIN QUARTER NOTES

Introduction

In the early 1920s, writers, artists, playwrights, stage designers and musicians crowded in legions to the Latin Quarter, and combined to produce the greatest output of artistic endeavor of this century.

As the Paris-based correspondent for two English-language newspapers, P. S. recaptured much of the excitement of those years in his feature columns. Those appearing in the *Chicago Tribune* were titled "Latin Quarter Notes" and "Stage Commentaries," while the articles he wrote for the *Italian Mail* were called "Paris Letters" or "Rambles in Paris."

Starting in November 1924, the "Latin Quarter Notes" appeared each Thursday in the *Tribune,* and complemented, in a lighter vein, the Sunday *Magazine's* scholarly articles on theatre, art, and other cultural matters by the paper's senior writers such as H. L. Mencken, Burns Mantle, Sidney Dark, and B.J. Kospoth. Eugène Jolas, with his "Rambles through Literary Paris," was covering the activities of the brilliant, aspiring novelists of the period.

At first P. S. was assigned to cover the myriad of Latin Quarter art shows, and he haunted the studios of the hopeful artists who crowded into Montparnasse. By the summer of 1925, however, P. S. had also become an habitué of Sylvia Beach's bookshop Shakespeare and Company, and his columns covered more of the literary field. As he became increasingly at home in the Latin Quarter, his column provided a vivid, well-rounded picture of the writers, artists, and musicians of Montparnasse.

But it was James Joyce who stood head and shoulders above them all. Thanks to the persistence of Sylvia Beach, the shy, unassuming, but absolutely determined daughter of a Princeton University theologian, *Ulysses* was given to the world in a cheaply printed paperback edition (the best that Sylvia Beach could afford) in 1922, and the battle of the censors was on. P. S.'s "Notes" are enlivened regularly with items concerning *Ulysses* – its bannings, confiscations, and burnings – and also with reports of Joyce's failing eyesight.

In early 1926, the *Tribune's* drama critic Simone Heller moved to London, and the signature of Paul Shinkman began to appear on the columns entitled "Stage Commentaries." His play reviews and the "Latin Quarter Notes" were both regular features of the Paris edition of the *Chicago Tribune* until late 1926, when he took a long vacation in the States. Shortly after his return to Paris, P. S. was made city editor of the *Tribune's* European edition.

Much of the material appearing in the articles written by P. S. for the *Italian Mail** duplicates stories appearing in the *Tribune;* however, the Italian newspaper gave him scope to write in greater detail, and with considerable literary charm. The following pieces, selected from articles appearing in both the *Tribune* and the *Mail,* between 1924-1926, reflect a sample of P. S.'s work during this period.

E.B.S.

*   *   *

* *Editor's Note:* The *Italian Mail*, a weekly, was one of the many English-language newspapers published in Europe in the 1920s. Recent inquiries at the Library of Congress, the British Museum Library, and the National Library in Rome failed to uncover any copies of the paper, which ceased publication in 1932.

A request made to Dr. Lee, present rector of the Episcopal Church in Florence, where P. S.'s good friend Canon Killian Stimpson was rector in the 1930s, however, produced results. Dr. Lee contacted a librarian, Virginia Caprio, consultant for the Syracuse University student year abroad program, who succeeded in finding the files wrapped in brown paper parcels in the basement of the Marucelliana, one of Florence's great libraries. One of her students researched the files and produced photostats of fifty articles written by P.S. from Paris.

Paris is a city of magic spots ...
the Champs-Elysées at midnight ...
a path of romance between
two golden chains of boulevard lamps.

October 16, 1924 – Paris is a city of magic spots. And these spots should be visited at varying hours of the day or night if one is to come fully under their spell.

Some evening after the theatre step into a taxi or one-horse fiacre and ask to be taken to the Place de l'Etoile. You will descend before the great shadow of the Arc de Triomphe. Walk around the side from which extends that enchanted thoroughfare – the Champs-Elysées. A path of romance between two golden chains of boulevard lamps, it seems to extend down through miles of space into the infinite. Up and down, in endless streams, move the flickering lights of taxi-cabs and carriages, all speeding towards – Romance!

Behind you, the perpetual flame flutters on the Tomb of the Unknown Soldier who lies buried beneath the Arch, and throws ghostly shadows upon the grey walls. It reminds you of a fearful experience that you had almost forgotten.

There is a rumble on the pavement and you stand aghast at the incongruous spectacle which appears. Slowly around the Arch and down the Avenue of romance comes a caravan of huge two-wheeled carts piled high with fresh produce of all sorts. A muffled figure seated silently on the very top occasionally calls a "Hué!" to the plodding horse, who seems lost in his own reverie.

The French peasants are on their way to Les Halles, the great markets of Paris.

November 5, 1924 – One of the very first things the American buys himself in Paris is a cane.

Secretly and somewhat shamefacedly, he will slip into one of the shops specializing in these particular implements, and pick out the style that seems best to suit his own type of masculinity, wardrobe, or pocketbook.

He will come out twirling it consciously and feeling much like a drum major leading a procession down the street for the first time in his life. He will blush as he recalls the jeers he directed back home at those who "affected" such a useless foible. He will picture with some apprehension the reception he will receive from the "old gang" when he returns, and decides that the cane must be left behind with Paris.

But he learns to carry it nonchalantly through Notre Dame and up the Eiffel Tower. Until one day he finds that he has accidentally left it at home – and his sensations are those of a man who has forgotten to put on his collar and necktie!

November 20, 1924 – Excitement was in the air at Abel (Buck) Warshawsky's studio yesterday afternoon. There was much crating of pictures, scribbling of addresses, final handshakes, and a lot of good wishes for the popular artist who leaves today for a four-month sojourn in sunny Spain.

To add to the festivity of the occasion, Bob Eskridge dropped in with an original from the etching he had just made of Warshawsky.

Buck says his first stop in Spain will be Mallorca, but his later itinerary depends upon the whim of the moment. He adds that he may attend a few bull-throwing contests, but they won't be the kind that take place in arenas.

November 23, 1924 – Foujita, a young Japanese artist whose work for the Ballet Suédois, now showing at the Théâtre des Champs-Elysées, has caused considerable comment, is exhibiting at the Galerie Devambez, 43 Boulevard Malesherbes until December 2.

* * *

"Garrets don't develop art – but they sometimes hinder it," according to Director Methven of the American Art Association. "In fact, I could name a number of young students who would undoubtedly have accomplished some great things, if they could have had the wherewithal to give their talent a chance. But unfortunately they have been denied an opportunity to develop any genius they may have had. As for the opposite type of case – well, everybody knows too much about them already!"

November 27, 1924 – *"Vive Jaurès! Vive la paix! A bas la guerre!"*

A throbbing army of French citizens swarmed the streets of Paris Sunday, carrying the streaming red banners of Communism, singing snatches of the "Internationale," and invoking the gods of peace to perpetuate the memory of Jean Jaurès and crush war for all time.

From the Chamber of Deputies to the Panthéon they marched. At the head of the procession moved majestically the huge funeral car draped with the tricolor and bearing aloft the casket containing the remains of Jean Jaurès. The great day had come!

Ten years after his assassination and martyrdom in the cause of peace, the eminent scholar was paid the supreme tribute of the French Republic, "Aux grands hommes la Patrie reconnaissante." His bones now rest with those of

Voltaire, Zola, Victor Hugo, and Rousseau in the hallowed Panthéon – France's Westminster Abbey.

Military honors were omitted, as Jaurès would have wished. But instead there were the honors of the vast proletariat in abundant measure. Scores of miners in working clothes formed a guard around the casket. Workers representing all parts of France and even Germany rallied to the shrine of the champion of labor and socialism, carrying the banners of the League des Droits de l'Homme.

The man who pulled the fateful trigger ten years ago in a café on the Grands Boulevards is still at large. It is probable that he was an interested spectator of the ceremonies.

November 30, 1924 – "My dream is of the Spanish Republic!" Señor Blasco Ibanez (author of *The Four Horsemen Of The Apocalypse*) told me with a tremor in his voice as we discussed a recent speech he had made in the Latin Quarter.

"Not a republic like France," he explained. "I like the United States. It must have a constitution similar to the United States."

His new book on Alphonse XIII will appear this month in French and English, with a Spanish edition of two million.

December 4, 1924 – Some day, after perhaps many years of wandering through strange countries, they will return to their "Promised Land" – Russia.

That is the dream of the Russian refugees who have found shelter in Paris from the ravages of the Bolsheviks. And, as their last possession by means of which they feel the goal may be attained, they are clinging desperately to their church.

The other afternoon, I talked with one of their number, the Prince Boris Wassiltchikoff, a distinguished but quiet-mannered, elderly gentleman. He told me that now, by what seems the very essence of irony, they are threatened with the loss of the church itself.

It has been pointed out that, like the Russian Embassy, the church was originally the property of the Russian Empire and consequently now reverts to the new and succeeding government. And so it will doubtless pass into new hands shortly after the arrival of the new Soviet ambassador and his colony.

The pastor of a wealthy English-speaking congregation in Paris recently informed his Grace Archbishop Eulogius, head of the Russian Orthodox Church in Western Europe, that his church was at the disposal of the refugees in Paris, should they find themselves without a place to worship.

"When the Archbishop told me about it," said the Prince to me, his voice filled with emotion, "there were tears in his eyes."

As I left, he smiled rather painfully and indicated a pathetic little group of photographs on the wall of his modest apartment.

"That is what remains of my own estate," he said.

*   *   *

Artists and critics continue to tear and split hairs over the "new" art, futurism, modernism, and the other "isms." But there is a young sculptor on the Left Bank who works quietly day to day, following his own intuition and, incidentally, building up what is probably one of the most significant schools in and out of the studios.

The young pathfinder is Roy van Auken Sheldon, who has given to his modern tendencies a personal character that has resulted in some sculpture of not only rare poesy, but distinctly Sheldonesque individuality as well. He has just completed a small study entitled "Maternity," which is an excellent example of his work. Others of his more recent studies are "Fatigue," showing a laborer seizing a moment's respite from his toil, and "Jazz Fantastique," which expresses the barbaric rhythm of the jazz age.

Along with his tangible creations, Mr. Sheldon finds time to evolve his own particular theory of "monumental sculpture" which has already attracted considerable attention. The idea is based on the assumption that the modern American skyscraper forms an ideal base for a gigantic sculpture of heroic proportions which, properly placed, would make of the edifice a colossal monument of aesthetic as well as commercial significance.

*   *   *

Neither England nor America can boast the equivalent of the French concierge. He is a hybrid character somewhere between a caretaker and a master of ceremonies. His importance to the community (particularly the building under his own domain) simply cannot be overestimated. And nobody realizes this more fully than himself!

It was none other than Ethel Mortlock, the celebrated English portrait artist, who recently convinced me of the extent of the concierge's power. I had called upon Miss Mortlock in her studio. (By the way, she is middle-aged, and a sight to behold! Fat, messy, and dressed in a brocaded satin affair, and adorned with many trinkets.)

"You see that distinguished gentleman?" she said as she pointed to an unfinished portrait reclining in one corner of her studio, within speaking distance of a life-size likeness of His Highness the Prince of Wales, and a half-dozen other notables. "That senatorial-looking personage is our concierge!" she continued, amused at my wonderment.

It seems that Miss Mortlock's companion, an elderly French woman who fluttered around with a purple velvet tam perched jauntily on one ear, recently had become engaged in "words" with her concierge over some apparent incivility. In the denunciation which followed, the concierge was referred to as "Voleur!" This was altogether too much, and as a result, there was an immediate severance of diplomatic relations.

At her wit's end for some means of restoring amity, the artist finally offered to paint the concierge's portrait. Needless to say, he at once capitulated in a radiance of smiles, and Miss Mortlock reports that Anglo-French relations are once more flourishing happily at her address.

December 18, 1924 – Some time during the past few weeks, a magic wand must have waved over Paris!

For there has sprung up in all parts of the city, bits of Christmas fairyland and the most marvelous sights imaginable. And *petits* Jean and Marie, like their little brothers and sisters in other lands, are in "the seventh heaven" of bliss!

Inside the great building, one finds even more dazzling sights. Galloping horses which prance back and forth beside miniature racing cars, cows which romp roguishly while tiny bells tinkle at their throats, and magic fish ponds in which sad-eyed fish swim rhythmically about to the strains of a tinkling xylophone until the young angler finally hooks them.

From early morning until long after the lights have begun to twinkle along the boulevards, Paris hurries busily along its way preparing for a *Joyeux Noël* and *Bonne Année!*

December 25, 1924 – Not all of Paris' holiday shopping is done in the *magasins* or shops. This time of the year finds the boulevards adorned with what would probably be tolerated in no other city in the world of the same pretentions as Paris –lines of hawkers are rigging up little wooden shacks along the Grands Boulevards. In another few days, fat, red-faced old women and shrewd-eyed men will be tempting the crowds with dazzling displays of Christmas and New Year's gifts. New Year's Day is the big gift-exchanging day in France. There is a special name for presents given on this day. They are called *étrennes.* Christmas is observed more particularly as a religious festival.

No Frenchman would think of letting Christmas be ushered in except with the midnight Mass and *Réveillon.* Seats are reserved in all the great churches, and the eager crowds who will occupy the unreserved sections begin lining up three hours before midnight. For it is the midnight Mass that heralds to the French the greatest of all religious festivals – *Noël.*

There is a great deal of hushed coughing, whispering, scraping of feet, and re-arranging of chairs and kneeling-benches. Just as the church clock chimes the eventful hour, the first soft strains from the organ flood the dim church.

The candles have been lighted. Slowly through the great sacristy gate files the colorful procession led by a gorgeously robed priest bearing the Host aloft. The male choir takes up the age-old Christmas hymns. Here and there in the vast cathedral, a bent old man or woman adds a cracked, feeble voice to the swelling chorus, heralding the birth of the Savior.

No more beautiful Christmas carol was ever conceived than the old French hymn, Noël!

By one o'clock the services are ended. Slowly the crowds pass out of the historic temples and through the narrow winding streets to their homes, or perhaps to their favorite cafés, for something to drink and the exchange of good wishes.

In other parts of Paris, strangely different scenes are enacted. Hundreds of revelers gather in Montmartre and along the boulevards for a night of feasting and dancing. While waiters scurry in and out bearing trays, and the jazz orchestras outdo themselves in syncopated symphonies, the merry throngs likewise exchange good wishes. In the Latin Quarter, students from every corner of the world bend over their *cafés crèmes* and exchange dreams while the great day dawns.

January 1, 1925 – A myriad of fantastic birds of gigantic proportions hover lightly in position ready for flight at the vast Grand Palais.

France's ninth great international aviation show is on, and the cream of the world's aircraft has been assembled in the spacious galleries which are crowded each day with admiring enthusiasts.

The amazing strides which the industry has made are shown most graphically by the exhibit of the Air Union. Here may be found one of the huge passenger planes which fly the air between Paris and London. A steady stream of visitors passes through it, admiring the cozy little passenger compartments. But perhaps the *dernier cri* in passenger accommodations is found in the great Farman ship with its brocaded salons and old blue velour upholstery.

However, one must not gather from this that the great air lanes are to be given over entirely to pleasure craft. The formidable bombing ships and trim little scouting planes should make nations pause long before going to war once more. Besides France herself, England, Holland, and Italy are represented at the show.

First day visitors were delighted with the opportunity to take a "whirl through the air" in a great swerving plane, from which they viewed the vast moving panorama with the "Eiffel Tower" and "Arc de Triomphe," and the "Tuileries" whirling by in rapid succession. And the surprising thing about it all was that they were alighted in exactly the same spot as that from which they had embarked two minutes before!

January 29, 1925 – "Not modesty, but scorn."

Such is the scathing announcement which greets the caller at the door to Cheever Dunning's humble little studio at the top of a narrow flight of stairs, just off the Rue Notre Dame des Champs.

The poet will tell you that it is not his scrawl. And, as a matter of fact, Cheever Dunning's attitude towards the world he writes about is far from scornful. True, he counsels in "The Hermit" to "hide thee by the roadside out of sight." But, in the next breath, he adds that, to himself, human association is vital.

Men have a right to scan the poetry that is put before them, he will tell you. If it is obscure, let them ask the poet, "Is your involved style due to inability to handle great subjects simply? Or do you wish to throw a glamorous haze about the commonplace? Both are legitimate queries.

Perhaps the most recent of Dunning's verse to appear in Paris is the group of twelve short poems in the *Transatlantic Review* for last November. He is now

Cheever Dunning
(sketch by Herman Foster)

conceiving a series of poetic translations, but managed to find a few spare moments to pose the other evening for Herman Foster, a neighboring Quarterite, who turned out a remarkable sketch.

* * *

The Jolly Dogs, under the leadership of M. Galy, have decided that hot dogs would do much to raise the aesthetic standards of life in Montparnasse. And so they have arranged to open what will be known as Jack's Quick Lunch at No. 127 Boulevard Montparnasse. *Vernissage* to be January 31.

* * *

Three Mountain Press announces Gertrude Stein's *The Making of Americans* is in the offing. The work, part of which has appeared in the *Transatlantic Review*, will be turned out in four to six volumes.

On the presses at the moment is Robert McAlmon's *Distinguished Air*, described as "three long short stories of post-war life in Berlin, dealing with social misfits and neurotic cases with an unastounded realism."

February 7, 1925 – An hilarious little travesty was enacted on the romantic Ile St. Louis in the heart of Paris the other day, on which all the good citizens gravely assembled to sacrifice their little island for the payment of the war debt to America. The first act depicts President Doumergue, the American ambassador, and an economic expert, arranging the details for the transfer of the island. The expert is not easily persuaded that the island is actually worth as much as the debt. However, he is finally convinced when the names of Voltaire, Baudelaire, and others (all former citizens) are recalled to him.

The treaty is signed. But alas, the burghers will have none of the arrangements worked out by their representatives. There is a revolt.

Act two shows the siege of the island at its climax, with the valiant citizens bravely defending their birthright. Suddenly, St. Louis himself descends upon the scene to assist his beloved Lucovisians in the struggle to retain their island. The day is saved!

The piece is now being printed. It will be sent to Senator Borah with the compliments of the pious islanders.

February 14, 1925 – *The Artist's Cinderella*
To the Cinderella who can slip her dainty foot into a tiny suede slipper which

rests in the Latin Quarter, will go the honor of serving as model for a huge portrait of the queenly Mrs. Frank Gould, wife of the famous American financier.

And thereby hangs a tale.

Pilides Costa, the young Greek artist, was commissioned several months ago to paint the portrait of Mrs. Gould. It was to be finished in April.

Meanwhile, the young artist has been working busily at his little studio just off the Boulevard Montparnasse and now has the work finished – save for the two dainty feet.

The subject has found time to pose but four times for her portrait. Now she has left for her villa in southern France and the painter has been unable to find a model in all the Quarter with feet as small as those of Mrs. Gould.

Only a brown suede slipper remains for him to work from. And the young lady whose foot would fit it, could bring joy once more into the life of Pilides Costa.

*   *   *

A Masquerader in Montparnasse

Montparnasse (and its artistic habitués) awoke one morning last week with a start, scratched its head, and began to wonder whether it had been talking to a certain young lady who had become more or less well-known on its boulevards.

With a shock which resounded throughout the entire Left Bank, the news broke that *La Garçonne,* often seen in the student cafés where she attracted much attention, was in reality Monsieur X, a deserter from the French Army, who shortly after the war assumed this disguise to escape prison.

Now, with the recent enforcement of the Amnesty Law pardoning political offenders, Monsieur X decided to abandon his feminine wardrobe and step forward in his true role as the husband of the woman with whom *La Garçonne* was known to live.

Electrolysis, according to the masquerader, solved the matter of a beard during his feminine existence. A few months were sufficient to provide a hair bob of the most approved style. But the womanly walk, gesture, and voice were matters that required one year before Monsieur X felt that he could trust himself to step forward into the world.

La Garçonne no longer appears along the boulevards of Montparnasse. But she will long remain a memory, and there are those who are still wondering what confidences they may have entrusted to the dashing young woman during her several years' existence in their midst.

February 26, 1925 – Marguerite will not stand enraptured midst a myriad of pink and white tissue paper flowers while a red velvet Méphistofélès whispers seductive messages into her ear. Nor will Dr. Faustus be revealed poring over huge tomes in a book-lined studio, when the curtain is rung up on the premiere of Gémier's *Faust* at the Odéon next month. The piece, which is by MM. Louis Forest and Charles Robert Dumas, is based on Goethe's version of *Faust,* with German music of the fourteenth and fifteenth centuries.

Walter René-Fuerst, the modern young master of *décor,* has, with a few telling strokes, evoked an expressionistic setting for the masterpiece that is as vivid as it is simple. "A minimum of minutiae with a maximum of expression," Fuerst told us, as he modestly went over the designs for us at his Left Bank studio the other afternoon.

America is still unknown to this young modernist of the theatre, but he is far from unknown in America. He has already been fittingly introduced with some acclaim through the columns of *Theatre Arts.* And when M. Gémier took his Odéon troupe across the ocean a few months ago, Broadway was introduced to Fuerst *décor* through *Le Bourgeois Gentilhomme, L'Homme et Ses Fantômes,* and *Taming of the Shrew.*

The artist's latest book on stagecraft is due in Paris within the fortnight. Meanwhile, he has seized a moment from his busy labors to sketch a caricature of himself.

Walter René-Fuerst
(self-caricature)

February 28, 1925 – France, of all the powers, with the possible exception of Italy, was sure to preserve the ceremonious dignity of her *déjeuner* and *dîner*!

Imagine, then, the terrific shock we received the other day when, on crossing the seething Place de l Opéra, we suddenly came head on to that abomination of epicures – the Automat lunch!

Neatly tucked into a little hole in the wall, as though still fearful of the consequences of its daring, the little lunchroom looked fantastically out of place on the Grands Boulevards.

Still incredulous, we investigated further. Sure enough – the Automat lunch of the most deadly Chicago species. Rows of little glass cases into which slugs were breathlessly thrust in order that a sandwich, slice of pie, or plate of beans might mysteriously slide out before the hungry shopper. Huge containers before which thirsty multitudes stood waiting for a chance to insert a coin in order that their rations of coffee, tea, or chocolate might flow forth without delay.

No English and Americans filled the place. The breathless lunchers were Frenchmen for the most part. And we sadly realized that the millennium has come! France, too, has fallen victim to the New World efficiency!

*　　*　　*

Canoeists and the Seine

What's to become of those gruesome French novels that invariably contained at least one harrowing scene where the heroine clapped a thin white hand over her eyes and then made a frenzied leap from the trail of a Paris bridge into the treacherous waters of the Seine? The police have ruled that nobody can jump into the Seine hereafter without a little white slip of paper duly signed by the Prefecture of Police!

Ask Lieutenant G. C. G. Smyth, the bold young Canadian who is paddling his own canoe from America to Rome and is just now passing through Paris. He will tell you that he was obliged to make several attempts to secure the little white slip before he could coolly fling his flimsy craft over his head and leap from the Pont des Invalides into the most celebrated river in the world.

A great crowd had been disappointed earlier in the week when the preparations for the dive were suddenly forestalled by the arrival of the *gendarmes.* Last Tuesday, however, the little paper was waved in their faces, and they willingly assisted in the preparations for the event which hundreds had gathered to witness.

"It wasn't very warm," is all that the young canoeist is reported to have said when he had clambered out of the icy water into his canoe and paddled ashore for a change of clothes. He will leave this week for Rome by way of the Seine, the French canals, and the Mediterranean, where he will collect first prize in the 10,000 franc stakes.

April 2, 1925 – Sylvia Beach invited a group of writers and newspapermen to her little bookshop Shakespeare and Company, in the Rue de l'Odéon, the other afternoon, to hear the first gramophone record of James Joyce reading from *Ulysses.*

59

There was something of a thrill about hearing the patron saint of the little shop whose walls are hung with several of his portraits, fill the room with his clear, ringing voice. Incidentally, the novelist selected a portion of his book to read which should clear New York customs without difficulty.

Joyce, Miss Beach tells us, recently underwent his fourth eye operation, and there are prospects of a fifth. Small wonder that he is in a highly nervous condition and can see but few of his friends.

Sylvia Beach
(sketch by Fred Pye)

April 11, 1925 – Ants have their soviets and a communistic form of society that would do credit to the human world, Dr. William Morrison Wheeler, the eminent American entomologist, stated the other afternoon, delivering one of his lectures at the Sorbonne.

For example, the busy little insects are never troubled with the problem of what to do with the profiteer. He doesn't exist. Those whose work it is to collect food, place it in a common storehouse for each to use freely as he needs. More than that, of course, the loyal ants are not expected to take.

As for birth control, here again, the little crawlers have solved their own problems. When the food supply is low, the birth rate is automatically low. Propagation is the function of a particular group in the colony, the other castes having to do with fighting the battles of the clan, procuring food, or perhaps merely decorating the miniature settlement with their beauty. Though drones, we are told, are in disrepute among their fellows. Yes, an interesting subject, says Dr. Wheeler.*

*   *   *

High up on one of the loftiest peaks of Montmartre, in a shadow of the great dome of the *Sacré Coeur,* lies a little square modestly hemmed in on all sides by rows of ancient houses, one of which bears the inscription, La Mère Catherine.

The other evening, as the latch of the little door turned after a breathless climb up the interminable steps of the Butte Montmartre, a wave of youthful gaiety burst out upon the silent square under the tranquil stars. A fragment of the great city down below had stolen quietly up to the tiny retreat for a few hours of feasting and merriment.

Between the rude tables under low rafters and soft lights, a handful of waiters hurried back and forth, while two Frenchmen twanged gaily upon their guitars over in the corner. On all sides, a flood of happy conversation. One heard no English here.

A little later the tables were cleared and foaming *bocks* and *cafés filtrés* appeared, while the room slowly filled with the haze of cigarette smoke. Here and there a shiny-eyed young French couple extricated themselves from the tables crowded in friendly proximity, and danced between the rows as well as in an incredibly small space at one side.

Towards midnight, the guests began to drift slowly away. As we stepped out in the little square once more, there twinkled far below us the lights of the great city – Paris!

April 16, 1925 – Should you be strolling along the serene Rue Vicomte on the Left Bank one of these afternoons and hear a mighty crash of chords overhead, you will know that Colin McPhee, the young Canadian composer, is at his Steinway, perhaps tossing off a concerto or two without the aid of a symphony orchestra.

There is a harmonic glow about the McPhee compositions, particularly his recently completed *Sarabande,* which Clara Rabinowitch is to introduce to Paris at her recital at the Salle Erard next week. Incidentally, two of the composer's concertos have been performed by the Toronto Symphony Orchestra, and the similar organization at Baltimore.

*Editor's Note: Many years later, when P.S. lectured on journalism at leading schools and colleges in the U.S., he would tell student audiences how the *Tribune* had sent him to get this story from Dr. Wheeler. At the start of the interview he realized that he had not the slightest idea of the meaning of the term "entomology," but succeeded in getting his story without giving his ignorance away!

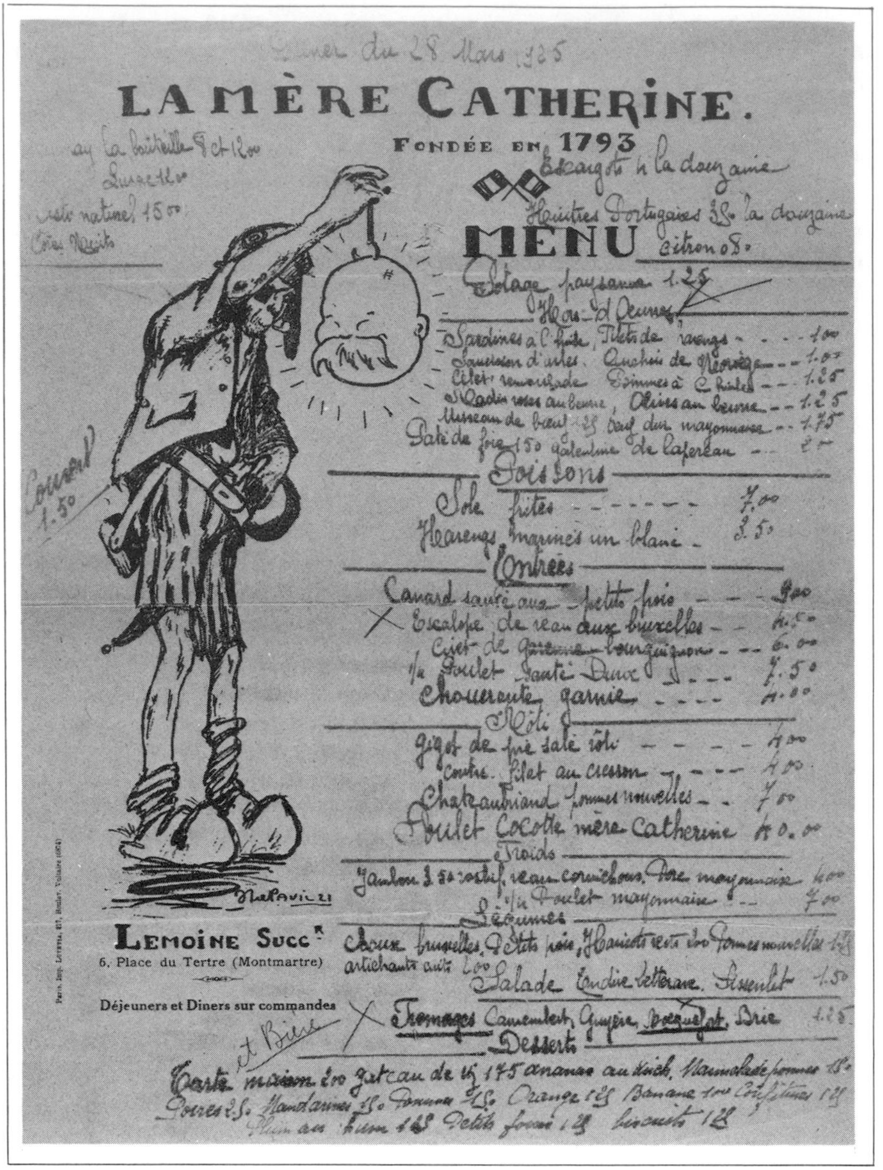

concertos have been performed by the Toronto Symphony Orchestra, and the similar organization at Baltimore.

* * *

Norman Bel Geddes is the second of the distinguished group to find their way to the Left Bank in preparation for the coming presentation of the De Acosta version of *Jeanne D'Arc*. Eva Le Gallienne, whose acting quite equals her father's poetry, is slated for the title role.

Norman Bel Geddes

Mr. Geddes' *décor* for the play is said to have been conceived with the spacious stage of a New York theatre in mind, and consequently will require a bit of condensing for the Paris production, which M. Gémier of the Odéon will direct.

* * *

D. F. Meziki is busy these days on mural decorations at the British building of the Decorative Arts exhibit. If "Mizi" is as good on walls as he is on canvas, the British exposition has nothing to lose. The artist has just taken a studio off the Rue Notre Dame des Champs and will be in Paris most of the summer.

* * *

Eric Scott, whose etching propensities carried him off to Oxford, England, has just returned with the fruits of two weeks' work. Christ Church, Pembroke, New, and several other colleges supplied him with a wealth of materials, he says.

April 25, 1925 – Count and Countess Tolstoi, relatives of the famous novelist, are the latest of the Russian nobility to embark upon a business career in Paris.

But instead of directing a Russian tea room, singing at a Russian cabaret, or fashioning smart clothes for the *beau monde,* they have turned to a field that has fascinated them both since childhood – horseback riding.

In the Rue d'Orléans in Auteuil, a short distance from the spacious Bois de Boulogne, may be found their smart new riding academy, together with a score of beautiful mounts from Arabia, Morocco, and other far countries. If you are interested, Colonel Huebner, former officer of the Russian Army, will modestly take a few turns around the arena and put one of the handsome thoroughbreds through a few of its high school accomplishments.

"I was instructed in riding ever since I was a child," said the Count the other afternoon, to which the Countess (formerly Eleanor McCormick of America) added that as a girl she too had made use of her father's stables, considered among the finest in America.

And so it was perfectly natural that the Tolstois should turn to horses as a means of livelihood. Surely the old writer himself would be the last to object to members of his family setting out to work for their living.

May 14, 1925 – Dynamic dissonances, fantastic fugues, writhing rhythms. One sometimes suspects they constitute the entire cosmos of the day's musical torch-

Grégoire Gourevitch
(sketch by D. F. Meziki)

bearers – particularly those of the latter who grace the melodic sector of the Left Bank.

Which is quite as it should be, so long as an occasional Beethoven or Chopin of yesterday is not entirely forgotten in the outpourings of musical modernism.

One Montparno who reveals a curious dual sympathy for the Left and Right of music, is Grégoire Gourevitch, the young Russian pianist. A product of his country's Imperial Conservatory, he now studies at the Paris Conservatoire.

Just to show his classical-modern tastes, the pianist is giving a recital at the Salle des Concerts du Conservatoire next week, for which the program lists the composers as follows: Beethoven, Saint-Saëns, Chopin, Borodine, Scriabin, Debussy, Prokofiev.

The impressionistic sketch of Gourevitch is by D. F. Meziki, also of Montparnasse.

*　　*　　*

Ulysseans of the Latin as well as the other three Quarters will be relieved to learn that James Joyce is on the road to recovery following his eye operation. His friend Sylvia Beach says, however, that it will be some time before he turns to his writing again.

May 30, 1925 – Arthur Symons, the Cornish poet, was one of those gathered about the log fire in Sylvia Beach's bookshop the other morning. The author of *Charles Baudelaire, Days and Nights, Silhouettes,* and a host of others, is busily making plans for his fourthcoming book on Eleonora Duse, the Italian tragedienne.

He tells us it is but half completed although already accepted for publication in America where it will be brought out this fall. Warm friendships with both the actress and her friend Gabriel d'Annunzio are the basis for what should be an interesting piece of work. In view of the author's other personal friendships with Réjane, Sarah Bernhardt, and Ellen Terry, his estimate of the Duse should be as accurate as it is enlightening.

*　　*　　*

The United States Students' and Artists' club, 107 Boulevard Raspail, will wind up its Sunday evening musicals with a flourish tomorrow night, to resume them again in the fall. Miss Frances Morgan will be the recitalist, using her rare Amati violin.

For the past ten days I have walked across Paris every morning at three o'clock. My route takes me along the tinseled Rue du Faubourg Montmartre, through Les

Halles, the city markets, across the glistening black Seine at the Pont Neuf, and into the sleepy Latin Quarter.

Three a.m. comes the closest to being the dividing line between two Paris days. At midnight the twenty-four hour cycle is far from finished. Those last three hours provide the romantic climax without which it could never be called a Paris day.

Three in the morning finds the Rue du Faubourg Montmartre flashing with the lights of the night clubs, swarming with cruising taxis ready to take the exhausted revelers home. The subways, trams, and buses have given up long ago. Here and there a *poule de luxe* flashes a dazzling smile and draws her ample mink wrap around her neck. Her business is to catch the lonely celebrant who has by some miracle escaped Venus all evening.

The cheery optimism of these maidens is a subject of perpetual wonderment. A steady succession of curt shakes of the head, smiling refusals, or mere icy silence, seems not to dampen their good spirits one whit. They are always ready with a pleasant "Au revoir, monsieur" or a laughing "Ecoute, mon chéri ..."

The shadows grow blacker down towards Les Halles. The peasants and laborers of the markets are clattering busily about in the half-light getting ready their products for the kitchens of Paris.

All traffic has been re-routed and the converging streets are piled high with beautiful green and white pyramids of fresh cauliflower, green and orange prisms of carrots, and symmetrical mounds of turnips, cabbages, and other produce fresh from the soil.

A bundle of rags suddenly stirs in the shadow of old St. Eustache. It is an old hag gnawing at a loaf of bread. Beside her is a half empty bottle of cheap white wine. They say these wretches are positively happy in their squalor so long as they are ensured enough bread and wine at odd hours of the day and night.

From under the ancient church, another old woman climbs the stairs to the sidewalk. She is dragging a basket of apples which she bargained for at the fruit stand located in the basement. Across the street, a tattered gang of black-moustached workers crowds about the only hot dog stand I have ever seen in Paris.

For two francs they receive a huge chunk of fresh bread, slashed down the middle and filled with sausage and French fried potatoes. They wander off in all directions munching contentedly at their collation.

Here comes a party of American sightseers. Evening wraps and white shirt fronts. A handsome young Arab in filthy corduroys smiles at the youngest of the girls. She smiles back and helps herself to a fresh carrot from his stock. Her escort slips a five franc note to the boy. They smile and pass on.

June, 1925 – There is a schism in the ranks of Montparnasse ... A new group of Left Bank intelligentsia has sprung up in the shadow of the Sorbonne, and bids fair to sweep all before it.

The first children's library in the history of France was recently opened.

Halfway down the little Rue Boutebrie on the edge of the Latin Quarter, stands L'Heure Joyeuse, gathering place for the Left Bank embryo book worms established by the Book Foundation of America. Scores of youngsters assemble every day for literary investigations, their subjects ranging from *Mother Goose* to *Treasure Island* – all in French, of course.

The young readers who visited the place in the early days were thrown into a frenzy of delight. It was the first time they had seen so many books together outside of a bookshop. And when they learned that they could actually handle and read the beautiful new volumes, the librarian told me they became almost beyond control!

Little Mlle Perrine Morel is one of the leaders of intellectual thought at L'Heure Joyeuse. In fact, she recently decided that articulate expression of her devotion to the new group could only be found through her facile brush.

As a result her *chef d'oeuvre*, in the form of a colorful, modernistic fresco, appeared at the library recently, announcing the Thursday afternoon story hour.

*   *   *

There is one ceremony of everyday life that is meticulously observed by the French. It is that of eating. Business may come and business may go, poverty may come and poverty may go, but eating still remains a fine art with the Frenchman, whatever his station in life. The sooner the visitor from foreign shores learns to regard it likewise, the happier he will be.

There are no Maison Lyons establishments to facilitate the process of taking sustenance. And an American cafeteria with its efficient "two-minute" service, would render the Frenchman aghast. Eating is the one thing we are obliged to do as we remain on earth, he says. *Alors,* why not make it a leisurely, enjoyable event?

And he forthwith proceeds to throw an *éclat* about the most modest repast that, somehow, makes of it a distinguished occasion. *Soupe, hors d'oeuvres, pièce de résistance, légume, fromage, dessert,* and *café noir,* must all be given the proper position in the sequence of the meal. To alter the order would be disastrous. Meat and potatoes together? Ah, oui, Monsieur, if you wish, but why not meat first, and, when that is finished, potatoes?

Wine or beer of course. It would not be a complete meal without *boisson* of some sort. And you will see the humblest laborer draw out his bottle of *vin rouge* in order that his noon meal may preserve something of its historical dignity.

Only breakfast is immune from this pomp and circumstance. But I half suspect that the reason for this is that the Frenchman has not yet fully recovered by that time from luncheon and dinner of the day before!

June 6, 1925 – Sam's Place has long been one of the favorite gathering places for Anglo-Saxon visitors to Paris. Situated in the heart of the city on the Boulevard des Italiens, its tempting English breakfasts, American griddle cakes, Boston baked beans, ham and eggs, and ice cream sodas have served to cheer many a downhearted visitor whose nostalgia has developed nearly to the bursting point as a result of an unsatisfied longing for a taste of his own home fare.

June 12, 1925 – Montparnasse is staging its own Decorative Arts Exposition these warm summer afternoons and evenings. Should you stroll past the Café du Dôme, for example, you will see a decorative *ensemble* gathered on the *terrasse* that is quite as picturesque, if not as esoteric, as the Place de la Concorde show. Sketch books and portfolios are much in evidence, to say nothing of foaming *demis* and frothing *bocks*.

Some of the Quarterites who were basking close by were: Cheever Dunning, the American poet, Nina Hamnett, the British portrait artist whose show is now running at the *Galerie Sacre du Printemps* in the Rue Cherche Midi, David Darling, American painter, Sergey Maslenikoff, whose hand-painted shawls are the despair of the feminine sector, "Lady Betty" Foster, who directs concerts, and "Mizi" himself.

*   *   *

Ivan Opfer, the portraitist, is about to begin work on two studies of Scott Fitzgerald and Pierre Loving. The former recently passed through the Quarter on his return from Côte d'Azur. The latter has a comprehensive review of the Paris stage in a recent number of *Drama*.

*   *   *

A familiar face to reappear in the Quarter was that of Buck Warshawsky, back from Mallorca ... "the most beautiful place in the world," says he.

Buck is busily making arrangements for his coming exposition at Anderson's in New York, which will open October 1. A number of his Mallorcan canvases will figure in the show.

*   *   *

And now that intrepid Stage Society of London announces that it will do James Joyce's *Exiles* next month. It was this group, it will be remembered, which dodged the censors back in 1902 and exposed Shaw's *Mrs. Warren's Profession* to a gasping public.

Apropos of the production of his opus in Paris last fall, and of the raising of the ban by his fellow countrymen, Shaw writes, "I could have reached the venerable age of sixty-eight in the odour of sanctity, but the Lord Chamberlain let loose that terrible play written thirty years ago. A play which I was depending on him to keep locked up so that I might end my days in peace."

* * *

Cecil Deighton, one of the Quarter's trustiest Britishers, has put by his *café crème* and crossed the Channel homeward bound, after nearly a year on the Left Bank. He has one more year at Oxford and promises to do what he can to stem the tide of the Oxford bags.

* * *

There is one more vacant chair on the Boulevard Montparnasse these days, and Broadway is feting the return of her prodigal prodigy, young Mr. Norman Bel Geddes, *enfant terrible* of the American theatre.

Paris, it will be remembered, was rendered virtually *hors de combat* last month by the Geddes production of the de Acosta play *Jeanne de'Arc.* Pulsating mobs swept across the stage with all the colorful harmony of a Florentine canvas, creating something of a thrill, and the wiseacres agreed that the Geddes setting and *décor* were the individual triumph of the entire venture.

An obstreperous mob, innumerable costume designs, and a colossal production, however, were not too much for the young producer. At any rate, he could usually be found of an afternoon dreamily surveying the passing show of Montparnasse over a *café crème* or *apértif.* As to who will succeed to the chair, nobody knows. Elmer Rice, the young American playwright and a Quarterite for the nonce, has been suggested.

* * *

July 25, 1925 – Swaying lanterns . . . countless bands and orchestras . . . gay dancers . . . scurrying *garçons* carrying huge trays of *bocks* and *demis* . . . and all over, the fluttering tricolor of the Third Republic!

Such was the throbbing scene that was enacted in the middle of practically every square and boulevard intersection of Paris last week in commemoration of the one hundred and thirty-sixth anniversary of the fall of the Bastille. From high noon on Saturday until the dawn of Wednesday, July 15, the city was given over to continuous revelry. Business was at a standstill, save for those whose duty it was to cater to the revelers.

We paused Sunday evening for a moment while the festivities were in full swing at a corner in the drab first *arrondissement.* A little orchestra, whose work was far more enthusiastic than it was artistic, poured forth the popular street songs and dances that the people have come to consider their own. Beneath the strings of colored lanterns stretched across the narrow street from café to café, swayed lighthearted revelers. Grey-haired old men who looked like teamsters cut nimble capers with old women. Swaggering young boys dancing at breakneck speed with the dark-eyed belles of the neighborhood.

The grand military review up the Champs Elysées was followed by affecting ceremonies at the Tomb of the Unknown Soldier.

July 31, 1925 – The Chair on the Boulevard doesn't get much chance to gather dust these days ... and it's Frank Harris himself who holds forth, for the nonce, in Montparnasse.

The waggish *raconteur,* whose autobiography is still costing the censors their sleep, may be seen of a summer's evening, serenely basking in the glare of a Left Bank café, while an admiring throng of Quarterites listen to memories of Oscar Wilde and all the rest.

Meanwhile, the autobiography continues to travel jauntily along the boulevards, tucked snugly under intelligentsia arms and resting carelessly on café tables. It is said to make the notorious *Ulysses* look like *The Vicar of Wakefield.*

Frank Harris
(sketch by Arthur Zaidenberg)

70

Arthur Zaidenberg, a new arrival in the Quarter and former art editor of *Public Opinion,* dashed off today's sketch of Harris while the other was reminiscing the other evening.

*   *   *

H. L. Cook is back for his sixteenth visit to the Left Bank, and says he is still writing poetry. Which is what a great many are doing, although all do not have their brain children published in *Harper's, The Nation, Poetry, Spectator, London Chap Book,* and the *Westminster Gazette.*

Cook says he will continue to write only for the magazine *World* at the present. Robert Frost once told him that no poet should publish a book before he reached the age of thirty.

*   *   *

And still they are begging for copies of *Ulysses.* Sylvia Beach tells us the sixth edition of the Joyce opus is due off the presses tomorrow. Meanwhile, his health somewhat improved, the author is occasionally seen on the Left Bank, his last literary appearance being in *The Criterion* for July, where he is represented by a *Fragment of an Unpublished Work.*

Sylvia believes that she is entitled to a well-earned rest and is leaving Monday for the Savoie – not to write a book, she says. The bookshop will remain open, however, until its guiding spirit returns about September 1.

*   *   *

Elmer Rice, the intrepid young American playwright, found the Left Bank so attractive that he took an apartment for himself, Mrs. Rice, and the children, and remained most of the spring. Now he is leaving for Switzerland to spend the rest of the summer, until he is called back to Broadway this fall to assist in the staging of his new play, *The Subway.*

If the new opus has half the success of *On Trial, The Adding Machine,* and a few other Rice dramas, the playwright will doubtless be back soon on a de luxe cruise around the world, like all the rest. Meanwhile, he says he likes America best because the writers for the theatre and their co-workers are permitted to try about anything they like in the way of experiments.

August 14, 1925 – Sylvia Beach writes to Mlle Myrsive Moschos, who is so ably managing the shop for her, that she is having a splendid time in Savoie, and that she only regrets that the new edition of *Ulysses* has been delayed.

*   *   *

71

George Antheil, the pianist composer, is going to Tunis next week in search of new rhythms. He says he is interested in no music but the ancient African and the modern European. There are whispers, too, that his opera will be played in London this winter.

*　　*　　*

James Joyce, after a long sea voyage for his health, is once more back in France. He is staying with his family at Arachon, Gironde.

August 28, 1925 – Now that Elmer Rice has packed up his Underwood and hied himself off to prepare for the much heralded arrival of *The Subway* on Broadway, Melpoméne's Montparnassian mantle has fallen upon young J. Gordon Amend.

Gordon looks like a product of Harvard's Baker's 47 Workshop, but he says the only bakers he knows are the ones who make croissants. At any rate, the latter delicacies seem to furnish him inspiration aplenty, with the result that he says he will stay and write plays indefinitely.

Which would not be remarkable, were it not that the producers seem to like Amend's opuses well enough to occasionally ring up the curtain on one. For example, *The Inghams* saw the footlights in Boston last year and may see Paris

Gordon Amend
(sketch by Arthur Zaidenberg)

this season. *Pandora's Box* will be danced in New York this year, it already having taken tangible form in Pierre Loving's volume of *Ten Minute Plays.*

And now Gordon says the great American psychological drama is in the offing. It is an unnamed, three act affair dealing with mother love.

Arthur Zaidenberg, one of the newer Quarterites, did today's sketch of the playwright ... an excellent likeness, marcelle and all.

* * *

During the customary migration of the Quarter's brush-workers, a small army of their brother artists who work on ladders and scaffolds have been busy keeping alive the old traditions.

The paint is flying hot and heavy at the United States Students' and Artists' Club on the Boulevard Raspail, and when Canon Stimpson announces open house this fall, the artists are promised completely refurbished quarters. At the American Art Association, also recently repainted, order once more is restored, and the resultant elegance is enough to frighten any ordinary Left Banker.

* * *

Ethel Mortlock, the English portrait artist, sends word from Dieppe, that she is in the throes of an extended vacation, and has learned to perform cowboy stunts on a loose-saddle in astonishing fashion. Her portrait of Carrie Swain Wisler hung in the last Spring Salon.

* * *

Baskerville, whose name is synonymous with covers for *Theatre, Vanity Fair, Vogue,* and other magazines, left the Quarter last Monday to return to his stomping ground in Gotham.

Charles Baskerville, Jr., has acquired a new pseudonym since we last saw him and now is known as "Top Hat" above which *nom de plume,* he writes accounts of Broadway after twilight for the *New Yorker.*

* * *

The London typesetters have arisen in righteous indignation at certain passages in the latest James Joyce opus and flatly refuse to have a hand in its publication.

Meanwhile, the *Calendar,* which had contracted to print the chapters including scarlet passages in its October issue, is tearing its hair and wondering what the author of *Ulysses* will say. "According to manuscript or not at all," thunders Joyce ... and the intelligentsia wait with bated breath.

* * *

73

Ezra Pound is the author of a discussion of "Mr. Dunning's Poetry" in the current number of *Poetry*. Cheever Dunning has already made several bows in the *Transatlantic* as well as in *Poetry* and is to be included in a new fall anthology soon to appear.

* * *

That frantic Ballet Mécanique conceived by George Antheil, which had its first public audition earlier in the week, is to be repeated this afternoon for a small group of thrill-seekers. As Sylvia Beach says, "It simply picks you (up) and drops you down with a bang."

September 25, 1925 – The etchers have their Moret ... and the writers have Antibes.

At any rate, the little seaside city must be athrob with the literary lights that are reported as assembled there. There's Scott Fitzgerald and his wife, Floyd Dell, Max Eastman and his wife, as well as a score of others. Harold Cook, the young American poet, has just returned, and John Mosher, whose short stories appear in *Smart Set,* is said to be due within the week. Charles Brackett, author of *Week-End,* is heading the other way, to spend a brief period in the Antibes.

* * *

September 26, 1925 – Mysterious tales of strange messages from the great beyond kept Paris is a state of nervous apprehension during the recent week given over to the International Spiritistic Congress.

Ghostly visitors are startling enough in themselves, but when they are given the stamp of reality by the testimony of such eminent men as Sir Oliver Lodge, Camille Flammarion, and Sir Arthur Conan Doyle, it is small wonder that the public works itself up into a frenzy.

The last-mentioned gentleman was a distinguished visitor to Paris during the conference and consented to open the week's program with an address on spiritism illustrated with several alleged spirit photographs. Owing to a super-abundance of excitement, however, the lecture broke up in confusion and was given a second time later in the week.

Felicia Rudolphina Scatcherd, of London, former editor of the *Asiatic Review,* recounted the strange details of the super-normal photographs which she took in London just before leaving to attend the Congress.

One of the photographs, she declared, bears the ectoplasmic likeness of the late Sir William Crookes, the world-famous spiritist. The other reveals a similar likeness of a spirit body supposed to be that of Sir William Barrett. Both were shown on the screen by Sir Arthur Conan Doyle at his second public lecture at the Salle Wagram.

"Just before I left London," stated Miss Scatcherd, "I supervised the taking of actual photographs under conditions that permitted an accurate check of their authenticity." These "spirit photographs" were interpreted by some as indicating the desire of the departed spiritist leaders to get into communication with the Paris conference. Outstanding among the week's gatherings was a charming *soirée* given at her hotel by the beautiful Duchess of Hamilton, an ardent spiritist. Several eminent French scientists as well as several prominent British spiritists were also present. The duchess told me of a curious healing power which she had discovered herself to possess some time ago. In an effort to give relief to a sick friend, she recounted, she had resorted to spiritism and the power of psychic concentration. Shortly after, her friend, given relief, discovered that her watch had ceased to run at the moment when the duchess' treatment was being administered. The watch was taken to a jeweler for repairs and, after an examination, the latter declared that the difficulty was due to the timepiece having been subjected to an electrolyzing force!

October 10, 1925 – What with the lurid lyrics of the newest Joyce opus, which are appearing serially these days; the scarlet Beasley memoirs; the sex-sprinkled autobiography of Frank Harris; and a score of others, there are those who say our literature has come to a pretty pass... Though Sylvia Beach reports no decline in sales at her Left Bank bookshop.

But if you think it's a "pretty pass" in Paris, you will find it's a riot in little old New York, says Arthur Zaidenberg, a Quarterite of this year's vintage.

October 16, 1925 - "Who is Sylvia?" queries the great Schubert in one of his pensive songs. If Franz had lived on our own Left Bank, in our time, he never would have confessed ignorance on this score. Sylvia, as every good Quarterite will tell you, is the young lady who constitutes "Shakespeare" of Shakespeare and Company's little book shop in the Rue de l'Odéon.

It is Sylvia Beach who enjoys the reputation of being able to produce anything between two covers, from a copy of Chaucer to the latest literary outpouring of our contemporary *enfants terribles.* Her log fires are famous these drear days, and among those who occasionally stop to warm their hands before the little fireplace are James Joyce, Arthur Symons, Ernest Hemingway, Marsden Hartley, Robert McAlmon, George Antheil, Eugène Jolas, and a score of others.

It was about Shakespeare and Company that Robert Forrest Wilson wrote in a recent *Bookman:* "This bookshop disputes with a Paris café the honor of being the chief focus of American culture in France, if not in Europe."

Fred Pye dashed off today's sketch while Sylvia flitted from room to room. The subject looks rather tense — somebody just asked for a copy of the *Odyssey* by James Joyce.

October 25, 1925 – Word filters out that the impending number of *This Quarter* is to contain some "best seller" material in the shape of another tract by James Joyce, as well as some music by George Antheil.

* * *

Cheever Dunning, one of the Quarter's few poets, has just been awarded the twelfth annual Helen B. Levinson prize in New York, for best poem by an American. His *Four Winds* captured the judges' fancy. He is at the present time confined to the hospital, and the little studio in the Rue Notre Dame des Champs presents a forlorn appearance.

* * *

Help! Help!

Customs inspectors in New York Harbor have been so flooded with wayward copies of *Ulysses* nestling shyly in the bottoms of trunks and bags, that at least one of them has succumbed and is now a Joycean.

Shakespeare and Company report a letter from a recently departed Quarterite who claims he penetrated the customs line with several of the exiled copies. Upon announcing that he was acquainted with the author and possessed a certain knowledge of the latter's works, the homecomer succeeded in striking so responsive a chord in his examiner that he was obsequiously directed to pass through without even opening his luggage.

* * *

In Our Time by Ernest Hemingway is the latest opus to cause a flutter among the author's fellow Montparnos. The book was put on the stands just last Monday and is the target of literary bouquets tossed by Sherwood Anderson, Gilbert Seldes, Donald Ogden Stewart, Ford Madox Ford, Waldo Frank, and John Dos Passos.

* * *

Eugène Jolas, the Left Bank poet who is known for his writings in English, French, and German, is represented in the current number of *Creer,* by two short studies entitled *Sion* and *Notules.* The latter included "Matin sur le pont du carrousel," "Nocturne," and "Images."

October 30, 1925 – Which brings us to George Antheil ... that concentrated Left Bank composer, who recently returned from a hectic hunt for heathen hymns in darkest Africa. He sails next month for New York to fill an engagement with Paul Whiteman's syncopated symphonists.

*　　*　　*

The Nation devotes several pages in a recent issue to a discussion of James Joyce by Edwin Muir, whose article deals with "those young authors of today who are in the process of being established."

And speaking of Joyce, there are deep rumblings and the flash of lightning that seem to betoken a storm on the literary horizon.

Two Worlds which, we are told, is a "Literary Quarterly Devoted to the Increase of the Gaiety of Nations" published in New York by Samuel Roth, glibly announces that its first number contains not only a *New Unnamed Work* by Joyce, but has been jointly edited by Ford Madox Hueffer.

Which is all very nice, except that the two gentlemen declare they have never heard of the publication, and are anxious to know where Mr. Roth obtained permission to use their works and names.

November 1, 1925 – "Vegetables and jewelry, rightly displayed, have an equal amount of fascination."

Sings Robert McAlmon in this month's *Poetry.* The Left Bank poet has contributed several short pieces, but the song dealing with vegetables is probably the finest picture of Les Halles that you can see, unless you are willing to call around some bright morning at three.

November 6, 1925 – "How much wood would a woodcutter cut, if a woodcutter could cut ..."

As a matter of fact, Howard Simon can not only cut wood, but he can cut it in such an intriguing way as to entice many a blasé gallery-goer down into the *caveau* of the *Café Sélect,* Montparnasse, where some of his choicest pieces of work are now to be found on exhibition.

Simon is perhaps the only Quarterite to find his forte in wood-engraving, that virile medium that is as ultra modern as it is ancient. Several years in New York

Woodcut by Howard Simon

have prepared him to turn out some work that has brought hearty approval both at home and at hand.

The banks of the Seine, as today's reproduction indicates, are a favorite haunt of the artist and the engraving of the Pont Royal was only recently completed.

*   *   *

While the festivities were at their height at the Students' and Artists' weekly tea dance yesterday afternoon, something of a syncopated stampede was suddenly precipitated by so simple an occurrence as a taxi driving up to the door.

Out of the groaning coach, however, there slowly staggered one base drum, half a dozen horns, fiddles, and clarinets, and a raft of the little knickknacks with which the trap-drummers like to tease the steppers!

It was the Rowland Collegians in all their jazzy jubilance, suddenly dropped unannounced from nobody knows where, to offer their services for the weekly terpsichorean teas. Line forms to the right!

*   *   *

Paul Robeson, the distinguished American Negro actor, was a celebrated visitor to the Quarter this week. The actor (who thrilled his alma mater in his

78

undergraduate days by being picked by the Rutgers University football team to grace the All American eleven) was the honored guest at a tea given by Sylvia Beach and Adrienne Monnier, of Shakespeare and Company's bookshop and Les Amis des Livres respectively.

Robeson sang several of his beloved Negro spirituals which he is to sing for America on a transcontinental tour this winter. He says he will then likely return to the stage, where he achieved such success in *All God's Chilluns Got Wings* and *The Emperor Jones.*

Adrienne Monnier

November 20, 1925 – ... and speaking of pounds," writes a fair correspondent anent the recent discussion in this column of British "quids" and pounds, "How about that famous Pound called Ezra?"

According to last reports, Madame, Ezra Pound was basking in the sun at Rapallo... occasionally seizing the moment to pound out another diatribe against the American passport and visa evil.

November 27, 1925 – *The Making of an American* requires 925 good-sized pages, according to Gertrude Stein, whose colossal book on the subject has just been brought out by Contact Editions.

And speaking of Contact Editions, Robert McAlmon returned recently from London with a sheaf of new poems soon to be published.

Gertrude Stein

November 28, 1925 – The spinsters of Paris had their fling last week. It was Saint Catherine's Day.

According to tradition, it is the day of the year when the *jeune fille* or flapper slips quietly into the background and leaves the stage to her older sister. Unmarried girls of more than twenty-five summers may roam the festive thoroughfares on this day and publicly receive the kisses of amorous *messieurs* with perfect propriety.

The only stipulation is that each must don a gay paper hat and wear it throughout the day. Otherwise, how should gallant Gaston ever dream that mademoiselle was beyond the quarter century mark? This year, as previously, there were a number of startled conjectures at the number of Paris spinsters. In fact, a large number of the young Catherinettes looked suspiciously young for their alleged ages.

The famous couturier establishments with their thousands of models and shop-girls are a center of activity on this occasion. Practically all of the more famous houses turned over the day to the *midinettes* and contributed champagne and dance music to the merrymaking.

*   *   *

Paris still gasps with astonishment when the curtain arises at the Champs Elysées Music Hall and, with a crash of bewildering jazz, the first *Revue Negre* to visit Paris swings into stride.

Jazz in itself is not unknown to the French capital, but the accompaniment of beautiful dusky maidens and their chocolate beaux, dashing breathlessly back and forth across the stage in one continuous whirl, was something new to Paris theatredom.

Completely swept away by the bizarre nature of the entertainment, the theatre-going public has jammed the music hall at every performance, and the *Revue Negre* has become one of those subjects upon which one simply must be posted. Several of the newspapers have printed long and learned discussions of "the art of *la Revue Negre*," the "philosophical aspects" of the matter, and "the finesse" of Josephine Baker and others of the stars. The engagement, which will come to a close this week, opened a couple of months ago with a brilliant special midnight performance to which several of the literary and theatrical stars of the French capital had been invited. To Americans in Paris, the *Revue* was simply an amusing spectacle, far from approaching several similar entertainments in America and much too elemental to require any philosophical analyses.

December 1, 1925 – Should you feel the need of a little color stimulus these drab days, permit us to suggest dropping in at the galleries of M. Bernheim. The veteran Quarterite, who signs himself "Hiler," has here gathered some thirty-five quaint studies of *bistros* and barmaids in the first formal exposition of his career. Just inside the door you will be confronted by the buxom Marguerite, who, you will observe, is taking no chances on losing that foaming *bock* which rests before her. She will point the way to a series of taxis and *terrasses*... barbershops and balalaikas.

December 4, 1925 – *L'Art d'Aujourd'hui* is the all-inclusive title selected by the international band of painters for their startling show. At the *vernissage* Monday evening, George Antheil and Olga Rudge played a few of the Antheil opuses for piano and violin.

Due to our inability to be present it has been necessary to depend upon the report of Sylvia Beach. Sylvia informs us in hushed voice that some of the painters have simply evolved in their mad modernistic march, until there is actually nothing left but a terrifying expanse of white canvas!

*　　*　　*

81

Having weathered the stormy censorial seas of America and England, as well as an occasional typesetters' walkout, Mr. Joyce's *Ulysses* is ready for a French cruise, where, it is safe to say, the sailing will be much smoother.*

Auguste Morel, the French writer, informed us yesterday that his translation of the book will be completed in about one year. The French *Ulysses* is to be brought out by Adrienne Monnier of La Maison des Amis des Livres, who hopes to do for France what her neighbor Sylvia Beach did for America and England.

Adrienne Monnier's Bookshop

December 25, 1925 – Eugène Jolas, Left Bank poet whose latest French verses in *Creer* caused some comment, has bade farewell to Paris, his "first love," and is en route to New York. Jolas is of the trilingual school, writing with almost equal facility in French, German, and English. Several of his studies will appear in the forthcoming *This Quarter*.

January 1, 1926 – Bonne Année!

And should you, by any chance, feel that the prospects are not too rosy for a twelve-month to come, reflect that, after all, you might be in the Maison des Pauvres, the *Mont de Piété*, or the hospital – perhaps the American Hospital in Neuilly.

For it may surprise you to know that a sector of the Latin Quarter has actually been uncovered in one of the cheery white rooms of the American Hospital. Quite by accident, we stumbled upon the little artist colony the other afternoon and found that it has been headed by Lawrence Porth, the young Chicago illustrator,

---

* *Editor's Note:* It is interesting to note that the *Tribune* had carried a recent article with the headlines "French Will Ban Naughty Books; Minister of Justice Gives Order to Police."

and E.W. Dubuque, the American mural painter.

Porth has just recovered from a nine months' session with malaria fever, while Dubuque likewise claims a serious ailment, although both find time to settle weighty art problems between the arrivals of the trays.

All in all, the nurses are having a little *salon des malades* all their own, and there is some talk of founding an annex of the Café du Dôme.

*　　*　　*

Walter René-Fuerst sends word of the formal opening of his Franco-American Stagecraft School at ten o'clock tomorrow morning, 37 Rue Froidevaux. Further, the young stage designer is the author of this year's book *Du Décor,* as well as the designer of a number of maquettes exhibited at the *Exposition des Arts du Théâtre* and the *Exposition des Arts Décoratifs.*

*　　*　　*

Joyceans will learn with regret that the author of *Ulysses* has been suffering greatly since his last eye operation, which proved to be a severe nervous, as well as physical, shock.

For this reason, it is doubtful whether the holiday season has held much pleasure for Joyce, although if any Christmas or New Year's Day gift were to please him, it would be the news that Sylvia Beach has just brought out the seventh edition of *Ulysses.*

This latest edition, in accordance with the wishes of the author, has been bound in blue paper, as was the original edition, instead of white as were the intervening ones.*

February 9, 1926 – Some little excitement prevails at the studios of Raymond Duncan on the Boulevard St. Germain, where *Artistes et Artisans,* the Duncan group, have just selected an American artist to be featured in a gratis exposition at the Duncan *atelier.*

J Paul Ninas has been selected for the honor after a canvass of the studios, and the opening of the exposition is scheduled for Thursday afternoon, February 18. The showing will include both oils and watercolors and is to continue for three weeks.

Meanwhile, *Artistes et Artisans* continue to hold their weekly Thursday teas for the discussion of the arts and crafts, as well as life in general.

Editor's Note: A copy of the seventh edition, in its blue paper cover, printed again on the cheapest paper, which was given to P.S. by Sylvia Beach in 1926, is now in such fragile condition that it cannot be handled without the edges flaking at a touch.

February 13, 1926 – When Debussy wrote his "Afternoon of a Faun" he must have had in mind the figure of a mere man in one of the great Parisian fashion salons during an opening.

For if ever a startled, shrinking, misplaced creature were to be found among the masculine sex, it is at such a time and place. It is the moment of supreme triumph for femininity. The couturier's salon becomes sacred ground, consecrated to womanhood. With the passing of the barbershop, man can boast no hallowed territory to match it.

The week before last, Paris had its spring and summer openings at all the smart fashion establishments (Worth, Jacquet, Pacquin, Poiret, Lanvin, Lelong). I was present at both Jacquet's and Worth's. Jacquet is a new couturière here and this was her first opening. And how swanky it was! An evening affair with brilliant cream and gold crystal chandelier salons, with everybody in evening clothes, stunning models strolling through the rooms, and afterwards champagne, sandwiches, and cakes. Of course it is strictly invitational.

Seated uneasily in the cream and gold rooms of M. Worth in the Rue de la Paix the other afternoon, a distinguished, ruddy-faced Britisher gazed sympathetically across at me in a sort of mute alliance against the enemy. Around us sat blasé French and foreign feminine buyers, ready to pounce upon a creation that tickled their fancy, or rather that they thought would tickle the fancies of their respective clienteles.

There was an arching of eyebrows and a not too obvious turn of the head as one of their fashionably gowned number occasionally passed through the room in search of a point of vantage. At promptly two thirty o'clock, a vision of dull pink and old cream lace suddenly appeared without warning and floated through the room.

Immediately there was a deathlike hush. Worth's 1926 spring fashion show was on.

If it is your expectation to read here an analysis of what Paris (led by Worth) has prescribed for feminine elegance during the coming spring and summer, I deeply regret your disappointment.

No mere man without a command of the "flounce, gore, fichu, crêpe, taffeta" vocabulary could possibly tell you.

As near as I could recall after the staggering parade of feminine loveliness had finished, the only impression I had received was one of some half a hundred indescribable creations worn by about a dozen of the capital's most ravishing *jeunes filles.*

Still, if you insist, I do recall that lines were generally straight, with flares only at the sleeves and occasionally at the skirt. The latter are short, just below the knee, and pastel shades are decidedly the thing. If you have any extra material to put into your sleeves, it must come below the elbow to be modish. Skirts are short, and for tailored wear, dark blue, trimmed with scarves and ties of blue and white checks and dots, must not be overlooked.

At this point, a young child of fortune and her mother from across the Atlantic, who sat next to me, began an inspection of pink silk lace of a more or less intimate design. This, I cannot and will not describe.

February 26, 1926 – In these days of Left and Right, whether it be of politics, literature, art, or music, it is a little distressing to be asked point-blank to which school or group one proffers his devotion.

There is, for example, that estimable Left Bank writer who, when asked if he were a Dadaist, fervently replied, "No, thank God, I believe a man should have but one wife!"

One ingenious solution to the problem has been found by Elliot Paul,

Elliot Paul
(sketch by Howard Simon)

American novelist, who joined the American writers' section in Paris during the past year. Paul is neither Left nor Right, at least so far as Paris is concerned, inasmuch as he lives serenely on the Ile St. Louis between the two extremes.

Which is not to say that Elliot Paul is a neutralist (still another "group"). No reading of *Indelible, Impromptu,* or *Imperturbe* could leave any doubt as to the author's definiteness of conception. Each was sufficient to cause a little flurry of nervousness among the Fundamentalists.

Howard Simon, the Left Bank artist of woodcut fame, offers today's pencil impression of Paul.

*   *   *

Howard Simon's new book *La Rive Gauche* will be off the presses during the coming week, it having been turned out by James McCullin at The Abbaye, 6 Rue Saint-Benoît.

Outside of an introduction by Elliot Paul, the book will be made up entirely of woodcuts and drawings from the prolific and sensitive pencil of Simon, numbering some fifteen in all.

February 27, 1926 – Duels in France

Duels continue to be fashionable in the twentieth century France, whether it be behind the footlights or in real life, and they generally reach about the same degree of seriousness.

Not long ago, we had the startling spectacle of Mistinguett, the veteran music hall star, furiously challenging one of her feminine enemies to a match of steel. The former at once began dueling practice, was photographed for the newspapers with a foil in her hand, and things looked serious. When the public had learned the story by heart, the matter was suddenly dropped, the closest approach to a foil having been the dear public itself.

Next M. Rouche, director of the Opéra, and M. Ravel, one of the foremost French composers, attacked each other with an interchange of heated dialogue concerning a certain operatic production which seemed to call for a duel as the only solution to the difficulties. Seconds were chosen, arrangements were made, but then it was discovered that the injured party had received restitution orally, which was quite as much a triumph as running through his enemy with a blade.

Now comes M. Jacques Sadoul, recently re-instated to the Paris bar after having been acquitted for treason. While passing through the Palais de Justice for the first time the other day, M. Sadoul heard himself referred to as a traitor by M. Galfucci, lawyer and son of the former president of the French chamber.

M. Sadoul punched M. Galfucci's face. There was an exchange of cards. A duel, it is said, will take place.

March 2, 1926 –
> "Light as a robin's song falling
> Were yet too heavy ... too heavy ...
> Lighter than a falling peach petal's push against air,
> All these were far too heavy and too fair."

So sings Bravig Imbs in his poem *Eden: Exit this Way,* which supplies the title of his slender volume of poetry just issued. This particular poem is dedicated to George Antheil, the composer, and is followed by some thirty-eight others of varying degrees of excellence.

As far as we know, the volume is Imb's first, but undoubtedly is not to be his last. There are fragments of sheer beauty beneath the glowing covers of *Eden,* many of them shot through with a melancholy charm that rings true.

As far as the rest of the volume, "Chartres Within" and "Two Songs Before Death" alone are worth several readings.

March 6, 1926 – There was a heavy sigh and a sorrowful shake of the head as Jean and Pierre discussed the day's happenings over their *petit déjeuner* at the bar of their café in the morning.

La vie chère was the theme of their perplexed cogitations, a subject which has now usurped the place of the weather itself as the Parisians' favorite topic of conversation, not because it is less changeable but rather because its changes are all in one direction and far more disastrous.

For now it is the lowly, democratic *croissant* which has been given a rude jolt by the unceasing upward march. The little pastry crescent, which every true Frenchman so dearly loves to soak in his *café crème,* has been raised in price from 25 to 30 centimes.

One sou is, in itself, not a great increase in price. But when it is recalled that it constitutes a 20% increase upon an article of food that is as national as the tricolor, some idea of the significance of the jump in price may be obtained. One French newspaper predicts the decline of the *croissant.* Other quarters predict its gradual evolution into the French pastry category, i.e., an article of fancy diet for the wealthier Frenchman and the tourist.

In any case, the "crescent," like the great lunar body from which it was named, seems well on the way to a total eclipse.

March 16, 1926 – A survey of the Left Bank's celebrities would not be complete without a word concerning the chap whose headquarters are at No. 107 Boulevard Raspail.

Canon Killian Stimpson, founder of the Left Bank Students' and Artists' Club

"Doc" Stimpson, as the Quarter knows him, or Canon Killian A. Stimpson (D.D. as the other three Quarters know him) is the man who runs the United States Students' and Artists' Club, as well as St. Luke's Student Chapel, just round the corner.*

Editor's Note: Canon Stimpson, himself a young man, had a remarkable flair for guiding the younger members of the American colony in Paris. He kept a concerned eye on the alcoholics and drug addicts, and is known to have prevented suicides.

His club was a boon to the Left Bank Americans, especially the more impoverished students, who could enjoy an inexpensive, but hearty Thanksgiving or Christmas dinner, followed by dancing, and forget their homesickness. Through rummage sales he helped them solve their clothing problem, but in extreme cases, when all else failed, he contacted their families in the States, and made arrangements to send them home.

Killian Stimpson and P.S. became close friends, and several years later, back in the States, the Canon baptized all three of the Shinkman infants.

Incidentally, Doc is said to be the only man who has ever brought students, artists, and chapels together upon an amiable basis. It might surprise you to see some of our deepest-dyed Montparnos in the little chapel of a Sunday morning.

Doc is also the man who has been kicking up all the disturbance in the Boulevard Raspail during the past winter with his Sunday night singing festivals, upon which occasions the brush and chisel wielders, hanging from every available corner in the place, took the opportunity to show that their lungs were quite as good as their powerful right arms.

In fact, so lusty were some of the ensemble renditions of "Lil Liza Jane" and "Swanee River" that startled Frenchmen, gathered in whispered conference outside, decided that another war had been won. Doc has consented to keep his club open during the summer.

* * *

March 18, 1926 – *Dédale,* which you may have seen mentioned in these columns a few weeks back, is to have another hearing at the hands of Raymond Duncan and his own disciples, whose Left Bank studio captures attention on the Boulevard St. Germain.

Dédale is described as a *kinema archaïque* dedicated to the nine muses and danced by twenty corybantes. It is to be performed Saturday afternoon at the Théâtre Femina with solo work by Aia, Beatrice, Maurice, and Robert (all members of the Duncan artistic family), as well as Raymond himself.

Lavinia Darvé of the Manhattan Opera will open the ceremonies, and this will be followed by *Prométhéus Crucifié,* a *tragédie orchestrique,* by Raymond Duncan, *Hymne à Apollon,* danced by the latter, *La Tentation de St. Antoine, Les Sept Contre Thèbes et Antigone,* a *tragédie synthétique,* and *Les Trois Rêves,* a pastorale.

March 19, 1926 – "There are many other theatres that should also burn down," wickedly observes Bernard Shaw anent the recent destruction of the Shakespeare Memorial Theatre at Stratford. To which might be replied with equal venom, "And a great many of them are housing your shows, Mr. Shaw."

In all fairness to the Bard of Shannon, it must be admitted that the cases where one is most tempted in the direction of arson have to do with the so-called "interpreters" of Shaw, and not with the septuagenarian playwright himself.

And with further regard to Shaw, it is interesting to note that we are to be introduced to a French adaptation of *The Devil's Disciple* from the pens of M. and Mme A. Hamon.

March 26, 1926 – Not the least important of the "groups" which constitute the fabric of the Left Bank culture is "Artistes et Artisans," the little band which rallies around Raymond Duncan at his studio in the Boulevard St. Germain.

The idea, as we understand it, is that abstract art in itself is all very well. At the same time, there is no reason why art should not occasionally step down from Parnassus and make its appearance in everyday life. It is Mr. Duncan's artisans who announce that they have taken up the banner in the latter cause.

Furniture, books, shoes, pictures, clothes, rugs, and drapes constitute a few of the everyday articles which are turned out by hand from the Artistes et Artisians workshops. Lest the group seem to lean too heavily towards the utilitarian, we have an occasional ballet, drama, opera, or poem produced by the same circle.

*　　*　　*

Dédale opened as promised at the Théâtre Femina last Saturday afternoon.

If there was any suspicion that the affair was to be a fantastic revel of the ultra ultras, it was quickly dispelled when the performance began with nine invocations to the muses chanted in a beautiful voice by Lavinia Darvé, soprano from the Manhattan Opera. To the evident astonishment of a large part of the capacity audience, the ceremonies continued with a series of beautifully arranged classic dances performed in absolute silence against a simple background of grey velvet. There was nothing of the bizarre or fantastic. The effect was that of sheer rhythm of form and movement expressed for the eye rather than the ear.

With one exception the ballets cast a spell of breathless silence over the gathering. *Prométhéus Crucifié* was the one departure from the rhythmic and harmonious spirit of the whole. This number introduced a jarring, distraught note that bordered on the ridiculous and was completely out of place.

*   *   *

It will be just ninety-five years ago next Sunday that Heinrich Heine came to Paris. There will be no Quarterite to whom that day will mean more than it will to Michael Monahan, the illustrious, silver-haired gentleman who has come to be a beloved figure in Montparnasse.

"A tribute of love and admiration to a writer who has possessed me from my youth up," writes Monahan, who is as Gaelic as his name, in the preface to his book on the great German poet. "A writer with whom I have had some of the best hours that can befall to a reading man, and of whose charm I am still unwearied."

March 27, 1926 – The democratic autobuses, unassuming tramways, and lowly undergrounds of Paris, have come up a notch or two in the social world. Monsieur and Madame Chic Parisien, who never before were seen in these humble convey-ances, have taken a sudden fancy to them, with the result that a certain *éclat* has been thrown about them.

All of which is the result of Paris' revised taxi rates which, to most Parisians, are now sufficiently high to constitute an unnecessary luxury and make the more modest modes of travel much more attractive.

April 4, 1926 – When you next visit Paris, it is quite likely that you will decide to attend Sunday morning Mass at the great Notre Dame de Paris.

But when Mass is over and you are wondering whether to have another look at the windows of the Sainte Chapelle or stroll up the "Boul Mich" to the Sorbonne, take a little turn around the corner to the wide expanse which stretches in front of the Caserne.

Here, on a bright, sunny morning, you will find row after row of small bird cages, each with its occupants chirping merrily in the sunshine in as many different tunes as there are kinds of birds in the collection. For this is perhaps Paris' most popular bird market.

Everything from the lowly guinea hen and her mate to the gorgeously plumed warblers that come from tropical shores, may be found on display. Crooning pigeons stalk peacefully about, not far from loquacious parrots. Trilling canaries flutter in cages close to iridescent pheasants.

And up and down, stroll the merchants – old men and women, small boys and girls, each displaying his stock to the best advantage, while little Jean and

Madeleine tug excitedly at Maman's arm and beg to be allowed to take home at least one feathered pet.

*   *   *

The scene on the Ile St. Louis when we were coming home late the other night – a little café with a group of taxi drivers gathered in the back room, one of them gaily playing an accordion and the rest looking on fascinated while a little old chauffeur in a long coat glided back and forth in time with the music, the while he balanced a bottle of wine on his head! At intervals, he added a flourish to his dancing in the way of an amazing outward kick or a brief poise on one leg, the other extended gracefully behind. Behind the counter, the patron with beaming face shook an empty bottle containing coins, or something, that rattled in time with the music.

April 23, 1926 – One of the most interesting events of the past week in the Quarter was the opening Tuesday evening of the Walt Whitman Exposition at Shakespeare and Company in the Rue de l'Odéon.

The exposition was organized by the Walt Whitman Committee of Paris, of which Sylvia Beach is an active member. First editions, original manuscripts, autographed letters, and early photographs were loaned. Included is a beautiful sculpture of Whitman done by Jo Davidson, the American sculptor.

May 7, 1926 –
"Ideas exist
As bleak, conceited hopes within the mind.
The will to cast themselves
Upon the outer visage of some form
Gives way to talk of semblance,
Or of friends."

Thus sings Virgil Geddes, the American poet, in the prologue of his new book of *Forty Poems*. Geddes, one suspects from no more than a casual survey of his works, is a wanderer, one of those wanderers in the realm of fancy who senses poignantly the tremors of emotional experience, who now smiles faintly at its whirlings and arabesques, now cries out at the rumblings of its divine tympani.

Geddes is in Paris for the moment. The volume, which is just appearing, is made up of poems written over a period of two years, many of which have already appeared in American literary reviews. There is a revealing preface by Elliot H. Paul.

May 15, 1926 – "C'est une question sérieuse, vous savez!" "Mais c'est une bonne expérience!"

Paris throbs with excited speculation upon the general strike which finds its center of activity in the sister capital across the Channel. In the autobuses, trams, on the streets, discussion is rife as to the outcome of the monster "walk out" and just what its significance to the rest of the world may be.

Paris feels a particular concern and is practically an actor in the drama, since its contact with Great Britain is probably closer than that of any other city outside the island. Communication between the two continues, but under vastly changed circumstances.

The flood of travel across the Channel to England has been checked, and since the air service seems to be the only method of travel left intact, fares have doubled in price.

May 19, 1926 – Nathan Asch, a well-known Quarterite who is now in New York, is represented in the current number of *The Nation* by a review of the memoirs of Frank Harris (another familiar figure in the Quarter).

Asch is none too easy on the veteran reminiscer and seems to resent a certain self-consciousness in reading Harris. He finds him neither a "Pepys writing to amuse himself nor a Casanova trying to pass the time away in dull surroundings." It is the last chapter, which forms a sort of apologia, that Asch finds the best in the book.

Meanwhile the young author of *The Office* (which seems to be enjoying considerable success) is also represented in *The New Masses* for May by a brief study called *The Bus-Boy*. It is realistic characterization in the manner of those which make up *The Office*.

*   *   *

William Carlos Williams is another well-known figure on the Left Bank whose name appears in the current number of *The New Masses*. His story is called *The Five Dollar Guy*.

And while on the subject of literature, it is interesting to know that Ernest Hemingway's new novel, *Torrents of Spring,* is due off the presses this very minute. As a result of the author's permanent arrangement with Scribner's, the new book is being brought out by that house.

*   *   *

The April number of *Le Navire d'Argent,* the little review published by Adrienne Monnier at La Maison des Amis des Livres, is the subject of considerable comment in the current number of *The Bookman.*

Michael Joseph speaks highly of this "American number," which includes French translations of the works of Ernest Hemingway, Robert McAlmon, E.E. Cummings, and William Carlos Williams, as well as a hitherto unpublished work of Walt Whitman.

*   *   *

Speaking of Walt Whitman, the exposition devoted to the Bard of Camden is still in progress at Shakespeare & Company in the Rue de l'Odéon.

The proceeds of the exposition are to go towards the erection of the Whitman monument which they are planning across the ocean. The exposition will continue through June, according to its sponsors, Sylvia Beach and Adrienne Monnier.

May 21, 1926 – At least three-quarters of the Quarter (which makes three/sixteenths of Paris) assembed at the behest of Kid Hiler, the American artist, Wednesday night in a gathering that must surely be memorable in the annals of Montparnasse.

The occasion was the welcoming of Harzberg, Senior, father of the artist, who had just returned from America. As a matter of fact it proved also to be a rallying of Left Bank forces that bathed the Palais d'Orléans in an effulgence of Old World brilliance.

Mme Isadora Duncan, the dancer, dropped in for a moment and this fact alone was responsible for the crimson glow. Then there were Don Byrne, whose *Messer Marco Polo* still lives, Gilbert White, the painter-raconteur, Cheever Dunning, of poetic repute, Roy van Auken Sheldon, whose sculptural menagerie still grows, Cedric Morris, Walter René-Fuerst, Hasoutra, Ivan Opfer, Lady Duff Twisden, Sybil Vane, the Countess de Bonis, "Lady Betty" Foster, Pierre Loving, Gypsy Rhouma-Je, H.S. Cresswell, Gwen Le Gallienne, and several score more.

May 22, 1926 – Paris awoke happily last Thursday morning to find that the sinister strike which has been worrying England as well as her allies throughout the world, has come to an end. The French capital, in particular, was already beginning to feel the effects of the labor tie-up.

Thousands of tourists headed towards London had changed their plans and remained in the French capital or continued their travel on the continent. News from England was almost cut off and the great London dailies, which are widely read through Paris each day, had disappeared.

There were one or two signs of sympathetic labor movements in France but they were not serious and consisted chiefly in refusals to perform labor that would hurt the cause of the strikers.

With the return to normality, travel is being at once diverted back towards the British Isles and the world breathes easily once more.

June 15, 1926 – Scores of swan songs have recently been written about the premature finish of *Le Navire d'Argent,* the little review published on the Left Bank during the past year by Adrienne Monnier of La Maison des Amis des Livres. This notice is not a swan song because we believe that nothing dies that shouldn't.

What has died in *Le Navire d'Argent* is a certain lack of that worldly wisdom that supplies the clay from which masterpieces are modeled. This can be acquired.

What has not died is the inner wisdom that made *Le Navire d'Argent* one of the finest reviews of its time. This cannot be acquired, and that is why it must re-assert itself in a second volume of *Le Navire d'Argent* this fall that will even surpass the first.

*   *   *

Meanwhile La Maison des Amis des Livres continues its throbbing career as one of the world's most significant centers of contemporary French letters. The writers who have taken the stimulus from Adrienne Monnier's little bookshop since it was born eleven years ago are sufficiently important and numerous to entitle it and its guiding spirit to a permanent place in the history of literature.

*   *   *

And speaking of poets, Pierre Loving announces that he is preparing a volume of his long and short poems which have appeared during the past few years in *The Dial, The Nation, Voices, The Smart Set, The Independent Anthology, Measure,* and others.

Among them, he says, will be the following verses, written in Monterey, California, some four years ago. They are called, "Between Them Came Doubt."

"Between tall cedars and the iron sea
Where the beach grass runs and straggles out
Dark, dark, they stumbled knee to knee
On sand. The wind brought salt, and wind brought doubt.

The world has changed: the stars are late
And late two limber bodies lie
With knives of sand between them – hate
Under a rindgold sun, a metal day. . .

The sea bore the look of whitened bones
Where the wind had bitten, and the gust

Cried omens up: sulphur mist on dunes
Like old crones burnished by a phantom rust.

And over the cedars flew a bird
That eyed them as they measured sand.
They rose at last. An unseen herd
Came trampling, led by one who raised his hand."

February 1927 – With the 1926-27 holiday season tucked safely away in history, Paris has forgotten the mistletoe and holly and turned to the more prosaic activities of the post-holiday lull. For the early months of the new year are always the quietest on the calendar of the French capital.

Although never without her share of foreign visitors, Paris is perhaps the closest to becoming a strictly French city during the months of January, February, and March. The fall and holiday guests have departed, and it is yet too early for the arrival of those who love the city when the chestnuts have begun to bud along the Grands Boulevards and the fountains in the Tuileries and Luxembourg have once more been turned on.

It is the Parisians' open season in their city, and the vast majority of the foreigners here are merely *en passant* on their way to and from the various resorts and capitals of Europe. The sightseeing buses have disappeared from the Boulevards, theatre tickets are no longer at a premium, and Sam's, that epicurean oasis for homesick American and British, has temporarily closed its doors.

* * *

CHAPTER 4

SKETCHES FROM EUROPE

1924-1926

Introduction

When Paul Shinkman left Paris in the late summer of 1924 and started out on his journey through Europe, his love affair with *la ville lumière* was already well under way. Even as he thrilled to his first glimpses of England, Germany, the Rhine, Switzerland, and Italy, he looked forward to his return to the Latin Quarter. The Place de l'Odéon had already become his second home.

The Alps, Lake Lucerne, and the Bay of Naples were "wonderfully beautiful," but P. S. was essentially a "people person," and it is his encounters with students, artists, street singers, nuns, an Italian naval officer, a Spanish padre, hotel proprietors, a lady in distress, and other tourists like himself that give his travel letters and diaries their charm.

*   *   *

During those years it was sometimes difficult to remember that World War I had ended less than a decade earlier. Life on the Left Bank as lived by American expatriates had little connection with the grim events of 1914-1918, yet the work of restoring the battle-scarred areas elsewhere in France was steadily progressing. At regular intervals, front page stories by P. S. describing the dedication of a war memorial, a new hospital, or restored ruins in cities such as Rheims and Saint-Nazaire appeared in the *Tribune*.

American generosity was never more lavishly displayed than it was in France at that time. In the early 1920s there was also a steady flow of Gold Star Mothers coming to France from the States to locate the graves of their sons who had fallen on the battlefields of Ypres and the Somme. This was part of a program instigated by the Comtesse Constance de Caen (a member of the Bourbon family, and cousin to the Pretender to the throne of France). Her account of this work, given in an interview with P.S. over radio station WINS in New York in 1934, gives a vivid picture of the way in which French and Americans reacted to the war and its aftermath. Her sentimental comments are typical of the spirit of the times.

E.B.S.

*　　*　　*

It's all a wonderful dream now,
just as I feared it would be ...
though perhaps that isn't such a bad outcome.

July 17, 1924

Dear Family,

Is it possible that I really am in London! I just stepped to the window again to look out at the wet pavements with lamplights reflected in them, and it sends chills all over me. It simply can't be true. However, I want you to hang on to these letters so that when I get home I shall have some tangible evidence.

I left Paris behind last night after two weeks of paradise. Positively, that is a magic city. People seem to be happy and thoroughly contented in every walk of life. As a young Italian told me on the train this morning, "Paris offers happiness to suit every pocketbook." There is no envying the millionaire.

The trip across the Channel was unpleasant, but I thoroughly enjoyed the ride through northern France in the twilight last night and through southern England with a beautiful sunrise this morning.

London is far different from Paris – it lacks that romance of the Latin Quarter, the Boulevards, terrace restaurants. But don't think that it has no appeal. There is a sombre mystery about its crowded streets that is charming. It is historic in a very dignified way. I should say Paris was historic in a romantic way.

Outside of wandering around Westminster Abbey this morning and riding along the Strand on top of a bus this afternoon I haven't done much so far. The principal thing was to find accommodations, and I think I have succeeded very well. This seems to be a very high grade, almost aristocratic, residential hotel. My room at $21 for the week seems high, until you realize that it covers all meals – four a day, including tea at 4 o'clock.

Dinner tonight was very good – soup, fish, roast lamb, potatoes, greens, bread, and pudding. And – oh Susie, what a blow! When I nonchalantly asked the maid for black coffee, she very politely informed me, "In the drawing room later, sir." Another faux pas like that will kill me!

I shall only remain in London one week. From here, if my finances permit, I shall go through Holland, Belgium, and Switzerland, and from there through Italy during August. That would bring me to Rome the early part of August for my first stop after London.

Pembroke House
Oxford, England
July 27, 1924

Dear Susie,

Would you like a few lines from Oxford? It's positively magnificent. Why can't we have schools like this in America? Of course it's the centuries back of them that give the buildings and grounds their charm.

I spent Thursday here, and together with a chap from Philadelphia strolled from one college to another positively captivated. Imagine coming upon the former rooms of such students as Shelley, Ruskin, and Samuel Johnson. In the latter's I was surprised and a bit irritated to find the trunks of a young American. Desecration! (The trunks should be mine.)

The climax came in the grounds of New College – through a great iron gate into an exquisite secret garden with beautiful lawns, flowers, and ivy-covered ruins of the original Oxford city wall.

Friday I made the grand pilgrimage to Stratford. I won't try to describe my impressions before Shakespeare's grave. It was a precious moment. His house, the church, and Ann Hathaway's cottage are all beautiful. I have some lavender flowers for you from the latter. (Some youngsters gave them to me.)

When I learned that an excellent company is playing Shakespeare in Stratford, I had no alternative but to stay overnight. I am glad I did, as I not only saw *Richard II* and *Hamlet*, done to the Queen's taste, but met a fine chap from Chicago who is a graduate of the famous drama course given at Harvard by Professor Baker. He had been over since October writing for the *Christian Science Monitor*, and returns to America next week.

I returned to Oxford last night to break the trip to London as accommodations here are not only excellent but very reasonable. I have a charming room on the third floor of this old house with three small-paned windows looking down upon a narrow little street lined with half-timber houses and interesting gables. This, together with a capital breakfast of bacon, eggs, tea, toast, and marmalade cost me but 5/6 a day, or five shillings and sixpence (about $1.35).

The first day I strolled into the deserted library of Christ Church (one of the twenty-seven colleges) and found an old man browsing over an original edition of some seventeenth century songs. He seemed pleased by my interest, as he took me upstairs and opening a window, showed me the original garden of *Alice in Wonderland*! The private garden adjoined the Dean's house where the author used to tell stories to Alice, the Dean's young daughter.

This afternoon I took a bus ride through Merrie England very nearly to Gloucester. It was a beautiful trip past vine-covered walls, thousands of roses, and hillsides covered with sheep. To make the trip truly British, it rained coming back.

At breakfast in Stratford yesterday morning I was bewailing to my Harvard friend the lack of local interest in Shakespeare. Turning to the sturdy maid who was serving our breakfast I asked her if she had ever been inside Shakespeare's house. She had not. I groaned in anguish, caught my head, and rocked back and forth until she had promised to make speedy amends. My point was proved!

Brussels
August 6, 1924

After England I spent six days in Holland which were crowded with interesting experiences, including the Peace Palace at the Hague, and the fashionable watering place Scheveningen,* where I had my first dip in the ocean. I also visited the Queen's Palace, the University of Leiden, took a trip to the island of Marken, and met an elderly American lady in distress.

The lady – a Mrs. Lewis from Kingston-on-the-Hudson, New York, fairly staggered into a restaurant in Leiden just as I was finishing my lunch. She had missed connections with her friends, and a persistent Dutch guide had been following her around offering his services and trying to get some money. She went on to Amsterdam with me and stayed at the same hotel, leaving for England Saturday morning.

The people here in Belgium speak both Dutch and French, but the city of Brussels is decidedly French – in fact they like to call it "la petite Paris." I plan to go to the Royal Opera Friday night to hear *Lakme*. By taking residential hotels I run into very few Americans and in that way get to speak a great deal more French. I spoke German entirely in Holland and had no difficulty at all. However, that doesn't go in Belgium!

Editor's Note: P. S. visited Scheveningen on a crowded weekend in late July, and decided that this was a suitable moment to try his first swim in salt water. A native of Michigan, brought up on the fresh water of the Great Lakes, he approached the experience with a biased mind. The crowds at the beach were dense, the water shallow, warm, and brackish, and his worst fears were more than confirmed. It took him at least ten years to get over his intense dislike of the taste of the salt water!

Mainz
August 10, 1924

You must have at least a few lines from Germany! Perhaps they'll be rather frenzied. I'm holding my tablet on my knee and sitting on the railway platform waiting for my train to Strasbourg, France, which means goodbye to Germany after a precious few hours. The train came and now I'm flying through German countryside (third class) which accounts for the ague effect.

I arrived at Cologne early on Sunday morning in time to attend Mass in the great dim Kölner Dom before taking the glorious trip up the Rhine by steamer to Mainz, where I spent last night.

It will interest you to know that I traveled incognito up the Rhine.* Upon boarding the steamer at Cologne I realized that such a step would be necessary. And so, turning the brim of my hat to a jaunty angle, and reversing on my finger the ducal ring (which as you know bears the family crest) I was no longer the Count Paulski von Boxheimer-Shinkman, but the Count Paul de Montmorency-Beaufort! Even then I was aware of the inevitable deferential glances which seemed to penetrate my incognito!

I like the German people immensely. They're as civil as any people I've met, and a great deal more so than many.

Hotels Savoy & National Interlaken
Switzerland
August 14, 1924

Switzerland is up to my expectations in every way, in spite of the fact that the weather has been unpleasant. There has been considerable rain, and tonight it is

---

*Editor's Note: A favorite Shinkman family legend concerned a pompous, wealthy relative who had taken the Grand Tour of Europe before World War I, and on his return, announced that he had traveled "incognito" up the Rhine.

quite chilly. There's a grate fire here in the lobby.

I reached Lucerne from Strasbourg late Tuesday night and had a merry time finding a place to sleep. I found a room in a private home in the top floor apartment of a chauffeur and his wife. The wife spoke no English, so all had to be arranged through a chap two floors below who acted as interpreter. After a rather excited conversation between them he announced that they had a room but that there was a telephone in it which the husband might have to answer in the middle of the night as he was on night duty. As a matter of fact it did ring about 6:00 a. m., but I went back to sleep easily. The room was very clean and comfortable and cost but 3 francs a night, so I stayed over until this morning.

Lake Lucerne is wonderfully beautiful, and I'll never forget the ride through the mountains to Interlaken this morning. One of the engineers on the mountain locomotive told me they made a grade of 12%. There is one locomotive pushing and one pulling, with a cogged rail between the tracks to do business. It was quite a thrill, and you can imagine the grandeur of the snow-capped mountains, misty clouds, and villages far below.

My visit in Lucerne was made especially enjoyable by my meeting three unusually fine chaps from Bavaria who were also taking a little boat trip on the lake to Wilhelm Tell's Chapel. One was a student of theology, one an art student, and the third a University of Munich graduate of the true genius type. It later developed that he has published a volume of poems and has been asked by the *Staats Zeitung* of New York to do some special writing. I was quite overwhelmed.

It was pouring when we got off the boat, so we went into a restaurant and had coffee in the true German style. After talking for some time we found that the weather had cleared a bit and so we started out for the Kapelle, which we enjoyed immensely. (I read *Wilhelm Tell* in high school and the doctor was getting ready to write an article on Tell.)

I hope you don't worry about me. I'm constantly meeting traveling companions like myself, but of course take no chances.

*   *   *

Genoa was my first stop in Italy. I then spent two days at Rapallo, a beautiful seaside resort overlooking the Mediterranean, and it was here that I had my first encounter with the deadly sex. The hotel was a first class family place up in the hills with several Italian and English families there for the summer. I was the only American and of course something of an object of curiosity. There were several fond Italian mamas with their marriageable daughters, and one papa who, particularly desperate, went after me in dead earnest. But your charming son wriggled out of the meshes and is still a grouchy bachelor.

From Rapallo, I stopped off at Pisa to see the Leaning Tower and then went on to Siena, one of the historic old communal cities. I arrived in the heat of high noon and there was a mad scramble for carriages that left me standing alone on the platform surrounded by my baggage. The last carriage had been taken by three nuns with those great white linen headpieces that stand out like wings and measure some three or four feet across. They beckoned to me to share the cab with them rather than wait for one to return. I was rather alarmed at the suggestion but my bags had already been hoisted up on the box. Since they couldn't understand English, I had no alternative but to climb into the rickety chariot beside them while they smiled pleasantly to put me at ease. I tried conversing in French until I am convinced one of them thought I was trying to flirt with her – then I hushed up. Can you imagine drawing up in front of my hotel in a tiny carriage surrounded by nuns with great flowing white caps!

*The delightful position of one
who cannot pay for his lodgings
and at the same time cannot move!*

Hotel Angleterre
Rome
August 24, 1924

It's impossible to tell you what a stimulus it was to reach Rome last Wednesday to find your letters waiting for me. I had no word from home since leaving London on July 28. I have an excellent hotel here and have settled down for a week.

My funds are getting a trifle low. I don't know what my cash balance is with you, but I imagine it is somewhere around $100. At any rate if you can scare up from $100 to $150 and send it to me care of American Express, 11 Rue Scribe, Paris, France, I shall be able to consider coming back home to you. I feel that my $400 has done pretty nearly all I can expect it to.

Perhaps you'd like to hear something about Rome. There is something very grand about it, in spite of the fact that it's the typical large city in a great many ways. I heard Mass in St. Peter's this morning. It was vast, and to me resembles a great public square with people crisscrossing in all directions. But so picturesque! Ragged women carrying babies, beggars kneeling to kiss the floor, nuns pausing to kiss the foot of the great statue of St. Peter, Franciscans with their rough brown serge robes, rope belts, shaved heads, and bare feet in sandals. Mass being said in some of the chapels, prayers being chanted in others. It's a wonderful place but it lacks the sanctity of the Notre Dame or the Kölner Dom.

I have an excellent hotel and have settled down for a week. It is conveniently located and I have quite a pretentious room with lofty ceiling, gilt mirror over the fireplace, upholstered chairs, and long flowered hangings at the big casement window which reach from the ceiling to the floor. No running water or bathroom, but what can you expect for the 16 liri (about 75¢) a day? The elaborate Italian tax upon travelers will raise this figure about 25%.

Hotel British
Lausanne,
September 7, 1924

I'm a bit excited tonight. Tomorrow I shall see Paris again! I left there July 16, so you see I have been gone nearly two months, and I guess it's a case of absence makes the heart grow fonder. The three weeks I spent in Italy were wonderful. I have seen nothing to compare with the Mediterranean – not even the Swiss lakes.

By the by, I hope you will have sent me some money in response to my letter from Rome by the time this reaches you. Otherwise, I shall be in a delightful position of one who cannot pay for his lodgings and at the same time cannot move!

*　　*　　*

The last night in Rome I went to hear *Rigoletto,* miserably produced but there were some fine voices. After a lot of peeking around the curtain, pounding, and other childish preliminaries, the curtain finally went up at 9:30. Things went along all right until about 11:30, when the performance was about two-thirds over. The lights suddenly went out all over Rome, and everybody had to go home and go to bed by candlelight.

From Rome I went to Naples. The Bay was one of the most beautiful sights I have ever seen, and the magnificent ruins of Pompeii were most impressive.

I took a boat trip out to the island of Capri, then to Sorrento, then a drive through the mountains to Amalfi. Florence was next on my schedule, but I could only afford to stay two days. I believe it's the most beautiful city in Italy, and it is filled with masterpieces. Did I tell you about the three German students I met in Lucerne? We became great friends, and you can imagine how pleasant it was to meet two of them again in Florence.

From Florence to Venice! Another dream realized. I had planned to make my arrival as romantic as possible. At the station I would step into a gondola and glide poetically down the Grand Canal under the stars to locate my quarters. Imagine then my anguish when an elderly Italian gentleman who had occupied the same compartment in the train, insisted on doing the honors for his country and led me briskly on foot across an ordinary bridge to the most matter of fact hotel. I could have thrown him over into the dirty canal with the greatest pleasure, and his gargles would have lulled me gently to sleep. I had visions of my entire visit to Venice being ruined.

Things took on a different aspect, however, when I discovered later that he was one of Italy's foremost writers on naval subjects, an ex-captain in the navy, and an acquaintance of Duse and D'Annunzio. We saw a good deal of each other.

We stopped at the Lido, a rather fashionable beach on the mainland just across from Venice (about ten minutes by ferry). The rates were surprisingly low. Hotels are so crowded that people are actually sleeping in bathtubs. The clerk at one hotel told me they had no rooms at all – not even a bathroom! I thought at first it was a joke, but he was in dead earnest!

The next morning, a luxurious little motorboat with racy lines and a uniformed engineer plowed up to the dock at the Lido with a great flourish. The attendant touched his cap as he assisted an illustrious old gentleman and a distinguished young chap in white duck to their places in the limousine cabin at the rear. Need I say that the two were none other than Captain Vittorio Vecchy, late of the Italian Navy, and the dashing Count Paulski?

Of course, I didn't miss taking a gondola ride and managed to get quite a kick out of it. You feel like a cross between Cleopatra in her royal barge, and an "extra" in a movie. Out in the middle of the Grand Canal were two gondolas brilliantly lighted with Japanese lanterns. In them were a stringed orchestra and singers. It sounded great across the water under the stars.

From Venice I stopped in Milan to see the famous cathedral and da Vinci's *Last Supper*. I leave here at 6:30 in the morning and reach Paris at about 3:00 in the afternoon. The little Hôtel Regnard will look mighty good once more.

*　　*　　*

A Little Journey in France

February 1926

Last week, one of the chaps at the office, Bill Shirer* from Cedar Rapids, Iowa, and I took two days off and made a little trip to Rouen, Amiens, and Beauvais. I

Editor's Note: William L. Shirer, author of *Berlin Diary.*

had never been to any of these places and should have hated to leave France without seeing the great cathedrals which are among the most famous in the world.

It was your Christmas present that paid for the whole thing, and I had a dollar left over. In other words, the whole trip cost me less than six dollars. I couldn't think of a better way to spend the Christmas present you sent me, and you can bet I made the most of it. Thanks heaps!

*　　*　　*

There is something delightful about embarking with a good companion upon a little two- or three-day trip into the provinces of a foreign country and then returning with a collection of charming memories to the Great City once more. The very act of pulling out of one of the great *gares* and then returning to Paris after a few days' absence supplies me with a peculiar thrill.

By arrangement, I met Bill one early grey morning at a little café on the Boulevard St. Michel. By 8:00 a.m., we were slowly drawing out of the Gare St. Lazare seated opposite each other by the windows of our third class compartment. Our fellow travelers were of the sturdy industrial class, although one grey-haired lady in fine mourning seemed to hold herself a little aloof.

The ride to Rouen was fascinating. It was the first time I had been outside of Paris for months, and Bill had not left Paris since he had arrived some six or seven months ago. The villages charmed us – little cafés with fantastic names beckoning to the new arrivals, sordid fiacres, women pushing carts.

We reached Rouen at about 10:30 a.m. and decided to stroll slowly to the center of the town. Rouen! Emma Bovary! Jeanne d'Arc! After a little leisurely walk down the main thoroughfare we suddenly stopped short in speechless admiration at a view down a little narrow street to our left – the Grosse Horloge of Rouen! A priceless stone archway spanning the narrow street and connecting the buildings on either side with a bond that has not been broken for centuries! Set in the arch, the exquisite dial of the old clock, with its dull rich coloring. I think our approach to this beautiful spectacle was one of the greatest delights of our entire trip.

After a few moments of contemplation, we decided to follow the little street under the arch. It carried us past a crumbling old house on the corner and then, very quietly and without ostentation, opened up one more priceless view to us – the facade of the cathedral itself.

Once more we paused in admiration before the indescribable stone lace-work, the intricate tracery, the filmy grandeur which is the front of this cathedral. We compared the dissimilar towers, and, of course, preferred the Tour du Beurre.

The afternoon, we decided, would be more appropriate for a visit to the interior of the church, so we turned our attention to the mundane subject of accommodations. Without difficulty, we found ourselves quartered Chez Paul, one of the town's best cafés, where there were a few rooms to be had upstairs. Our 24 franc room (for two) was of good size with a small dressing room, and from the large windows we gazed out across the square upon the memorable facade of the old cathedral. It was enchanting at night.

Down those narrow winding streets, with their centuries-old half-timber houses projecting intimately out over the street. I crossed to a stone-paved court to look at a room advertised in the window of the little café on the street. After climbing a narrow winding staircase of stone and beams, I encountered the *patron,* who pointed proudly at the beam work inside and spoke of its centuries of age.

The afternoon, twilight, and early evening we spent roaming aimlessly through these magic streets, inspecting old courts, the spot in the middle of the new marketplace where Jeanne d'Arc was burned, the tower where she was confined, and the small Church of St. McGlou. We laughed delightedly over the determined efforts of the sacristan to shut us up in the sacristy so that we could not leave, save through a narrow gateway, where he would be awaiting us with an itching palm. From one side to the other we dodged him, and spurred on by his challenge, slipped out without rewarding him for haunting us during our entire visit to the little church.

As we left the church, he playfully (?) shook his fist at us through the window, and then followed us out upon the porch to ask the beggars at the door if we had been as munificent with them as we had been with him!

We stopped in the cathedral during the afternoon and again at dusk as a little group of the faithful knelt in the shadows for Holy Hour. The occasional singing, the voice of the priest, and the dim lights, formed another of those unforgettable pictures.

Following dinner at the Restaurant de la Cathédrale we spent the evening strolling again through the dim streets and then heard the last selection of the orchestra at Paul's café before going upstairs to bed.

Early next morning, we were on our way to Amiens, via a wheezy little train. About ten, we reached our second point, a bit shaky from the quantities of hard cider we had drunk at Rouen and which, we later discovered, had amazing medicinal powers! Furthermore, we had not had time for breakfast, and so arrived in Amiens allowing that, cathedral or no cathedral, we would find a café and eat.

Thus we lounged luxuriously over coffee and croissants in a cheery café in the heart of town, discussing everything from politics to prohibition in America. Then to the cathedral, which we admired from the front for some time before entering. In fact there seemed to be a rich, delicately wrought uniformity about its facade that was missing in the cathedral at Rouen.

A little stroll about the vicinity and we decided that Amiens, outside the cathedral, had no charm for us – dull, drab houses that seemed all to be of the mid-Victorian era or worse. Bill suggested going on to Beauvais instead of remaining in Amiens. By the rarest fortune, we were able to secure third class rail accommodations that very afternoon.

Two delightfully ingenuous French soldiers climbed into our compartment somewhere between Clermont and Beauvais. One had been in the service about a year, while the other was a rookie. Quite naturally, the former was the more reserved, knowing, and deliberate, even when it came to accepting a cigarette. The other, however, a great country bumpkin type with a frank face and a rough figure, obviously of the soil, was more revealing in his actions, and gazed delightedly from first one side of the compartment and then the other at the country through which we were passing, offering ingenuous comments, and once or twice breaking into some little provincial song. Neither liked the military, but had no particular reason to offer.

The more sophisticated declared, in a rather unpromising tone, that Beauvais was *"pas beaucoup"* since it had practically no attractions save for one or two little movies. Walking up from the little station at Beauvais with our soldier friend, we inquired whether he were to remain long in the town. *"Oui,"* he replied very seriously, *"jusqu'à huit heures ce soir!"*

Beauvais intrigued us much as had Rouen. There were the same little narrow streets, each jog revealing an enchanting new vista of old houses and occasional towers. The broad marketplace took us across to the cathedral, which consists of only the two transepts. What a cathedral it would have been if it had been completed! The loftiest vault in the world! Some beautiful windows, rare Beauvais tapestries, and that wonderful clock which records the weather, season, time (in all parts of the world), and religious holidays, etc., and is wound once every hundred years!

A little old man was working furiously away at a platform which he was erecting in front of the sanctuary of the vast church, in preparation for a funeral to be held the next morning. "They keep me terrribly busy," he told us. "Sometimes two or three funerals a day!" He spoke of all this quite professionally, as I might object to the excess of assignments from my city editor. The funeral, he told us, nonchalantly, was a *"troisième classe."* He found time to show us into the clock room and explain some of its intricate workings, which he did with the proud air of the inventor himself and certainly the magnificence of a connoisseur proprietor or patron of the arts.

We were still in a rambling mood, and I wished to see a couple of particularly old houses nearby of which I had read. So we strolled about the little medieval town until it was quite dark, suddenly realizing that we had found no place to spend the night. I yearned to find quarters in one of those old houses, but luck was not with us and so we decided upon the Hôtel de la Poste, a modest, but clean place where we were quartered for twelve francs for the night.

We cleaned up a bit and then went out in search of a late dinner. Near the hotel is the Restaurant Chateaubriand, and what a dinner we had! We lounged idly over wine, cheeses, and dessert, and then strolled around to a café where we believed there might be music. The music turned out to be an impossible electric piano, so we continued our walk, discussing intimate subjects – the institution of marriage in particular – and then we stepped in at the town's leading café for coffee. Here we drank and smoked until nearly midnight, though the square was deserted and the café nearly empty long before that time, except for a few of the city fathers of Beauvais, in for coffee at the close of their weekly meeting.

Bed sounded wonderful, and around midnight, we found our way back to our little hotel, and called it a day and a trip.

Sketches in Rome*

August 1924

My visit to the Colosseum was about to begin. I returned alone to the shattered amphitheatre, sat down on a granite slab under the first tier, and forgot the twentieth century. Six lions come rushing through that gate over at the left. The little group of women and children in the center, surrounded by a circle of husbands and fathers, scream with terror. Fifty thousand spectators rise from their seats and scream with delighted anticipation. It was a gala day.

I shifted on my hard stone bench, and realized that it was twilight. This place must be magical under the stars. Besides it was gradually emptying and those still remaining seemed to be moving towards the exit with the exception of two girls and a boy seated high up on the second tier and myself.

The soft yellow light on the east walls suddenly disappeared. A chill seemed to drop over the place as it became quite dark. The trinity and myself alone remained, as I was aware from the faint white of a dress scarcely visible through the shadows. The end of a cigarette glowed and moved through the darkness towards the exit. They were all gone. The Colosseum to myself and the stars!

I sank back against the wall and reflected. There was the grating of footsteps on the gravel in front of me, and I could just make out a young Italian soldier, softly singing to himself as he strolled along. He saw me, touched his cap, and

---

* *Editor's Note:* While in Rome, P. S. wrote some sketches that he later showed to the editors of the *Italian Mail,* an English language newspaper published in Florence. As a result, they engaged him to do a weekly column from Paris.

stepped forward to ask the time in Italian. After some difficulty with the language, I responded and he sat down beside me to enjoy the surroundings after my own fashion. Conversation was as out of place as it was impossible.

Then I remembered that he had been singing in a singularly sweet voice. Would he be kind enough to sing a few more Italian songs? He understood and after a moment's hesitation, sang out in a clear sweet voice that was as truly Italian as his uniform. The Colossuem, the stars, the song! One's imagination is a more satisfactory medium than a feeble pen. It was beautiful.

"Biese!" I called several times after a few moments of silence between songs. He responded laughingly and then drew the words of a song from his pocket and, while I held lighted Italian matches and burned my fingers, he sang it with great enjoyment. I have since wondered at the picture we must have presented in the middle of the great arena. Two crouching figures on a stone bench, a flickering light between them, and an Italian song!

It grew late and I was reminded of army regulations. *Caffe*! before we part, I suggested. After a series of bibulous gestures, he understood, and we strolled slowly away to a nearby restaurant. Then we shook hands in the middle of the street, he waved good-bye, and I rattled away behind a gloomy cochère.

*　　*　　*

There is a partly burned candle on my dresser beneath the portrait of a young girl with brown eyes and a red hood. It is not the relic of religious devotions as one might expect. Nor is it burned in adoration before the shrine of the pretty girl. It lighted my way yesterday through the fearful subterranean passages of the catacombs of Saint Calixtus.

"Biglietto – L2" warned the sign at the end of the avenue of cypresses where one makes the descent. I stepped into the little shack, presented a two liri coin for a ticket and to my astonishment was handed a long slender taper. Some mistake. These are only for placing at the shrines of saints.

No, to each request for a *biglietto* the startled visitor received in return a candle, apparently of beeswax such as is used by the Church. Things were getting exciting and the little group stood in hushed expectancy until a Dominican in his white serge robe and black *cappa* came towards us and calmly directed us in English that we follow him.

Down several flights double file and then the little flame was passed along from candle to candle. From the head of the mysterious procession it passed slowly back to the entrance, far above.

Down – down – it grew damp, cold, and awesome. Several began joking uneasily about their lights going out or their candles burning down. Through low vaulted corridors, past niches in the rock, many torn open, others still sealed with

110

a marble slab inscribed with a dove, fish, or a sacred monogram X P (Christ).

Saint Cecilia's tomb, devoid of the holy remains but containing a sculpture of the Saint in the position in which the body was found, startling but beautiful in its reality. The arched vaults of the Popes, a tiny chapel, seemingly of another sphere, but heavy with the echoes of sacred devotions. We were ready to return to the world of today. Many of the candles were burned to the end and one lady was obviously nervous.

*   *   *

I have just come from Mass at Saint Peter's. There is music from a violin and guitar in the street below my window. I have no change to throw them. My money has vanished at an alarming rate, and Italy should take care of her own wandering musicians.

But it's really not bad music; in fact, considerably finer than any other street efforts I've heard, excepting the harp and cello in London. Supposing I take one glimpse at them. Perhaps they are playing for their dinner. I have seen musicians doing it before. I'll throw them a lira when they come beneath my window.

The music has ceased! Where are they? They must be walking this way. I'll be at the window ready to greet them.

I throw open the shutter. They are gone.

*   *   *

"Quo Vadis." I have always regretted not having seen the famous motion picture of that name. At any rate, I shall see the famous little church itself, possibly an effective substitute. Small, unpretentious, barren, it stands modestly on the Appian Way, quietly receiving the truckloads of tourists going and coming in steady streams.

A small Italian boy heralds the approach of carriages by turning innumerable handsprings along beside them – then looking up with a smile and extending his hand with the unmistakable gesture.

A hush falls upon the few who may enter the little tabernacle at one time. It was here, history records, that the Savior appeared to Saint Peter when the latter was fleeing from persecution. Just inside the entrance a square stone is embedded in the floor. It bears the impression of two feet – a reproduction of the sacred stone, since removed, upon which Christ is said to have stood.

Outside once more to find the young acrobat still performing with great gusto. As we drove away, I saw him puffing contentedly at a cigarette.

Castles in Spain

August 1925

Eleven days in Spain certainly have been profitably spent if they brought unforgettable memories. My itinerary took me by way of Orléans, Tours, Bordeaux, and St. Jean de Luz. This charming little French village in the shadow of the Pyrénées beside the Bay of Biscay, enticed me into staying three days, with several dips into the ocean, and an afternoon trip over to swanky Biarritz.

The excursion up Mount St. Rhun ... 2900 feet high. A beautiful view from the top, and tons of gnats. So I returned down on the first cable car, only to be bundled out half way down and be told that the electric current had been shut off. We waited for some time at the little mountainside junction while the passengers, notably two Englishmen (man and wife) stormed up and down. Finally somebody commandeered a limousine from a little mountain restaurant nearby, and with tears in my eyes and a threat in my voice, I induced the chauffeur to accept me as the eleventh passenger to cram into his car. We whirled down the mountain, and things went swimmingly until we were startled to look back up the hillside and find that the cable cars had resumed running.

(Meanwhile) the dear lady in whose car we were riding was marooned on the very peak of the mountain. Her chauffeur had considered this an excellent chance to make a little cash on the side, never dreaming that he wouldn't be back to the spot where she had left him before she herself returned! Ah, these French!

Burgos was my first stop in Spain. The interior of the cathedral resembled Venetian lace and I believe it made the greatest impression on me that any structure has, from Westminster Abbey to St. Peter's. It was priceless.

Madrid is perhaps my pleasantest Spanish memory, for it was on the way into the Spanish capital that I met Padre José Olea, who became a fast friend. He took upon himself the responsibility of making my first visit to Madrid an event to be remembered. That afternoon stroll through the park with a beer and a chat under the trees. My nose suddenly began to bleed, whereupon he summoned a waiter and instructed him to escort the *caballero* to a lavatory where he might check the flow.

The theatres in Madrid were moderately interesting but, of course, not of the best, out of season.

The bullfight was a real sensation. Four bulls and two horses, brutally killed. One horse led off with his intestines hanging out, unable to utter a sound. Their eyes are covered, their ears are tied shut, and their vocal organs are cut! God! The most degrading spectacle I have ever witnessed. A perfect reproduction of the pagan arena, with animals substituted for humans. As for the pageantry, it was exactly as one expects – bespangled *picadors, matadors, bandilleros,* bands, and smiling *señoritas* throwing flowers to the heroes parading about the ring.

Five men in velvet uniforms *(bandilleros)* and winged black caps are the first to appear in the ring. Then the bull enters and they spend some time waving their red cloaks before it. Next, two men on horses *(picadors)* enter and enrage the bull by prodding it with long spiked lances, while the five *bandilleros* continue their work. When either or both of the horses has been gored and perhaps killed, the *caballeros* withdraw and the five begin once more, while two new actors appear with grey darts which they throw into the back of the bull's neck. Each throws two at once until the bull is rushing furiously about, trying to shake several of them from the back of his neck.

Then, with a blast from the trumpet, the *matador* enters. With his spear and the continued assistance of the cloak wavers, he plunges the fatal spear into the vital spot in the back of the bull's neck. As a scientific result of this assault, the animal is exhausted, lunging at first one and then the other of two cloaks waving upon either side of him until he falls and is quickly stabbed to death. In a moment several teams of mules come tearing in, and the bull is unceremoniously dragged out by the horns as are any carcasses of horses which have failed to respond to the beating of rods or the ferocious pulling of their tail. An uplifting spectacle!

Valencia was a disappointment. Toledo, the ancient city that looks like the cities in the fairy tales ... perched on a great rock, with grey castles, monasteries, gates, and crumbling walls, limned against the sky.

Barcelona was made hectic by my financial status, but I found its very spruceness most engaging. And the cathedral at Barcelona with its great black vaults and shadows – is it what Max Reinhardt and Norman Bel Geddes had in mind when they created the cathedral for *The Miracle*? Beautiful jeweled windows, and an entrancing cloister with swans, palm trees, and trickling water. Beautiful in quite a different way from the fascinating cloister of the cathedral at Toledo, which was far more interesting to me than the church itself.

Left Barcelona, a 24-hour ride to Paris. And it was a wonderful morning ride through the streets of beloved Paris, even though I did have to haul my roommate out of bed to pay my taxi fare.

A Bicycle Trip in Touraine

July 1926

It was undoubtedly Helen Josephy who had the most to do with the crystallization of my bicycle trip project. She looked into my face sympathetically, seemed to see there the signs of enormous fatigue, heard with apprehension that my father and mother were soon to gaze upon their son for the first time in two years, and declared the trip and a coat of tan or sunburn indispensable.

Leaving Paris is not easy according to Helen, who said she once had the struggle of her life to pack her bags for a fortnight in the rurals of Entretat. Like a drowning man one grasps frantically at every straw that tends to hold him to the frenzied capital. *"Make* yourself go," she told me.

So I did, to the extent of sleeping scarcely a wink the whole night before, springing nervously out of bed when my gendarme-concierge rang imperiously to awaken me, and dressing, with a brown taste in my mouth, rushed to make the 8:08 train for Tours. (It should be added that the previous day and evening had been spent in those strange acts and reflections that I suppose occupied Charles I on the eve of his execution. A sort of preparation for another world.)

My ticket to Tours had been bought so there was no reneging without the loss of 36 francs. The train was jammed, but I managed to squeeze in between a fond French papa and a fat Italian and his wife who promptly made themselves at home by putting up the portable table and piling several bananas on it, which made quite a domestic picture. The weather seemed dubious, as usual, but there was enough occasional sunshine to give me faint hopes.

We arrived at Tours shortly after noon, and I began the quest for a bicycle. In my rambles I passed a very promising pension (Hôtel Pension Charluet) not far from the station, and it occurred to me an excellent idea to make a room reservation for the following Sunday night and thus have a place to leave my bag.

Madame seemed very charming and most understanding. The bicycle came next (there was no thought of such piffle as luncheon), and before I knew it, I had engaged a machine for three days at 8 francs a day. Thrown in was a little chat with Madame *la patronne,* who informed me that she had traveled much more than her husband although he was the kind who would enjoy going even to America. Further, she announced that women were definitely much more difficult to do business with than men. A man would turn the whole shop upside down waiting on her for a bicycle, she said.

Excited by the feel of the pedals and handlebars once more, I decided to dispense with lunch, bought myself a cap, and took to the road leading across the river and out of the city. This I followed in a state of feverish exultation, the wind blowing past me, a row of hillside châteaux looking down upon me from my left, and the winding Loire to my right.

It seemed but a few moments before I coasted around a pretty little curve and spied a grove of trees with a wayside inn – Vouvray, one of the world's most famous wine centers! Although I had passed a bit beyond it, it did not take long to reconsider and decide to pedal back to the gardens in the woods for a bottle of Vouvray 1919, at about 5.50 francs for a demi. I believe I enjoyed that little bottle of wine as much, if not more, than any I have ever drunk. To a dry bicyclist, it was bottled sunshine. A little French family was quietly enjoying luncheon at another table, but with that exception the gardens were deserted, save for the chirping birds and alas, the mosquitoes.

In a few minutes I was once more on the road and my next stop was Amboise. What a thrill to suddenly spy the towers and battlements of the old grey castle high up on the hill across the river. I whirled merrily across the bridge and into the little town which nestles at the foot of the steep castle walls. Then I found my way to the *Entrée du Château* and was shown through its enchanting gardens and halls.

Although I had planned to pass the night in Amboise, it seemed much too soon to put away my bike, and, besides, the lady at the *château* had suggested that I go on to visit nearby Chaumont.

Chaumont struck me as the typical picturesque little castle town. Nothing but a small group of plaster houses, a store or two, and a couple of inns, it rests peacefully at the foot of the hill upon which the romantic park and ducal estate are placed. Since the *château* was open until seven, it seemed advisable to make my hotel arrangements, clean up a bit, and then visit the castle before supper. I had noticed a sign recommending the Hôtel de l'Avenue du Château. The little inn, whose two main rooms opened directly off the street, attracted me. I was given a pleasant, small room one flight up overlooking the charming garden behind the building for 15 francs. With pardonable pride, Madame showed me the white enameled bathroom which seemed to be the place's only concession to the twentieth century.

I washed, made arrangements for supper in the garden at 8:30 p. m. (I was the only guest), and then mounted the beautiful shaded lane to the park which surrounds the *château*. Although the last party had just been shown through, Monsieur had no objections to taking me on an individual tour, and, with the aid of little Daniel, his three-year-old grandson and obviously the present lord of the castle, we inspected the charming old place. I think I was more impressed by Chaumont than by any of the other *châteaux* I saw. It is a castle lifted bodily from legends where King Arthur might have passed a night – castle of childhood fairy tales, like Warwick in England.

Dinner was served me in calm solitude in the beautiful little garden at a table under a bower of vines. A priceless rural repose of soft bird songs, farmyard sounds, and the quiet of the angélus or Gray's Elegy. And what a dinner! Only two tranquil cats and my silent old servitor were in the garden beside myself.

First there was a marvelous thick soup with bread and a large bottle of Chaumont white wine which has the effervescence of champagne, then a priceless omelet done to the queen's taste. Then, "It is a tournedos that one is going to serve Monsieur. How will he have it, rare or well done? And what a tournedos …

with cress and potatoes . . . then a huge bowl of fresh lettuce salad nicely dressed by my *garçon* . . . then a pot of coffee with a glass of Cointreau and cigarettes! The bill, including wine and liqueur, was some 20 francs.

Towards the end of dinner, my waiter became a bit more communicative and finally asked me without warning, whether I had passed through the dining room on my way to dinner! This strange question concerned me some. Was some of the silver missing? Did they suspect me of being another Jean Valjean and the candlesticks?

I replied guardedly that I had passed through the dining room on my way into the garden, whereupon the old man proudly announced that great people from my country had taken food in the little garden where I found myself. Yes, Madame Wilson herself, and daughter, had been visitors and found their welcome and their food so delightful that the former could not resist leaving a brief tribute in the form of a card bearing a kind word for the little inn. This card, it seemed, had been proudly framed with several other similar ones, and placed in the dining room that guests might understand that it was no ordinary house at which they were taking shelter.

The wife of the former President? I asked with interest in spite of my dragging eyelids (a large bottle of Chaumont). Yes, the wife of the former President. So I sat silently in the garden for about an hour puffing happily at my cigarette and dreaming while Madame and the little Gaston watered the flowers, then I passed in through the dining room for the old man to show me the famous card.

Sure enough! There it was, a charmingly penned tribute to the Hôtel de l'Avenue du Château, signed by Mrs. George F. Wilson and daughter Mae! I did not set the old man right.

I should like to be able to record that I slept the sleep of the innocent that night, but my frenzied exhilaration at finding myself on a bike once more had completely drowned my good sense and I was to pay the penalty. Now I began to realize what it means to grow old and rusty, for such an agonizing pain went from my thighs to my knees as I have never before known and hope never to know again. Sleep was practically out of the question and I tossed through the night, trembling at the thought of my enforced continued bicycling in the morning. (There are *no trains* at Chaumont.)

My worst fears were confirmed, as I painfully took to the saddle once more the next morning. *Petit déjeuner* in the garden cheered me a little, but after a friendly farewell to my host and a brief run on the road to Blois, I was writhing in pain and had to recline in the grass on the roadside to study my map for some time while passing motorists glanced curiously at me as though they penetrated my ruse.

Somehow I managed to get to Blois, for the pain seemed to ease a bit as I got under way.

I made straight for the great pompous *château* since I was not yet sure that I would remain in the city for the night. I checked the bike and made the trip through the building which I found grandly beautiful but without the intimate charm of Chaumont. After a rest in the little city park (under the walls of the castle) I decided to act upon the recommendation of a friend, the Comtesse de Caen, and take a room at the Grand Hôtel de France. After some little discussion with the not too friendly Madame at the desk (my dusty, unprepossessing appearance did not speak too well for me) we arranged for a room at 18 francs for the night, and the bike was wheeled grandly around the hotel garage by a boy in buttons.

The little room was clean and pleasant. Following a thorough cleaning up, I descended to the hotel dining room for an excellent, although somewhat expensive luncheon. The afternoon, I decided to give over to routine matters and the doctoring of my sore legs, so I lost no great amount of time in stopping at one of the city's most important pharmacies. Here, however, I had some difficulty in describing my suffering and explaining what it was that I wished. After my broken description accompanied by the rubbing of my hands over my sore thighs, the considerate young clerk at once assumed that I was suffering from the world's oldest ailment and tactfully guided me over to a corner that I might supply him with the details in greater privacy!

He finally fixed me up, however, and I found his ointment excellent, though it took me another day to get noticeable relief. I sent cards during the afternoon, tried what seemed the town's leading café just around the corner from the hotel, and became thoroughly disgusted with a querulous old American in a fantastic get-up whose principal talent seemed to be trouble-making.

Dinner at the hotel was equally good, and I spent the evening at my café listening to the music, and more especially to the amusing comments of three Frenchmen (two women and a man) at a nearby table apropos of the Americans. They were supplied with their theme by antics of the above-mentioned American, who succeeded in so stirring up a group next door that the gentleman with the ladies had begun to forcibly propel him along the street in the direction of his hotel.

After a good night's sleep, I strolled again in the courtyard and above the grounds of the *château,* taking a bus after lunch for the famous Château de Chambord which is about half an hour's ride from Blois. I found Chambord even more magnificent than Blois and far too grand for a hunting lodge, although deeply interesting and fascinating in its lofty battlements and galleries. From Chambord our motorbus whirled us through some charming little villages to Cheverny, the charming little *château* tucked away by itself and still a private residence. Because the family was absent, we strolled through a large part of the building which is the perfect country gentleman's house – beautifully furnished and enchanting in the glamour of its distinguished past. From Cheverny we proceeded back to Blois.

Madame of the Grand Hôtel de France was far sweeter once she had submitted my bill and heard the crackle of some bank notes. The idea of a journalist's discount shocked her, however, and in short order, I had reduced the bill by 10% and wrung a most unctuous smile out of the lady by my reference to the Comtesse de Caen.

At Tours, I found my way to the Pension Charluet where Madame regretfully informed me that she had naught for me but a bathroom to sleep in! Would Monsieur mind? No, I was quite sure I wouldn't mind, at 20 francs for the night, dinner, and breakfast the following morning. In fact, it turned out to be very agreeable and I had a quick bath into the bargain.

After cleaning up, I went down to the dining room to encounter the eternal *pensionnaires* ... the middle class Englishman with his wife and their married son and daughter-in-law, the three English school teachers, charming, perhaps, but oh so unattractive, the middle-aged German tourist quietly eating alone, a young middle class French couple, and a young man who looked Italian (or at least Latin.).

In the evening I strolled about the beautiful old Cathedral of Tours and was delighted to come across Maybelle Anderson and one of her friends I had met at Blois. They had escaped from the rest of their party, and had had a most wonderful day along the way back to Tours. We walked in the evening and wound up in the little park in the center of the city which serves also as the terrasse of the town's leading café. Hundreds of townspeople assembled at the little tables beneath the trees to listen to the orchestra, sip coffee or beer, and watch the movies on a screen erected over the entrance to one of the adjoining cafés. It was an enchanting setting and we enjoyed it all hugely. As midnight approached, we strolled past a little Italian grocery store and inquired for *rillettes de Tours,* but he only had Italian ones. However, we bought fresh apricots and then went back to our respective hotels, and for me, the close of one of the most glamorous little trips I have ever made. I returned early next morning to Paris.

Resolving Beauty Out of Chaos

December 15, 1924 – Like a magnificent Phoenix rising from the ashes, the new city of Rheims * is rising slowly but steadily from the ruins which were practically all that remained to mark the site of the historic city at the close of the Great War.

While a little group of people knelt silently at Mass in a corner of the great shell-shattered cathedral last Sunday morning, the city fathers were convened in annual session to consider the work of reconstruction that has been done during the past year.

It has been a hard struggle for the little city. Of the 75 million francs spent on rebuilding, 50 million francs came from the state – the rest had to be borrowed.

118

And there are fears that the government will not be able to live up to its former promises of assistance.

In spite of the overwhelming task of resolving beauty once more out of chaos, the townsmen have shown that indomitable courage and power of recuperation which defy comparison in the world's history. Where not long ago, a huge pile of debris stood in the middle of the great cathedral may now be seen great expanses of concrete floor and walls designed to withstand the ravages of centuries for future posterity.

Where tragic ruins loomed like menacing skeletons against the blue sky, may now be seen beautiful winding roads lined with homes and gardens. Green blinds and red tiled roofs lend color to the former grey expanse of wrecked structures. The physical development of the new municipality has not been forgotten, and the beautiful natural park (the gift of the Polignac family) as well as two handsome swimming pools and a great stadium, promise well for the health of the future men and women of Rheims.

True, there is a vast amount of work still to be done. But Rheims has shown herself equal to the greatest catastrophes that can befall a city – and has won the undying admiration of the world.

Rheims Gets Hospital As U.S. Memorial

May 1, 1925 – High on a sunny hillside overlooking the grey towers and spires of ancient Rheims, a little group of French and Americans gathered yesterday for the formal presentation of America's gift to the shell-torn city – the American Memorial Hospital for Children.

In the middle of the spacious roof garden of the handsome structure and beneath the clear blue skies of Champagne, Ambassador Myron T. Herrick handed to the Mayor of Rheims the official title to this product of three years' ceaseless toil on the part of American women and the fruition of a promise made in 1919.

Editor's Note: Helen Josephy Robison and P.S. were reporters for the two great rival American newspapers in Paris – the *Chicago Tribune* and the *New York Herald Tribune* – and as such they should have been deadly enemies. Instead they proved to be extremely congenial companions, mainly, Helen insisted, because they were both busy and trying to avoid romance. This created a great bond between them.

They were together on a bus chartered to take a party of journalists to Rheims to view the rebuilding of the war-torn city that is recounted in this feature article by P.S. The bus was full to overflowing, mainly with rather scruffy French journalists, and neither Paul nor Helen could find a seat. Helen was the sole female journalist in the group, and Paul was incensed that nobody got up to give her a seat.

After a while he began vigorously gesticulating, and exclaiming in his best French, "Pour la dame! Pour la dame!" Eventually one of the Frenchmen most reluctantly responded, by which time Helen was reduced almost to hysterics by the comical aspect of the whole situation. And so a lifelong friendship began.

Where shells and shrapnel once whistled through the air, now will be heard the laughing voices of little children recovering from their sufferings. Where battle-scarred expanses once stretched, gaunt and menacing, now extend flower-lined walks and a sunken garden – a living tribute "to the memory of the American soldiers who fell on French soil."

Broad, sunny corridors, glistening white rooms flooded with light, and numerous spacious verandas are the inviting vista which greets the eye of the visitor. A group of entrancing nurseries, with bright colored walls and cheery rugs, have been fitted out with miniature tables and chairs, dolls, books, and toys, that will make the long hours of convalescence for the little patient supremely happy.

From all corners of America have arrived donations for the beautiful hospital. States, counties, cities, organizations, and individuals have chosen this means of preserving the memory of their soldier heroes, and in each room the artist, Saint-Hubert, has painted a fresco of happy children grouped about the inscription of the donor.

American soldiers, nurses, and military units are among those for whom memorials have been given. One room bears the simple inscription, "In memory of the happy return of my boy from the battlefields." Another touching memorial is to the fallen soldiers of Rheims, given by their American comrades. Still another is for the children of New England who did their bit at home.

"When our French children read over and over those patriotic lines, their little souls will bless their older American brothers who battled for them," said M. Guichard, head of the Rheims hospitals, in accepting the responsibility of the administration of the new institution.

American War Memorial is Dedicated At Saint-Nazaire

June 26, 1926 – Great grey battleships once more steamed majestically into the placid bay of Saint-Nazaire this morning. But the little group of hushed, war-torn townspeople who gathered to welcome them nine years ago was not there: instead, the entire population of the little seaside town was out in gala attire to dedicate the great pile of bronze and granite which will commemorate for all time the heroism of the American doughboys who fought in France.

The unveiling of the monument was one of the most touching post-war ceremonies in history. Early in the morning the little village became alive with expectancy of a great day. Smiling townspeople, many in picturesque Breton costumes, passed up and down the streets beside bronzed sailors in the white caps and red and blue tams of the United States and French Navies. Gold-braided admirals and silk-hatted statesmen hurried through the main thoroughfares making last-minute preparations for the ceremony.

Promptly at 10:45 a.m. a resplendent cortege swung down the drive from the prefecture and passed through a lane of American and French sailors along the sea front to the position where the great monument lay hidden beneath a huge canvas. Scores of red, white, and blue banners fluttered above the heads of the long line, in which marched Ambassador Myron T. Herrick, General Gouraud, Ministers Leygues and Vincent, Mrs. Harry Payne Whitney (the American sculptress who created the monument), General Pershing, General Rockenback, and scores of French senators, deputies, and military and civil dignitaries from all corners of the country.

When the gathering had assembled, surrounded by thousands of spectators, there was a pause while cameras and motion picture machines clicked. Then a roar of guns broke the silence and several hundred doves suddenly released on the beach circled about the monument and flew out of sight. As a marine band struck up "The Star Spangled Banner," the signal for the unveiling was given and the canvas which cloaked the monument slid slowly down amidst a chorus of admiring exclamations, followed by cheers and applause.

A series of bombs were sent spinning into the air only to crash high above the heads of spectators and release hundreds of glistening American and French flags. Other flags of all the allied nations followed amidst the cheers of the crowds.

Shortly after the close of the dedication, which featured speeches by civil and military dignitaries, including General Pershing, visitors were whirled in automobiles to the Salle des Fêtes du Chantier de Penhoët, where a lavish banquet was given jointly by the city and the Chamber of Commerce. It was late in the afternoon when the scurrying waiters were at last given a rest.

The evening was marked with a brilliant fireworks display on the water and band concerts in the decorated and illuminated public squares. There was also dancing in the hotels both at Saint-Nazaire and at La Baule.

Radio Interview with the Comtesse de Caen

Introduction: Eight years ago last fall, in 1926, my Paris editor directed me to call at a modest little hotel not far from the editorial offices of *L'Action Française* to interview a distinguished personage with the imposing name of Comtesse Constance Hillyer de Caen. I was somewhat awed by this first contact with French nobility but, to my astonishment, and delight, I was welcomed by a sweet-faced little lady with silver hair, sad eyes, but a smiling mouth. We talked for almost an entire afternoon.

That little lady from France is in the studio at WINS with me this afternoon, and is, in my opinion, one of the best friends America has in that country. She is still known to thousands of American doughboys as the "Little Mother of the

The Countess Constance Hillyer de Caen

American Soldiers." Her family has been connected with the house of Bourbon for many centuries. Her grandfather was the son of the Duc de Berri, who was himself the son of Charles X.

Comtesse: It is a great pleasure to be here, but I would rather not discuss the politics of France. My work has been outside the realm of politics. I am only interested in helping wherever I can, regardless of nationality or politics.

P.S.: How did you get started in this remarkable work?

Comtesse: When war broke out I wanted to do my duty to my country and I joined the Red Cross. When the Americans came, knowing the English language, I asked permission of the Red Cross delegate to give my services to the Americans. When the Americans arrived we introduced them into families where they were made completely at home. We visited the hospitals, wrote to the mothers of all the boys, and kept in touch with these mothers who were anxious to know where their sons were. From the bedsides of a great number of the boys we wrote to the mothers, sometimes giving them the last words before the boys passed on.

In December 1918 I began my first trip to America to carry messages from the boys to their mothers in this country. At that time the railroads were in the hands of the government, and at the request of the mothers, I was given passes straight through to San Francisco.

P.S.: Do you remember what the first message was that you delivered?

Comtesse: I shall never forget it, because it impressed me so deeply. The young American soldier didn't realize that he was dying, and when I asked him if he would like me to carry a message back to his mother in Los Angeles, he said, "Give her my love, and tell her I will see her very soon, and tell her I don't regret what I have done." He died shortly thereafter. That message was the first one of the 2,500 that I delivered to Gold Star Mothers.

P.S.: These messages must have carried you to many corners of our country.

Comtesse: I have been in every state except Colorado, and now I am going to visit Colorado, and later Canada. In 1932, I had traveled 12,000 miles, and as you see, I have still more to go. Some of my most interesting memories are those of visiting Indian families on your reservations. The Indians, by the way, actually made me a member of their tribes in Travers City, Michigan, Hominy, Oklahoma, and Pawhauska, Oklahoma, and in Mayatta, Kansas. Can you imagine a little woman like myself decked out in full chief's regalia, feathers and all? Of course, on these visits, I had no official status. Everything was done entirely through personal friendship and gratitude.

P.S.: What are some of the outstanding experiences that you have had in carrying out this magnificent work?

Comtesse: There are thousands, but I must tell you about the case of a German boy in the American Army who couldn't speak a word of English. He came from your far West, and as he was dying in my arms he thanked me in his own language, and seemed so happy to know that I would see his mother, even though he would not. On my next trip to this country I did find her in a little town in Texas, and you can imagine her gratitude when I gave her a picture of her son taken during his last days at the hospital. The mother has since visited her son's grave in France, and we are seeing to it that it, and several thousand like it, are kept green with an occasional bunch of flowers.

P.S.: I am sure you also had some less tragic experiences with the American soldiers.

Comtesse: Yes, indeed. I laugh even now to recall what was at that time a very serious problem. You see, many of these boys were away from home for the first time, and the sparkling wines of our country were a great temptation to them. Many of them became all too easily intoxicated, and we had to lecture them severely. I am glad to say that in most cases they responded good naturedly. Happy New Year to all the Gold Star Mothers, and to my dear American boys.

*   *   *

CHAPTER 5

OPERA AND THEATRE

Introduction

Opera and theatre were P.S.'s twin loves, and he was fortunate to be in Paris at a time when they held enormous glamour. Opera to him was totally romantic, and the opera stars were expected to be highly temperamental, both on the stage and off. Composers and authors, too, had their moments, and were prone to settle arguments by dueling.

Prima donnas were often motivated by professional jealousy, and an amusing incident was recorded in the *Chicago Tribune,* Paris edition, on May 16, 1925. It bears the graphic headlines, "Olczewska banned from Vienna Opera for expectorating on Jaritza during *Walkyrie.* " Two years later P.S. tells how this firebrand, playing Amneris in *Aïda* at Covent Garden, where she ends act IV, scene 1 by turning on the priests "in redoubled fury," was given a tremendous ovation, and was recalled some eight times.

P.S. had a special affection for the Puccini operas – *Tosca* being his favorite. He heard both Jaritza and Mary Garden in the part several times.

His favorite, however, was Mary Garden, with whom he had been infatuated, (in spite of the twenty years' difference in their ages) from the first time he had heard her sing *Monna Vanna* in Chicago. Mary Garden was sufficiently secure in her position in the opera world (from the moment of her spectacular debut in 1900 in the title role of Charpentier's *Louise* in Paris) that she does not seem to have felt the need to put on outrageous scenes to get attention. In 1925 she was the reigning queen of the American-French-Italian opera season at the Gaité Lyrique, on the Champs Elysées, where P.S. attended a gala opening performance of *Love of Three Kings.*

In the small, pocket-sized book of opera synopses that P.S. bought on arrival in Paris, are notations not only of opera casts, but of the many opera houses where he attended performances. Besides the well-known opera houses in the capitals of Europe, the list includes Wiesbaden, Nuremberg, Salzburg, Graz, the

Hague, Brussels, Milan, Munich, Glyndebourne, and others. In Berlin, in the 1950s, he heard operas in the Staatsoper in the Russian sector, the Stadlicheoper in the British sector, and the Opera House in the West sector. He made a hobby of "collecting" opera houses, and was frustrated by small opera houses, such as Venice, which were more often closed than open!

*   *   *

In 1926, when P.S. took over the *Tribune's* theatre column from Simone Heller, his secondary journalistic career began as a drama critic. For the rest of his working life he wrote theatre reviews and interviewed theatrical celebrities for *Theatre Arts Magazine,* for King Features Syndicate, and for various radio stations, always aside from his regular work.

The reigning stars of the Paris stage in the 1920s were, undoubtedly, the two husband-wife teams, Sacha Guitry and Yvonne Printemps, and Georges and Ludmilla Pitoëff. P.S. saw the former during his first ten days in Paris, and many times during the succeeding three years. The latter he saw at a later date in various plays including Pirandello's *Comme Ci (ou Comme Ça)* and the French translation of Shaw's *St. Joan.*

La Pitoëff, with her huge, luminous eyes, was considered by many to be the most inspired actress to play the part. She had several children, which never interfered with her career, and on Armistice Day 1926, P.S. saw her give an especially moving benefit performance of *St. Joan* when she was definitely *enceinte.*

Another unique figure of the Paris stage at that time was Raymond (nicknamed "Goatherd") Duncan, brother of the famous Isadora, who founded his own school of drama and attracted much attention to himself and his followers by wearing flowing white robes, his bare feet in sandals, and his long hair held by a Grecian headband.

From his earliest years P.S. saved theatre programs, and his collection spans two continents from the early days of World War I to the late 1960s. The Paris collection includes performances by Cécile Sorel in *l'Abbé Constantin;* Yvonne Printemps playing Mozart in a comedy of that name, written by her husband Sacha Guitry, Ida Rubinstein in Dostoyevsky's *l'Idiot,* Eva Le Gallienne in *Jehanne d'Arc,* Ludmilla Pitoëff in Jean Cocteau's *Orphée,* Silvain in *Tartuffe,* Josephine Baker as La Vierge Noire at the *Folies-Bergère,* and Mistinguett at the Moulin Rouge.

From his student days there are programs from the Whitney Theatre in Ann Arbor with Sarah Bernhardt, Sir Herbert Beerbohm Tree, Maxine Elliott, Mrs. Patrick Campbell, and others. When Walter Hampden gave a performance of *Hamlet,* P.S. and his college friend Dick Forsyth each donned a pair of moth-eaten green tights, grabbed a spear, and came charging on the stage as soldiers in the final scene.

126

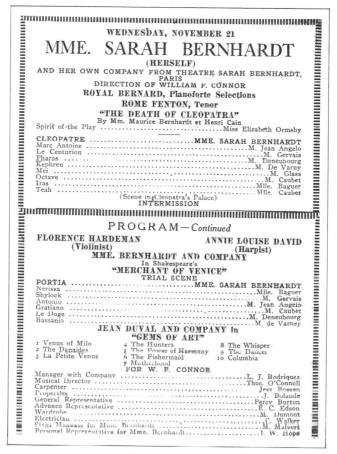

WEDNESDAY, NOVEMBER 21

MME. SARAH BERNHARDT
(HERSELF)

AND HER OWN COMPANY FROM THEATRE SARAH BERNHARDT, PARIS

DIRECTION OF WILLIAM F. CONNOR

ROYAL BERNARD, Pianoforte Selections

ROME FENTON, Tenor

"THE DEATH OF CLEOPATRA"

By Mm. Maurice Bernhardt et Henri Cain

Spirit of the Play .... Miss Elizabeth Ormsby

CLEOPATRE .... MME. SARAH BERNHARDT
Marc Antoine .... M. Jean Angelo
Le Centurion .... M. Gervais
Pharos .... M. Deneubourg
Kephren .... M. De Varny
Mei .... M. Glass
Octave .... M. Caubet
Iras .... Mlle. Baguer
Teah .... Mlle. Caubet
(Scene in Cleopatra's Palace)
INTERMISSION

PROGRAM—*Continued*

FLORENCE HARDEMAN   ANNIE LOUISE DAVID
(Violinist)   (Harpist)
MME. BERNHARDT AND COMPANY
In Shakespeare's
"MERCHANT OF VENICE"
TRIAL SCENE

PORTIA .... MME. SARAH BERNHARDT
Nerissa .... Mlle. Baguer
Shylock .... M. Gervais
Antonio .... M. Jean Angelo
Gratiano .... M. Caubet
Le Doge .... M. Deneubourg
Bassanio .... M. de Varney

JEAN DUVAL AND COMPANY in
"GEMS OF ART"

1 Venus of Milo   4 The Hunters   8 The Whisper
2 The Danaides   5 The Power of Harmony 9 The Dancer
3 La Petite Venus   6 The Fishermaid   10 Columbia
                      7 Motherhood

FOR W. F. CONNOR

Manager with Company .... L. J. Rodriquez
Musical Director .... Thos. O'Connell
Carpenter .... Jess Boesen
Properties .... J. Bolande
General Representative .... Percy Burton
Advance Representative .... E. C. Edson
Wardrobe .... M. Dumont
Electrician .... C. Walker
Stage Manager for Mme. Bernhardt .... M. Malvert
Personal Representative for Mme. Bernhardt .... I. W. Hope

Program presented by Sarah Bernhardt in Ann Arbor, Michigan, 1917

Taken together, P.S.'s reviews and informal commentaries concerning opera and theatre productions and personalities offer a refreshing on-stage (and off-stage) view of the unique blending of the old and the new that characterized the performing arts in Paris in the mid-1920s.

E.B.S.

*   *   *

M. Balieff in Rehearsal is Not the M. Balieff
Dear to Audiences

October 16, 1924 – I dropped in at the Théâtre Femina on the Champs-Elysées the other evening to watch M. Nikita Balieff conduct a dress rehearsal of the new *Chauve-Souris* which opened last Wednesday night. It was a rare experience.

"Change your mustache!" shouts the rotund director with a face like a full moon.

There is a scurrying of feet, and the magnificent Oriental prince disappears into the wings to return in a moment with a startling hirsute decoration turned smartly up at each end.

"Mais non, non, non!" wails M. Balieff, "It must turn *down*!"

There is another moment's pause and the prince returns with a drooping effect that will strike horror to the bravest heart.

"Bravo!" is his reward, and the rehearsal continues.

From orchestra pit to the stage, then back to the last row of seats, M. Balieff seems to be everywhere at once. One moment he is helping to move a huge platform into a better position on the stage, the next, he is calling loudly from the back of the theatre to turn off the blue lights and try an amber flood.

I stayed until three o'clock the next morning, and the drilling was still going on when I left.

As for the show itself, this Russian vaudeville de luxe is probably the most consistently beautiful series of stage pictures that has ever been seen. I liked it even better than the original edition. M. Archangelsky is again the principal composer and has supplied M. Balieff with a score that seemed to me to come pretty close to the great Tchaikovsky himself – though, of course, one musn't say so.

The plans call for a couple of months in Paris and then the usual migration to America, opening in New York early in January. Probably the first-night contingent there will be much the same as it was here: evening clothes from gallery to stalls with a peck of diamonds and some celebrities such as Premier Herriot on hand. During the entr'acte there was a bewildering parade of evening wraps on the Champs where the women repaired for a few puffs.

Kreisler Says His American Wife Is Best Critic
And Finest Inspiration

November 15, 1924 – "My dear, where *have* you been?" exclaimed an anxious-faced woman as the world's greatest violinist stepped into an elevator at the Hotel Majestic last night, and they were whirled, together with the *Tribune* reporter, up to their luxurious suite on the second floor.

Fritz Kreisler had just come from a rehearsal, but had been loitering along the way until a half dozen broken appointments had become tragic history. A telltale package lay on the table.

"More books!" cried Mrs. Kreisler in consternation as she drew out several beautifully bound editions of Anatole France.

The great artist walked meekly around the table to where she sat, and threw a caressing arm around her. He had brought her something also.

"Surely you didn't buy me those earrings?" she gasped as she turned an appealing glance towards the reporter. "I have everything I can possibly use – and still he brings me more! He simply won't stop buying."

In the seclusion of the next room, the violinist smiled whimsically at his interviewer. "I don't know what I should do without her." he said, "She's my best critic, my inspiration, and she knows more about music than anybody else in the world! Yes, she's American. I met her between two worlds – half-way across the ocean on the way from New York to Germany. She hadn't heard me play, and didn't know my name, she simply knew *me*. So, I guess I won her on the strength of myself alone!

And now what would you like to know? Jazz? No, of course that's not a ridiculous question. For a long time I thought jazz showed a real element of merit and would develop into something very much worthwhile. But I'm beginning to lose hope as it becomes so commercialized. It has rhythm and vivacity, but its artistic *élan* has been lost. Its present appeal seems to be primarily to the barbarian instinct that, I guess, is in all of us – a sort of vengeance of the jungles upon us in return for out modern civilization.

America is young, and all her efforts have been expended towards industry, commerce, and the things by which nations live. Art is the last development in the history of a country. It has already started coming in America, and the prospects are glowing."

The telephone jangled harshly in the next room and a long-suffering but adoring wife announced more callers. Hers is the hardest role in the world – the wife of a celebrity. But she plays it to perfection.

M. Fritz KREISLER

To Paul Alfred Shinkman
cordially,
FKreisler

Fritz Kreisler

November 18, 1924

Dear Family,

The cream of my musical interviews came last night – with Fritz Kreisler! However, it looked for a while as though it were going to turn into a pretty little domestic bout between Mr. and Mrs. Kreisler, with myself on the side-lines.

I had been trying to get hold of Kreisler for an interview all week, after hearing his first concert a week ago Sunday night. It looked as though luck was agin me, but I made one last desperate attempt to get him on the phone, and finally I found myself talking to the great man on the other end of the wire.

After I told him who I was and what I wanted, he invited me to call that evening at six o'clock when he would be back from rehearsal.

Of course I was there on the dot and called up the Kreisler apartment to be told by Mrs. Kreisler in no very sweet tone that her husband had not yet returned but that I should wait downstairs, let him come up when he came, and then come up myself later. I waited several minutes and sure enough, in he came, pulling his coat collar modestly up around his face to ward off celebrity chasers. I collared him and he smilingly asked me to come right along up with him, while he rang for the elevator. The door swung open and out came a feminine storm-cloud – the Madame herself!

"My dear, where *have* you been?" It seems half a dozen people had been there at four o'clock by arrangement but – no Fritz. He insisted he had been back earlier in the afternoon, but – "No you must be mistaken about that!" (in very firm tones).

Fearing the worst, I tried to beat a hasty retreat but Mr. K. insisted that I come right along with them to their luxurious apartment (I think he felt in need of protection). We escaped into the farthest room for our interview and when we came out she seemed still a bit miffed, especially when he announced that he had bought her a pair of earrings! She told me she simply can't make him stop buying her things that that clever dealers bring around, assuming he's good for any amount.

I felt rather sorry for the old chap having his gifts received like that so I took a hand in things and told her there were some pretty fine earrings in Paris and she'd better wait until she had seen them! "But I don't want them," she said positively. "I already have everything I could possibly need." It was quite a touching scene but things seemed to be all right again when I left – although there was another reporter waiting downstairs (can you blame them for getting peevish?)

January 1, 1925 – Paris is aghast at the *Ballet Suèdois,* now showing at the fashionable Théâtre des Champs Elysées.

Relâche, in particular, sent the critics scurrying for their most vitriolic ink with which to pen their anathema of the crazy creation. Here is a brief synopsis of what occurs before the eyes of the dazed audience:

Gendarme appears against a background composed of row after row of blinding white lights which vary in intensity while they change colors; fashionably gowned woman walks upon the stage from the audience and throws off most of her clothes, while the *gendarme* starts to pour water from one pail to another and back again, persisting in this exciting occupation until the end of the opus.

Elderly gentleman in evening dress and with flowing grey beard darts out from the wings in a toy automobile; he alights and goes through some weird steps with the maiden, after which eight young men similarly dressed march out and begin tossing her back and forth: the chorus of eight then casually remove their coats and trousers and step forth in acrobatic attire plus silk hats.

All concerned continue in eerie gymnastics, while the grand opera orchestra screams and moans the fantastic score, first in lyric simplicity and then in wildest syncopation – and through it all, the solemn *gendarme* gravely continues to pour water back and forth from one pail to another!

The performance was an invitational affair for the members of the French Chamber of Deputies. Which may explain why there was still an audience until the bitter end.

*   *   *

For the first time in history the pompous Opéra is to re-echo to the strains of an American musical composition.

To add to the novelty of the occasion, Mr. Blair Fairchild, the American composer, who is obviously of English extraction, told me his music is considered essentially French, due to his having received most of his training in Paris, although the inspiration for the present work was a group of themes which he uncovered while delving into the music lore of Persia! So the affair will take on something of an international aspect.

The piece, known as *Le Songe d'Isfendiar,* is a romantic ballet. M. Rouché, the major domo of the great temple of music, has promised to give it one of his typically colorful productions some time during the present season.

The composer already has the honor of being the first American to have a composition performed at the Paris Opéra-Comique. His ballet, *Dame Libellule,* was performed there in October 1921.

"I tell you Mimi still lives!"

January 28, 1925 – As the damp shadows fell over the dripping gables and chimney pots of the Latin Quarter last evening (sixty-four years after the death of Henri Murger) the little Queen of the Bohemians might have been seen fluttering excitedly along the boulevard, shaking the raindrops from her coat, and turning in at a student café for a rendezvous with Rodolphe.

"I tell you Mimi still lives!" a poet was saying at a corner table, while his friends speculated upon the Latin Quarter of Murger's immortal *Bohème* and that of twentieth century Paris.

"She lives in a grotesque garret, and she will die singing her death song from a straw pallet while Rodolphe clutches frantically at her departing spirit."

"No," says another. "The Quarter has changed during the century. Rodolphe no longer feeds the fire with his manuscript. He now rings for another basket of *boulets*. The straw pallet upon which little Mimi breathed her last has made way for the Murphy bed which folds up out of sight. Benoît is no longer made to forget the back rent due him by means of the sparkling wine of his impecunious tenants. Now he demands six months' advance rental in cash, plus twenty % *service*, and Schaunard learns to dicker with the movies, while his neighbor across the hall speaks of 'magazine rights'."

Where a festive dance in a neighboring café used to suffice as entertainment for the humble Quarterites, we now have the Mediterranean cruise, a jaunt to the Riviera, or a leisurely journey through Africa as an essential part of the year's program.

All of which is simply advanced in support of the startling proposition that "things are diff'runt" among the artists than they used to be.

But Mimi and Rodolphe still live – oblivious to the changes around them.

The Opera's Fiftieth Birthday

January 1925 – Paris' magnificent Opéra celebrated its half-century birthday last Monday.

The whole city and particularly musical circles, made great preparations for the event, which was marked with a grand festival of music with the elite of Paris in attendance. There was an opera ballet, *Le Triomphe de l'Amour,* one act from *Les Huguenots,* the mad scene from *Hamlet,* and the ballet *Sylvia,* the four pieces representing the four principal periods in the history of the Académie Nationale de Musique et de Danse.

In January 1875, the beautiful temple of music was inaugurated with great pomp and circumstance. What a brilliant scene it must have presented with the Empress of Russia, the Queen of Spain and her son, the Lord Mayor of London, the

Count and Countess of Paris, the ex-King of Hanover, and officials from all the great capitals of Europe, gathered around the crimson and golden horseshoe beneath the huge chandelier of flashing crystal!

Monday evening did not see a gathering of such royal proportions, but, just as fifty years ago, the President of the Republic was present, together with the French ministers and the entire diplomatic corps, as well as a distinguished gathering of notables from various parts of the world.

April 3, 1925 – Surely the English-speaking drama is gaining support in Paris.

In addition to the various Shakespearean plays which are regularly played at the Odéon and the Comédie Française, there are the annual visits of companies from England and even America.

To add a still more interesting note to recent developments, we now have the distinguished Italian company of Ruggero Ruggeri arriving to present a season of Italian drama, with a production of *Hamlet* at the top of the list.

Signor Ruggeri, who has already been acclaimed in Paris as one of the world's most important theatrical figures, was the guest of honor at a brilliant reception on the eve of his opening performance last week. Scores of the leading theatrical and literary personages of the French capital gathered in the foyer of the beautiful Théâtre de la Madeleine to extend a hearty welcome to the distinguished Italian actor and the members of his company.

Hamlet, Tragedy in Six Acts by William Shakespeare, presented in Italian at the Théâtre de la Madeleine

Hamlet, in the dulcet accents of the Latins, is not an easy combination to imagine. The idea takes on, at first blush, something of the unpleasant aspect of a Verdi opera sung in English.

If, however, there was any sense of the incongruous at the Théâtre de la Madeleine Thursday evening when the curtain rose on an Italian-speaking court of Denmark, it was almost entirely dispelled as the tragedy once more began to unfold about the outstanding figure of Ruggero Ruggeri.

This Hamlet is not Italian. He is a Hamlet of careful repression whose emotional crises are few, but who, when they come, hurls himself into the maelstrom. He is not handsome or romantic. There is nothing of madness. He is a cool, calculating intellect, trying desperately to penetrate the cataclysm that whirls about him.

By the grace of Signor Ruggeri's inspiring acting, which amounted to pantomime under the circumstances, the Italian *Hamlet* venture was saved, and has become a noteworthy event of the dramatic season.

April 18, 1925 – Paris now boasts what is undoubtedly the Queen of the Music Halls throughout the world.

In a burst of glory, with the élite of Paris on both sides of the footlights, the new Opera-Music-Hall was formally inaugurated last week at the Théâtre des Champs Elysées. After a somewhat checkered career as the home of grand opera, concert, and drama, this most beautiful of Paris theatres is now to become a vaudeville house *de luxe.*

Glittering Paris society was out *en masse* for the inaugural occasion, and the great horseshoe of crimson loges was brilliant with the exquisite gowns and wraps of the ladies, against the more sombre black and white background contributed by their escorts.

And Paris will long remember the distinguished group, representing the artistic and literary *crème de la crème,* who were on hand to make the *première* a truly gala affair. First, there was M. Jean Richepin, the celebrated writer of the Académie Française, who followed his discussion with a few readings from his poems. Next came Mlle Cécile Sorel, queen of the Comédie Française, who thrilled the spectators with her performance of the first act of *Maîtresse du Roi,* herself as the bewitching Du Barry, courtesan of Louis XV. Mme Nina Kochitz, stately soprano from the Opéra, Dorville, king of Paris clowns, and Billy Arnold and his real American jazz syncopators *par excellence,* were others who contributed to the impressiveness of the occasion.

Jazz And Giants, Beauty And Speed Characterize U.S.
"American a Creature of Happiness," says M. Bernard Fay

May 9, 1925 – Cloud-pierced skyscrapers . . . flaming youth . . . herds of buffaloes roaming interminable plains . . . swirling Broadway at midnight . . . throbbing jazz rhythms . . . roaring Niagara from a writhing airplane . . . the majestic Grand Canyon at dawn.

These were a few of the crashing impressions which were hurled at the bewildered group of Frenchmen who gathered at the little Théâtre du Vieux Colombier on the Left Bank last night.

They had come to learn of *Les Plaisirs et les Joies aux Etats-Unis* from M. Bernard Fay, fresh from America and still athrob, apparently with its dynamic imprint.

A burst of strident "blue" harmony from the seductive piano of Mr. Eugene MacGown opened the program. "To create ze American atmosphere," as one beaming French maiden announced.

M. Fay then began his clinical discussion of the American species. "A creature of happiness," he said, "with a love of the physical in beauty and joy . . . a child set out to conquer space instead of time . . . a pulsating being who yearns for physical expression but is quick to recognize intellect . . . an adolescent youth of exaggerated emotions." (Emotions that have created that pathetic American genus, "the nervous wreck.")

Kentucky and ragtime are vital phases of America, it is said. During the entr'acte, Mr. McGown sent a rhythmic thrill through his Old World audience with "Kentucky" and "Tea For Two," while an anonymous but unmistakably talented American Negro crooned a vocal accompaniment with some syncopated steps nicely synchronized.

The last half of the evening was given over to the mad cinema whirl through that New World that pulsated between the Grand Canyon of Wall Street and the Grand Canyon of the West. With a sickening tailspin from miles above Gotham down to the whirling earth, the picture was brought to a close – no, it was a huge golden sun dipping gently down into the cool, placid horizon of the West, that sent the audience serenely into the outside world once more.

*　　*　　*

The Théâtre Albert-Premier in the Rue Rocher nightly brings together an enthusiastic audience of English, Americans, and English-speaking French. The plays so far this season have included the most ambitious assortment, ranging from Sheridan's classics to the very modern *Juno and the Paycock* by the promising new playwright Sean O'Casey.

Thus indicating that if London is cosmopolitan enough to enjoy her English version of Molière's *Le Bourgeois Gentilhomme,* Paris has no intention of falling behind in the appreciation of British theatrical fare.

*　　*　　*

Terpsichore, however, has decided to shed some of her cosmopolitanism in the French capital. The Charleston, foxtrot, blackbottom, and similar importations, are in grave danger of losing their crowns.

From Montmartre comes word that the historic Butte has decided to hark back to the early days of France for the inspiration for her new dances instead of traveling across the ocean. Thus we have the Chibreli and the Morvandelle announced as the smart ballroom steps for the New Year.

Indeed, certain dancing academies have already undertaken to teach their followers the new dances, which have their inspiration in the old folk dances of the French provinces. Quite naturally, these colorful dances require special music,

136

and it is said that old-time fiddlers, and bagpipe and hurdy gurdy players, are now in great demand to take the place of the acrobatic trap drummer and the moaning saxophonist.

Back to Clothes Movement Strikes Montmartre Shows

Mad Montmartre, heretofore the world's center for undressed reviews, has hit the Sawdust Trail and is going to get dressed!

Such was the startling announcement made to the *Tribune* yesterday by Mr. Earl Leslie, American producer of the famous Moulin Rouge review, and already one of the outstanding figures of the French capital.

The American producer's pronunciamento came as a result of an inquiry as to his opinion of the recent stage reform wave sweeping America and believed by many to be sweeping across the Atlantic to Europe.

Ready to prove that his assertion is backed up with cold facts and is not idle newspaper talk, Mr. Leslie pointed out that his current review is not only more fully dressed than any he has staged in Paris heretofore, but makes current Broadway reviews look like the Garden of Eden in comparison.

"All this talk of Montmartre being the center stage of nudity is nonsense," he declared with spirit. "We are actually beginning to dress our girls and are going to continue to do so. The old days of placing the emphasis upon undressed girls, even in Montmartre, are over.

All this is for a very simple reason," the producer went on to explain. "Aside from all moral considerations, it is absolutely true that a beautiful girl gowned is far more alluring than any number of the other type. Figures prove this. Who are the girls who make up the so-called 'ten-strike' with the audiences? They are the girls who are costumed so as to best set off their particular type of beauty. The fact that they may be wearing several yards of costume has no detracting influence... *Au contraire!*"

Mr. Leslie did not deny that there are scenes in his review where beautiful *figurantes* wear practically nothing. At the same time, he insisted that Montmartre is taking seriously its "back to clothes" movement and that where the music hall reviews have been hitherto designed to appeal merely to the sophisticated, adult taste, they are now calculated to appeal to less mature tastes as well. "Why, they are actually bringing children to our matinee performances," he said, intimating that under old conditions, this would have been an incredible procedure.

"This is where New York makes its big mistake," he explained to the *Tribune*. "They have not yet learned that mere nudity is not a drawing card with the music hall audience. I have seen American producers order a wholesale *déshabille* on the part of their companies, merely to attract audiences. When these producers have learned the secret of our movement here in Montmartre, they will climb onto the 'back to clothes' bandwagon."

"Jazz is Music of Future,"
Says Mary Garden

May 14, 1925 – Mary Garden, queen of the grand opera divas, is the jazz fiend's latest and most eminent victim.

"Do I like jazz?" she repeated, in her flower-banked apartment within the shadow of the Arc de Triomphe yesterday afternoon, when the *Tribune* reporter asked her the fatal question. "Do I like jazz? I adore it! In fact I sing it!" And the countless jade bracelets on her slender left wrist rattled a rhythmic obligato.

"Jazz is a part of the march into the future," Miss Garden continued. "America lives in the future, not in the past. France has a glorious past, but she must not forget that there may be a dozen Napoleons in Paris today."

A beige tailored suit with a smart straw turban to match constituted yesterday's costume of Février's *Monna Vanna,* an operatic heroine who sways warrior princes from their purposes.

It was suggested that the presence in Paris of Director Johnson, of the Chicago Civic Opera, might have something to do with his wish to keep an eagle eye on his famous songbird.

The blonde head tossed defiantly above the tightly drawn collar of pearls, the size of chestnuts.

"I have refused invitations to sing at both the Opéra and the Opéra-Comique this year in order to give what help I can to M. Longone, of the American-French-Italian Opera Company at the Gaité-Lyrique," declared the diva. "He is an impresario with a real future. But it's not my company, I've had all the opera directing I want.

Four performances, then back to the Riviera for a rest before the fall season in the City Beside the Lake!"

May 17, 1925

Dear Family,

I must tell you about my chat with Mary Garden last week. She is here for the

American Opera season which opens Wednesday. She was charming over the phone when I called up to ask for an appointment. On the way to her apartment, I passed a flower stand, and decided to take a rosebud "in memory of that last wonderful performance of *Monna Vanna*," which I heard her sing at the Chicago Auditorium four years ago. When I knocked on the door, she called out to come in and before I knew what had happened I had given her a smack on the cheek! The first grand opera star I've ever kissed! She knew I was from Chicago and, of course, that struck a tender spot with her when I had phoned her. The poor French newspaper photographer, who was the only other one present, looked on in amazement. I think he is still trying to figure out whether I am her husband, son, or lover!

She just laughed and enjoyed it immensely – particularly the rosebud, which she immediately fastened to her suit. After we had had a little chat, she asked me whether I were going to be on hand for her opening performance. I told her not at $10 a throw! (price for best seats the opening night). She said nothing more about it, but a little later suddenly trailed over to her escritoire and pulled out two tickets for the opening night of *L'Amore dei Tre Re*, in the center of the first row, first balcony! Said she would listen for my applause, and, of course, I told her she would sure get it, in the good old American fashion. She is a delightful personality – full of vitality and dash.

May 30, 1925 – Amidst an unprecedented blaze of splendor, and with the cream of the French capital in attendance, Paris last week launched her American-French-Italian Opera season at the Théâtre de la Gaîté-Lyrique.

    Love of Three Kings was selected as the opening offering and, to add to the *éclat* of the occasion, Signor Montemezzi, the composer, was himself on hand.

Safe to say, no composer ever witnessed a more brilliant gathering assembled to do homage to his work.

Mary Garden, the American songbird, was queen of the evening. It was in Paris a considerable number of years ago, that the dramatic scene took place which made her a grand opera star overnight. Consequently, Paris has always felt a particular affection for her, and to say that it is mutual is unnecessary.

Cécile Sorel, of the Comédie Française, Lucrezia Bori, the operatic star, Dolores, former Ziegfeld Follies queen and now the wife of a millionare, and Giuseppe de Luca, the famous Italian baritone, were a few of those we noticed in the parade of European personages, including, of course, members of the diplomatic corps from England, America, as well as France itself.

Madame Nazimova, the Russian tragedienne, told us it was one of those affairs at which she "had to be present." She was sitting with the Baron and Baronne de Rothschild, her coal-black eyes and hair contrasting sharply with an ermine wrap.

After the memorable performance, we ventured backstage to renew a week-old acquaintance with Mary Garden. She was sitting quietly with two or three friends, still in her last act costume. Yes, she was entirely satisfied with the performance. And her audience – how kind they were!

How Chaliapin, Famous Baritone, Punched a Fellow Artist's Nose

June 18, 1925 – High up in a luxuriously furnished *atelier* overlooking the Trocadéro, a handsome, silver-haired gentleman, his eyes flashing with anger, suddenly sprang at the throat of his companion yesterday afternoon.

Feodor Chaliapin, world-famous baritone, was demonstrating to a delighted group of friends just how the report originated that he had turned pugilist and furiously pummeled the nose of a fellow artist on the stage of the Chicago Auditorium recently.

"We were rehearsing a scene from *Boris Gudounoff*," naively related the blue-eyed star, "and I asked the maestro to let us go through the part without music. Then, as Boris, I went through the scene where the fierce king seizes one of his enemies by the throat and shouts angry threats at him.

And next morning," continued M. Chaliapin, smiling ruefully, "I read that, in a fiery wrath, I had broken the nose of Monsieur X. Yes, the reporter, who had slipped into the auditorium, had seen me do it himself!"

Following his final performance of *Boris Gudounoff* at the Paris Opéra this evening, the opera star will take a few weeks' rest, before filling several European engagements. He will return to the Metropolitan Opera of New York for the coming season. In fact, Chaliapin declared that he has become so attached to the cause of American opera that he will be actively connected with the movement to establish a national operatic organization.

June 21, 1925

Dear Family,

Met Chaliapin the other day and he gave the *Herald* reporter and myself a fine-looking photograph of himself, personally autographed.

Saw the Diaghilev Russian Ballet Wednesday night. They are doing only modern stuff (Stravinsky, Poulenc, etc.) and the costumes and settings are most unusual. Throw themselves around the stage in the most grotesque steps you ever saw. In Stravinsky's *Le Chant du Rossignol,* they suddenly begin to play leapfrog while the music screams along in all sorts of discord. Makes you sort of wonder. Do you like the new music?

June 30, 1925

Dear Family,

Last Friday night, an American soprano, Madeline Keltie, made her debut at the Opéra-Comique in *Madame Butterfly.* After the performance, a friend of hers gave a supper party at the 400 Club here, which is one of the fashionable dancing restaurants. The *Trib* received invitations to both the performance and the supper party, and it was my rare luck to be given a couple of them. Two others went to Jay Allen, another reporter, whom I like very much. So I took Helen Josephy and he took his wife and we had one wonderful and memorable evening!

As for the supper, ooh la la! Everybody was in evening dress of course, and what gorgeousness! And what a list of celebrities had been invited. Sessue Hayakawa, the film star, Florence Walton, the dancer, Claire Luce, dancer from the Casino de Paris, Norman Bel Geddes, the famous American stage designer, etc., etc. And the opera soprano, the guest of honor, looking like a queen in one of those shining white and silver gowns, came in while the orchestra struck up "Un bel di."

Towards the end of the evening, we got up enough nerve to go over to her table and tell her how much we had enjoyed her performance. And then – I don't know exactly how it happened – I suddenly found myself gliding blissfully over the shiny floor with the great opera star in my arms! And what a dance it was! I

Feodor Chaliapin

shall never forget it. The rest at my table, of course, were aghast at my boldness.

The performance was fine. I like *Butterfly* music, in fact most anything of Puccini. He can put more pathetic beauty into a measure than a lot of so-called "moderns" can put into a page.

*   *   *

A *répétition générale* is to the Paris theatre what a dinner party at Buckingham Palace is to London society. Absence is no dishonor – but to be present is to scale the last dizzy heights of Parnassus itself!

At about nine o'clock, the crème de la crème begin to assemble. The majority are in evening attire of varying and independent conceptions. There may be two or three in velvet jackets, and a stray reporter or two in business suits.

Little groups of men and women gather informally in the aisles. Perhaps the playwright is among them. Over in the corner there is an animated discussion going on between two critics. The elderly gentleman with the distinguished Van Dyke beard must be a dramatist – or perhaps a professor from the Sorbonne.

Everything is gratis. For once, the omnipresent French *pourboire* withdraws discreetly before an occasion where art is, or is expected to be, paramount. The ladies at the check-room work furiously but smilingly without thought of reward. The program boys distribute their books with prodigal generosity. The ushers withdraw tactfully and without the expectant pause after escorting their charges to the stalls. In short, all effort is directed toward placing the thrifty Frenchman in the happiest possible frame of mind before the curtain rises on the momentous occasion.

Which may explain in some measure why but few Paris productions are sent prematurely to the storehouse!

November 30, 1925

Dear Family,

Saw Pavlova again last week . . . think of it, Pavlova on a vaudeville bill along with acrobats and trained seals! However, I got standing room for only 10 francs (less than 50¢).

December 12, 1925 – Pavlova, for the first time, has consented to appear on a music hall bill in the French capital, and is sending strangely mixed audiences into ecstasies of delight. Regular devotees of the Hall find themselves beside the elegant elite, who arrive just in time to see the great dancer and then depart when her "turn" is finished.

"The Swan," danced to the beautiful music of Saint Saëns, has proved by far the favorite number with the French audiences, and Pavlova has been obliged to include it on each of her two programs. Others which have found great favor in her audiences here are the Dutch Dance to Grieg's *Music,* the Pavlova *Gavotte,* and Schubert's *Moment Musical.*

Among the other celebrities which the music hall has gathered in its strange collection of entertainers during the year are: Cécile Sorel, Queen of the Comédie-Française, Paul Fort, the French poet, Nina Kochitz, soprano from the Opéra, the poets Maurice Rostand and Jean Richepin (the latter a member of the Académie Française), the Revue Nègre, Tahra Bey, the Hindu fakir, and now the incomparable Pavlova! What next?

January 26, 1926 – Met Raymond Duncan (the brother of Isadora) the other afternoon. He runs a couple of artist groups here and trots around in a white kimono, bare feet, sandals, long hair done up like a woman's with a band across his forehead, and all the other tricks. He wears this outfit all the time.

He weaves rugs and tapestries, makes furniture and sandals, and has schools in Paris and Nice. He is about forty-five years old, and they say is a terror when he is aroused – packs a powerful wallop (so a newspaperman told me who got thrown out on his ear). He invited another fellow and me to stop in Thursday afternoon for a little tea party at which an American artist will be selected to give a free exposition of his paintings at the Duncan studio. It will be lovely.

March 21, 1926 – *L'Ame en Peine. A play in three acts by M. Jean-Jacques Bernard, produced at the Théâtre des Arts.*

The Pitoëffs have returned to their Théâtre des Arts. They opened the new season Friday evening with a curious bit of dramaturgy called *L'Ame en Peine.*

As the title indicates, the piece is a total renunciation of material conceptions and aspects. It is an adventure in the realm of pure psychological phenomena –

the realm of Ibsen, Strindberg, O'Neill, and the Germans.

There is no plot.

If there is an actress in Paris who is best suited to the role of Marceline it is Ludmilla Pitoëff, of such tender Sainte Jeanne memories.

To say that Madame Pitoëff actually weeps before her audience is banal. But to say that she has caught the mystic haze and poignancy which envelop Marceline to the point of actually becoming the distraught creature herself, is to acknowledge again the gifts of dramatic understanding with which she was born.

Georges Pitoëff is Antoine and is a no less vibrating force in the one act in which he makes a speaking appearance.

April 10, 1926 – "It's tremendous! The first act is a woman's happiness; the second her sorrow; the third her depravity; and the fourth her redemption. It is a wonderful piece of art!"

The speaker was Mary Garden, Queen of the Songbirds, as she sat in her luxurious suite in a hotel near the Etoile the other afternoon. From time to time, the half dozen or so bracelets on her right wrist jingled merrily as she dramatically waved an arm in the recounting of the story of her new opera, *Resurrection*.

The American diva has reached Paris on her annual visit following the close of the Chicago season, which was marked this year by the sensational success which greeted the new work *Resurrection*, a lyric drama based upon the Tolstoi classic and with music by Alfono, the well-known Italian composer of Turin.

Plans are practically completed for Miss Garden's appearance at the Opéra-Comique as Mélisande in the famous Debussy work *Pelléas et Mélisande*, the role which she herself created a few years ago at this historic opera house.*

"Of course, I should enjoy singing this role at the Opéra-Comique again," the opera star told me." But how I should like a chance to sing *Resurrection* for Paris! That marvelous work with the magnificent score that Alfono has written!"

If plans underway are to develop, the star who began such a phenomenally brilliant career at the Opéra-Comique some twenty-five years ago, when she introduced *Louise*, may repeat that triumph in the role of Katousha.*

Editor's Note: An amusing story is told by Nigel Gosling in his book *The Adventurous World of Paris 1900-1914*. When Debussy picked the Scottish-American star Mary Garden to create the role of Mélisande in his opera *Pelléas et Mélisande*, it is said that Maeterlinck, on whose play the opera is based, who had wanted his mistress to sing the part, was so enraged that he challenged Debussy to a duel. But the affair blew over. It appears that the poet merely advanced upon the composer brandishing a walking-stick, whereupon Debussy collapsed and had to be revived with smelling salts.

Editor's Note: A year later Mary Garden returned for her regular spring season in Paris, and P.S. interviewed her again. This time she autographed for him a photograph of herself in the role of Katousha in Alfono's *Resurrection*, an opera that she made very much her own. Few singers seem to have revived it since.

Mary Garden

June 12, 1926 – Paris might be said to have given itself over to a great Russian festival during the past week.

In addition to the opening of the season of the Russian players at the Théâtre Atelier, there is being produced at the same time at the historic Théâtre Sarah Bernhardt, the famous *Ballets Russes* of Serge Diaghilev.

The ballets are meeting with great acclaim, although the opening performance of *Romeo et Juliette* was the occasion for a considerable turmoil. It seems that the two artists who were responsible for the *décor* and costumes, had switched over from their alleged school of Art to the opposition, and their former colleagues were on hand to boo, whistle, and hiss at the opening performance as a protest.

The disturbance was put down by the police, but not until the entire theatre had been thrown into an uproar.

*   *   *

Still another Russian item on the local artistic calendar is the series of symphony concerts which the great Russian conductor Serge Koussevitsky is presenting at the Opéra. His concert this week includes numbers by Stravinsky, Prokofiev, and a first audition of *La Préface du Livre de Vie,* by Obouhow.

July 17, 1926 – Vous aimez le jazz?

This seems to be the burning question of the day in Paris, for Paul Whiteman, proclaimed "Jazz King" is here.

The American jazz conductor and his band of thirty-two pieces are not only giving daily concerts at the beautiful Théâtre des Champs Elysées, but are also playing at the handsome newly-opened Ambassadeurs gardens.

While jazz harmonies and rhythms are far from being a novelty to the French, this is the first opportunity of hearing the kind of jazz that has been hailed by the critics as the precursor of a new school of music.

Worse Than Jazz

July 24, 1926 – Far from satisfied with the crashing which went on at the Théâtre des Champs Elysées a few weeks ago when his Ballet Mécanique was performed, George Antheil, the young American composer, arranged for another performance last Saturday.

Those who are familiar with the Antheil music, know that it is about the last word in the so-called modern school of "boiler factory" music. The score calls for sixteen

147

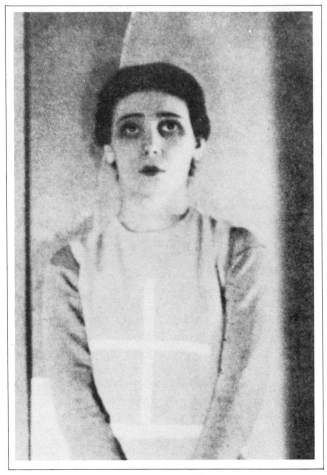

Ludmilla Pitoëff

electrically controlled pianos, half a dozen electric bells, and a couple of aeroplane propellers.

At the first performance, the audience broke loose in a pandemonium of mingled applause, hisses, whistles, and cheers.

France's First Family

November 1926 – "Maman, Maman, but you *must* let me grow my hair right down to my knees."

Thus pleaded little ten-year-old Aniouta Pitoëff, daughter of the famous French actor and actress, Georges and Ludmilla Pitoëff. She had just completed another of her fairy tale fantasies, and since she is chief performer, as well as author, producer, and designer for her own plays, it is imperative that her short curls be persuaded to extend themselves to her knees for the role of the fairy princess she had assigned herself.

The first couple of the French stage, Georges and Ludmilla Pitoëff are of Russian extraction, but they met and married while acting in Paris. They have acted together continuously for the past twenty years, and the family of six children, all of whom are on the stage, or have definite stage ambitions, were born and raised like little Aniouta, with scarcely an interruption to their distinguished mother's career.

Ludmilla Pitoëff is best known internationally as the creator of the role of St. Joan in the French translation of Bernard Shaw's play of that name. Anyone who saw her give a performance on Armistice Day, in aid of war victims, and watched her take up the special collection from the orchestra stalls herself between acts, with tears scarcely dried from the last scene, will feel that they have not seen a portrayal of the part of *St. Joan*, but Saint Joan herself. Her husband's distinguished production, and his own acting in the part of the Dauphin, made this production one that will live in the history of the French stage.

* * *

With the passing of Jean Richepin, one of the most glamorous figures of the contemporary French picture has gone. Those hot-blooded days when the youth was branded a profligate and his writings a moral menace ... wild lyrics of untrammeled gypsy life and unrestrained youth.

He who was once the lover of Sarah Bernhardt – "the French Jewess," writes Carl Van Vechten, "who defied the laws of society so flagrantly that on one still-celebrated occasion she permitted her actual lover, Jean Richepin, to enact the role of her stage lover in his own piece *Nana-Sahib.*"

149

Of late, Richepin had become the quiet, respectable old Academician that he was expected to be. I last saw him on a gala program at the inauguration of the Champs-Elysées Music Hall, in April 1925. He read some of his own poems, and Cécile Sorel did a gorgeous scene from *La Maîtresse du Roi,* with furniture, tapestries, and costumes from her own private collection.

More recently Josephine Baker, our own contribution, has graced the boards and sent Paris wild by introducing the Charleston.

* * *

CHAPTER 6

THE REGAINED GENERATION

Introduction

The average reporter writes for today's, or at the very latest, tomorrow's, edition of his paper, and for him, each day's news is dead twenty-four hours later. The idea of writing anything of more permanent interest is foreign to him, and the effort needed to produce enough material for a book is anathema.

P.S. always insisted on calling himself a newspaperman, rather than a journalist. He was proud of the fact that he had learned his trade in the old-fashioned school of hard knocks, as opposed to being a product of a school of journalism.

In spite of endless protestations in later years that he was "working on a book," it is not really surprising that the project never seemed to get off the ground. However, in the summer of 1959 two things inspired him to get some Paris reminiscences on paper.

The first was the catalogue he received from Paris of the exhibition organized by his old friend and colleague Morrill (Bill) Cody and staged in the Centre Culturel Américain, called *Les Années Vingt*. This brought the whole period to life so vividly, for someone who had been part of it, that he was finally impelled to put pen to paper with some recollections of his own.

The second was the stimulus provided by his son's Harvard friends, visiting at vacation time. For these college boys, to whom Paris in the 1920s was already a glamorous chapter in literary history, to listen to the stories of someone who had sat around the fire at Sylvia Beach's bookshop and been a part of the small group invited on Sunday afternoons to meet in Sylvia's apartment over the shop, there to rub shoulders with Joyce, Hemingway, and Elliot Paul, was an almost sacred experience.

So it happened that in August of 1959, when the usual family holiday at Bethany Beach was postponed, P.S. shut himself up in his study, sent out letters to some of the old Paris group of American authors, asking for quotes to include in his article, and finally went to work.

The resulting piece appeared in the Spring 1960 issue of the *Michigan Alumnus Quarterly Review,* and is reprinted here with their permission.

E.B.S.

*   *   *

Sylvia Beach saw the goal perhaps more clearly even than did those who were to achieve it.

It is time to make an important correction in Gertrude Stein's widely accepted designation of one of the most powerful groups in the shaping of American literary tradition. It was no "Lost Generation," to use Miss Stein's term, that fled the New World for Paris' Left Bank in the nineteen twenties. There was nothing "lost" about them, unless it was their patience with an era that just crowned Sinclair Lewis. Certainly they themselves were not lost to the homeland. Their alumni ranks, living and dead, include Ernest Hemingway, William Carlos Williams, Kay Boyle, T.S. Eliot, William Faulkner, E.E. Cummings, F. Scott Fitzgerald, Eugène Jolas, Robert Sage, Robert McAlmon, Bravig Imbs, and Gertrude Stein herself, who even achieved Broadway recognition with a musical version of her play *Four Saints in Three Acts.*

The spring of 1959 saw the first formal recognition, at the international level, of the group of young American writers who came together in Paris during the twenties. The occasion was a carefully compiled exposition of their works and memorabilia in the United States Cultural Center, recently opened in the Latin Quarter of Paris. The exhibit was called "The Twenties: American Writers in Paris and their Friends, 1920-1930."

If the word "friends" is to be used in its strictest sense, there were few such to be commemorated by this or any other succeeding generation. Four names which do come immediately to mind are James Joyce, Sylvia Beach, Adrienne Monnier, and Ford Madox Ford. It was Joyce, with his breath-taking *Ulysses,* who sounded the new note of daring in a new and benevolent climate far from his native Dublin; Sylvia Beach, who from her Shakespeare and Company bookshop in rue de l'Odéon, saw Joyce through his agonizing series of eye operations, while bringing out successive editions of *Ulysses* and encouraging a band of his young American admirers to develop their own literary talents; Adrienne Monnier, whose bookshop, La Maison des Amis des Livres, just opposite Shakespeare and Company in the rue de l'Odéon, published French translations of Hemingway,

McAlmon, Cummings, and Carlos Williams in its own review, *Le Navire d'Argent;* and Ford Madox Ford, whose *Transatlantic Review* found space for early recognition of Joyce and many of the Americans before it made way for Eugène Jolas' and Elliot Paul's *avant garde* monthly *transition.*

But in the minds of those who knew her, there can be no doubt that it was the gentle, self-effacing daughter of a distinguished Princeton University theologian, whose modest bookshop in the rue de l'Odéon was the central force in motivating from abroad the new trend in American literature. Sylvia Beach saw the goal perhaps more clearly even than did those who were to achieve it.

William Carlos Williams, in an unpublished letter dated June 23, 1959, writes: "When I was taken to see Sylvia Beach, her reputation was already well known to me through her association with James Joyce. Shakespeare & Co. and rue de l'Odéon were as well known to me as my own name. Sylvia Beach, coming from Princeton, was from my own State and all the stories I heard of this slightly-built woman gave me courage to proceed on my way in the arts, for if she had found the courage to do as much as she had done so should I. At least that remained always in my head. I was proud of her, her daring and accomplishments.

When I saw her, what a small woman she was, not particularly good looking. I looked at her hard among her books and was all the more convinced of the force of her way with her associates. She knew what she was doing and she had the loyalty and courage to persist in it, and a charm which made me feel instantly at home in her presence. I felt she was interested in me as a writer and as a writer only – but her warmth at once radiated out to me from that. She became at once my friend, I wanted at once to write for her. James Joyce must have felt the same attraction for her. The whole bookshop was filled with it and that was Sylvia Beach, a powerful spiritual force."

Sylvia Beach was the most powerful recognizable force behind the emergence of a distinct phase of American literature on foreign soil. Complementing the spiritual force attributed to her by William Carlos Williams, there was a quiet reserve of taste, judgment, and practicality that remains today to give life and authenticity to such historic events as the recent Paris exhibit.

In 1922 it was all of these gifts which went into the publication of *Ulysses* under the sign of Shakespeare and Company. Miss Beach recognized the work as an inspired effort in a new technique which could not hope to win easy acceptance. She was prepared to battle for her personal conviction. Three years later, Joyce lay suffering at Christmas time from nervous shock induced by his latest eye operation. His Christmas gift from Sylvia was a copy of the seventh edition of *Ulysses* – bound in blue paper, as was the original edition, instead of white, as were the intervening copies.

Joyce probably has been the supreme beneficiary of Sylvia Beach's unique genius for encouragement and effectuation. But those others who found their way to her bookshop included many with a mind for images and a gift for words, who were helped merely by an occasional chat with the quiet young woman in her plain, unstudied environment of books and inscribed photographs of the literary *avant garde* of two continents.

On occasion Shakespeare and Company extended its much-needed encouragement of the then ultramodern art forms by turning itself into a miniature *salon* for a chosen few. Here, silver-haired Arthur Symons, leader of England's symbolist poets and interpreter of Baudelaire to his countrymen, warmed his hands before the log fire as he passed through Paris on his way home to complete a book based upon his warm friendship with Eleanora Duse and Gabriel d'Annunzio.

Paul Robeson sang spirituals for Sylvia Beach, Adrienne Monnier, and their friends. On another memorable afternoon, a group of writers and newspapermen were invited to hear the first recording of Joyce's reading from his *Ulysses.* The absent author had just undergone his fourth eye operation and there were prospects of a fifth.

At one of the unforgettable Sunday afternoons in her small apartment above Shakespeare and Company, Sylvia had invited a small group to meet Joyce. Mrs. Joyce, the Hemingways, George Antheil, whose *Ballet Mécanique* soon was to rock Paris from the stage of the Théâtre des Champs Elysées, and a few others were there. There was great interest in a set of handsome portraits of Joyce (in the white suit which he always wore at home because of the failing eyesight) which had just come from the photographer for use in publicizing *Ulysses.* Sylvia and I were skimming through the lot, expressing approval or criticism as seemed called for, while the shy subject himself maintained a grave silence. Suddenly we came to a print in which the mane of iron-grey hair seemed to be even more tousled than usual.

"I am certain that I do not like this one," said Sylvia with unusual firmness. I concurred. We waited for the final judgment. It came in a measured monotone of solemnity not easily associated with the author of *Ulysses:* "Well, I've been making other people's hair stand on end for the past several months, I don't see why I can't be permitted to let my own do the same."

Joyce's great affection for the young Americans who owed so much to the stimulus which he and Sylvia Beach provided, was modestly exhibited. Even his affliction, however, could not prevent his attendance at the turbulent *répétition générale* of George Antheil's *Ballet Mécanique* at the spacious Théâtre des Champs Elysées.

Shakespeare and Company, despite its deep interest in the music of Paul Robeson and George Antheil, was first of all a bookshop and lending library, in addition to serving as "principal agency" for the new magazine *transition*. Contributors to a typical issue of the Jolas-Paul publication (No. 6, September,

1927) included Archibald MacLeish, Boris Pilniak, Carl Sternheim, Gertrude Stein, Virgil Geddes, Kay Boyle, Laura Riding, Yves Tanguy, Rainer Maria Rilke, Samuel Putnam, Robert Sage, Henri Monnet, Bravig Imbs, Man Ray, André Gaillard, Serge Esseine, Paul Eluard, and Robert Desnos.

For good measure there was included an installment of Joyce's *Work in Progress* (eventually to become *Finnegan's Wake*) and a surrealist manifesto entitled *Hands of Love*, signed by thirty-one writers, in violent protest against Mrs. Charles Chaplin's charges in an American divorce against her husband. An equally thunderous denunciation of another irritant of the contemporary scene was sent hurling back across the Atlantic one midnight during the same period by the grace of a *New York Times* correspondent and his leased wire. It, too, was in the form of a manifesto, drawn up by an enraged band of American expatriate writers and their European colleagues in answer to published reports of Sinclair Lewis' evaluation, following his return from a lonely visit in Paris, of American literary "genius" on the Left Bank. It was a great day when the first copies of the supercharged issue of the *Times* found their way back to the Boulevard Montparnasse.

To the south of Shakespeare and Company, on the Boulevard St. Germain, was the venerable Café des Deux Magots, made famous to Americans by Carl Van Vechten. Here, close to the Ecole des Beaux-Arts, one found younger and more disciplined artists rubbing elbows with students and professors oriented to the nearby American University Union.

It was this ferment of opinion with regard to art, freedom, and their own artistic integrity that cut straight across nationalist, racial, and religious lines to bind the young expatriates into groups of varying unity. The little band in the rue de l'Odéon, led by Joyce and encouraged by Sylvia Beach, was by far the most generally respected, if for no other reason than that it was so engrossed in its own affairs. Moreover, its international, though predominantly American, composition was a matter of printed record in the steadily accumulating files of *transition*. Added to this was the singular good-neighbor relationship with Les Amis des Livres, led by Valery Larbaud and encouraged by Adrienne Monnier.

But there was no lack of motion among young artists and writers gathered in groups all over the Left Bank, even when the Butte Montmartre began to lose the afterglow it had acquired from Heine, de Vigny, Berlioz, Stendhal, Renan, Toulouse-Lautrec, and George Moore. Halfhearted attempts to arouse an occasional *concours* between Left Bank and Right Bank schools of thought and artistic expression got nowhere. The Left Bank was too busy with its internecine clashes, some of which achieved the distinction of battered heads, shattered café tables and glassware, and the arrival on bicycles of the nearest *agents de police*. Revolt was in the air as it had not been since Zola fled Paris in 1898.

But just because the writers of the twenties were in revolt, it did not for a moment mean that they all agreed among themselves, as Kay Boyle has observed. Carl Van Vechten's little hotel in the Place de l'Odéon, just around the corner from Shakespeare and Company, was torn between café groups of students from the Sorbonne on one side and the international complex of Montparnasse on the other. Even Montparnasse itself observed subtle distinctions between the frequenters of the Café du Dôme, the Café de la Rotonde, and the *nouveau riche* Café Sélect. It was on the terrace of the Dôme that Sinclair Lewis favored a conspicuous but not overcrowded table during the ill-fated inspection of Montparnasse which generated the heated headline exchange previously mentioned. It was on this same *terrasse* that Frank Harris basked nightly in the adulation of a circle held breathless by the biographer's intimate recollections of his friend Oscar Wilde.

At the very moment, Harris' new autobiography was scandalizing the censors in Britain and America – while providing a distinctly sophisticated touch in the form of shiny new copies of the publication nestling under the arms of promenading Quarterites or placed conspicuously beside glasses of coffee or beer on the tables of Montparnasse.

Here, too, Flossie Martin for years kept green the memories of the American hinterlands as she made her buxom, bantering rounds of the tables, greeting old friends and making new ones. One day she vanished and the word went round that she had gone home.

Set apart from the categories into which the artists of the twenties in Paris were divided was yet another strictly off-beat minority, in many ways the most interesting group of all. These were the lonely individuals who courageously hewed to the line as true eccentrics, oblivious to both friend and foe. What mattered it if even in a twisted world they were called *poseurs*, crackpots, egocentrics, or mere self-propagandists? Nothing mattered except that they give expression to an inner spark that might be buried, but never extinguished. These were the Cheever Dunnings, the Stanislas Stockgolds, the Raymond Duncans, the Arthur Francks, the Grégoire Gourevitches, the Bernard Fays.

It was Cheever Dunning, earlier a contributor to Harriet Monroe's *Poetry: A Magazine of Verse*, in Chicago, whose twelve short poems in the November 1924 *Transatlantic Review* directed a flutter of attention to his door at the top of a rickety flight of steps leading from an obscure Montparnasse courtyard. Here the uninvited caller was repulsed with an inhospitable warning which had been indelibly scrawled across the door long before by a couple of admirers: "Not modesty, but scorn."

What mattered it to Dunning if Elliot Paul, in *transition* (October 1927), ridiculed a recently published *"tour de force* in *terza rima* by Ralph Cheever Dunning, whose doggerel lacks the crackle of Edgar Guest and the wholesomeness of Phoebe Cary." It is doubtful whether the poet ever had heard of Paul or seen a copy of *transition*. He did, however, in one of the memorable talks I had with him, once comment wearily upon the "stream of consciousness and interior monologue" style made famous by Joyce and exalted by Paul. Scorning the mention of names, Dunning described the new technique as "constipation of ideas and diarrhea of expression."

To the few of us who were privileged to enjoy an occasional *café noir* with the shy, frozen-faced man on the terrace of the Dôme, it was impossible not to be reminded of another American poet, whom he never mentioned. Dunning must have known his own "Annabel Lee." But now the exquisite perfection of his measures was dedicated only to abstract dreams and such symbols as the poppy.

Around the corner and in less obscurity was the vast, cluttered studio of Stanislas Stuckgold, Polish modernist painter and founder of a new school dedicated to what he called "Zodiac art." True to his word, Stuckgold achieved a formal one-man show of Zodiac art at the Devambez gallery on the fashionable Boulevard Malesherbes during the summer of 1925. His fellow-Quarterite Ivan Opfer was just beginning work on a more traditional portrait of a young writer from America, Scott Fitzgerald.

High among the Stuckgold gallery of portraits hung a recent study of the then French minister of fine arts. Other canvases had traveled to exhibits in Munich, Berlin, Copenhagen, and Tokyo. Contemporary technique of the old man had evolved in the direction of what was described as the "fourth dimension." By placing his subject behind him, as he himself sat at his easel facing in the opposite direction, Stuckgold (whose long white hair and ghostly physiognomy gave him a startling resemblance to Svengali) found that the "waves" of personality thus sensed enabled him to achieve a much truer portrait than the human eye could possibly reveal.

Less bizarre than the Stuckgold *atelier* but equally graced by celebrities was the studio of the young American, known only as Hiler, who made Latin Quarter history in the twenties with a fabulous soirée honoring Isadora Duncan. The aging but still queenly dancer appeared in dazzling green satin topped off with a mass of flaming red hair. Her entrance was characteristic and appropriate. Surrounding her was her "court" of handsome, raven-haired young men representing half a dozen nationalities.

Two Métro stops to the North, but still in the Quarter, the great Isadora's brother, Raymond Duncan, moved rhythmically back and forth, in flowing white, among his young acolytes, their looms and cobbler's benches, all dedicated to art in the everyday life of man. Bare feet encased in hand-fashioned sandals and shoulder-length hair held in place by classic bands at forehead level were the outward symbols of a cult that had little in common – except a strange, groping instinct of new art forms – with its American brethren similarly huddled on the banks of the Seine.

Of Raymond Duncan's group *Artistes et Artisans* one chronicler of the period wrote: "Abstract art in itself is all very well, but it presents no reason why Art should not occasionally step down from Parnassus and make its appearance in everyday life."

Down the Avenue des Champs Elysées, at the Salon des Artistes Indépendants, a young American, Arthur Franck, was showing his collection of "cubi-classic" canvases designed to "reverse the artistic gesture in the direction of construction rather than destruction" and to express the classic theme and color in terms of modern forms.

Arthur Franck was not alone in his combined passion for the new and love for the old. Grégoire Gourevitch, pale and emaciated in the wake of his flight from the scourge of Bolshevism in his native Russia, found solace at his piano in the little Left Bank Hotel which now was his home. Between Sunday night concerts at the United States Students' and Artists' Club, provided by young Canon Killian Stimpson of the American Pro-Cathedral of the Holy Trinity, Gourevitch probed the intricacies of his former master, Scriabin, with a burning passion close to idolatry.

"Not a composer, but a builder," was the young Russian's description of his own creative-interpretive role as an artist. At a single concert at the Salle des Concerts du Conservatoire his program included the works of Beethoven, Saint-Saëns, Chopin, Borodin, Scriabin, Debussy, and Prokofiev.

Without ever learning a word of English, Gourevitch loved the Americans for their devotion to the old and their enthusiasm for the new in art. A few years later, true to the cult of his master Scriabin, who strove to unite music and philosophy, he became the first artist to fly the Atlantic in a dirigible – his beloved grand piano with him – so that he might draw inspiration from the boundless sea beneath. Wild acclaim in New York, shattered hopes and promises of gaining recognition and a living in the New World, a benefit concert to pay his bills at the Savoy-Plaza, and eventual retreat back across the Atlantic to his little corner of the Latin Quarter in Paris: this was Grégoire Gourevitch's own Appassionata Sonata.

Complete and uninterrupted absorption of the artist in his own work – despite occasional outbursts between opposing groups and cults, mostly in print – was the blessing gained from a supreme tolerance toward the artistic principles and techniques of others, no matter how eccentric they might be. This was the unwritten law recognized by serious artists who came from every corner of the world to Paris in the twenties.

It is doubtful whether Grégoire Gourevitch ever heard of the nearby recital of Antheil's "percussive music" as represented by the *Ballet Mécanique*, scored for some sixteen electric pianos, a pair of electric bells, and an airplane propeller. If he had, he would have dismissed the event with a bored but tolerant shrug of the shoulders. On the other hand, the partisans in the audience at that frenetic ritual were aroused to such ecstasies of approval and contempt that the resultant bedlam virtually drowned out the deafening music itself. A typically French touch, never to be forgotten by those who were present, was the *jeu du théâtre* of a portly gentleman in the second row who, when the score called for an all-out passage by the airplane propeller, hastily pulled up his coat collar and dramatically raised his umbrella to fend off the icy blasts from the stage.

Sinclair Lewis, Scott Fitzgerald, Ludwig Lewisohn, Homer Croy, Elmer Rice, and Frank Harris were but a few of the literary lights who sojourned on the Left Bank for varying periods of time during the twenties – not so much to work, perhaps, as to enjoy the fruits of literary successes in the United States and Britain. Eva Le Gallienne arrived from New York with Norman Bel Geddes and Mercedes de Acosta to take up residence in the Latin Quarter while preparing their lavish production in French of the de Acosta play *Jehann D'Arc*. But these notables were regarded more as spectators than as habitués of the Left Bank. If noticed at all, they were treated with respect or at least tolerance, but rarely envy.

The "Lost Generation," as such, now has passed into history. A new generation, far from being lost, includes Paris on a summer swing through Europe or wins fellowships for formal study at the Sorbonne. It may have been Adrienne Monnier who, with the realism of her people, knew that the Latin Quarter as it existed during the twenties could not survive more than a decade. The last issue of her *Le Navire d'Argent*, in 1926, at the close of its eleven-year existence for the encouragement of young French writers, contained these words from a letter to a young poet:

*"Si vous devez rester inconnu, et si vous avez su, néanmoins goûter les joies qui sont réservées aux poètes, vous trouverez cette résignation heureuse qui fait dire au Dominique de Fromentin: Je dois, peut-être à ces essais manqués comme beaucoup d' autres, un soulagement et des leçons utiles En me démontrant qui je n étais rien, tout ce que j' ai fait m'a donné la mesure de ceux qui sont quelque chose."**

          *   *   *

---

*Editor's Note: If you are to remain unknown, and if you have nevertheless been able to partake of the joys reserved for the poet, you will attain that happy resignation of which Fromentin writes in *Dominique*: "Perhaps like many others, I owe to these unsuccessful attempts a soothing peacefulness, as well as some useful lessons. In showing me my own insignificance, what I have done gives me something by which to judge those who have been more successful."

.

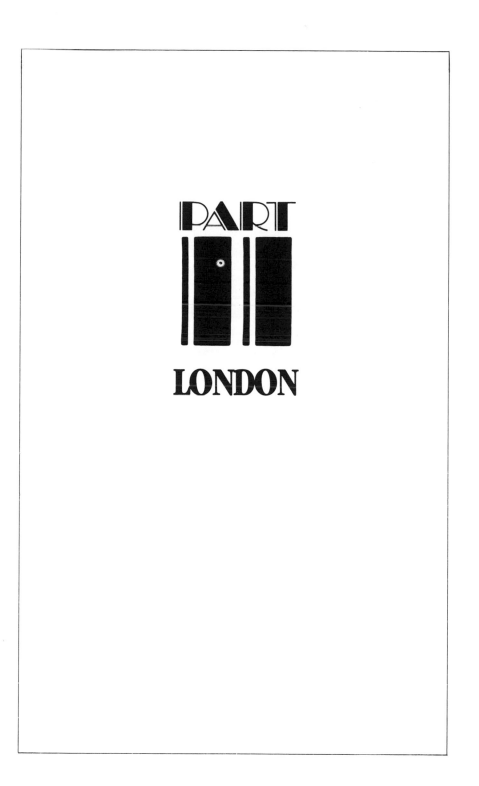

PART III

LONDON

INTRODUCTION

In April 1927, Paul Shinkman was offered a choice by the *Chicago Tribune* – to become an assistant correspondent in Berlin or in London. It was a doubly agonizing decision that had to be made almost overnight: first, whether to leave his beloved Paris, and second, to decide between two important news centers. In the end, he chose London.

The move was important in many ways, but principally because he would now be working for the parent paper in Chicago, rather than for one of their European editions. Furthermore, since his supervisor John Steele, the senior *Chicago Tribune* correspondent in Europe, was constantly traveling, P.S. had more responsibility than he had held in Paris. He found the challenge stimulating, and soon after the Lindbergh flight, which came less than a month after P.S. had started his London assignment, his career as a foreign correspondent took a giant leap forward.

Although the move to England did not present a language barrier, the atmosphere in London in the 1920s was almost as foreign to an American as it would have been in Berlin, Moscow, or Rome. It took P.S. more than six months to break through the crust of English reserve that met him on all sides. He found that he had exchanged the free and easy life on the terraces of Montparnasse for the frigid atmosphere of residential hotels in Bloomsbury. In England at that time, nobody spoke to a stranger.

In fact, nobody spoke very much at all. Silence hung like a pall in the high-ceilinged hotel dining rooms and lounges. Almost the only sound at tea time or at after dinner coffee, was the tinkling of spoons on cups and saucers. P.S.'s imitation of the timid, sporadic conversation, made in subdued tones between deathly silences by elderly spinsters recounting what "Lady So-and-so" had said to them over lunch, was a classic.

P.S. decided to make the most of his stay in England by taking regular week end trips to places of interest. England is small enough so that he could travel all the way from the south coast to the north of Scotland without being absent from his desk for more than a few days. By taking his bicycle on the train to his destination, he could spend leisurely days exploring the English countryside. The English classics are so closely associated with *places* that he found himself taking informal literary pilgrimages to Canterbury, Stratford-on-Avon, Oxford, the Lake District, and to such country inns as "Ye Olde Hostel of God Begot" in Winchester.

His love of theatre led him to do some play reviewing, but his first reaction to the London theatre was not enthusiastic. He found the comedies of Londsdale and Coward unbearably affected and superficial. Fortunately, there were plenty of good American plays and musicals for consolation.

But nobody as gregarious as P.S. could be lonely for long, even in England in the 1920s, and the ice was finally broken when he met Durand Smith, a fellow American correspondent in Fleet Street at the end of 1927. The two met at the press table at a luncheon given by the Chicago Subway Commission for officials of the London Underground. Durand Smith, whose home was in Lake Forest, Illinois, was newly down from Cambridge, where his athletic prowess at tennis and ice hockey had earned him the rank of a "blue." He also had many friends. He asked the toastmaster to point out to him the correspondent for the *Tribune,* and at the end of the luncheon, after filing their stories, he and P.S. went off together for a drink at the nearest Fleet Street pub.

It so happened that Durand had found some enchanting "digs" in one of the old Inns of Court, just off Fleet Street, and he was looking for someone to move in with him to share the expense. Although from a wealthy Chicago background, he was extremely parsimonious, and kept meticulous accounts, much to the amusement of P.S., whose money came and went in the most casual manner. In a matter of weeks the two newspapermen had moved into the charming, low-ceilinged rooms at Clifford's Inn, where in 1872, Samuel Butler had written *Erewhon.*

London in 1927 was the mecca of the top hat, white tie, and tails set, and Fred and Adele Astaire were the idols of everyone from the Prince of Wales on down. P.S. himself was an excellent ballroom dancer, and as his circle of friends widened, he found himself invited to dances, both in town and at country house week end parties.

While P.S. kept his sense of humor vis à vis the more stuffy, stiff English conventions, so unappealing and ridiculous to the average American, he nevertheless conformed sufficiently to ensure that he did not make himself conspicuous, either by speech or dress, as did so many of his countrymen at the time. When he started to take riding lessons from a strict old riding master in fashionable Rotten Row, he went to a London tailor to be measured for the correct attire – ill as he could afford it. Durand Smith, on the other hand, turned up one day for a lesson from the same riding master (who had instructed P.S. on the correct deportment in the event that he should meet King George V riding in the Row) wearing plus fours, and in no time had allowed his horse to bolt with him.

Two of Durand's best friends at Cambridge were John and Glanvill Benn, sons of the publisher Sir Ernest Benn, and P.S. recounts how he was roped in at the last moment to pinch hit for a defaulting guest at the twenty-first birthday party of their younger sister Betty. After dinner and the theatre, the party repaired to the Benns' flat overlooking the Thames at Whitehall Court, for dancing to the gramophone and charades. These last two activities were the staple fare of the social life of the young generation in the 1920s. Later, P.S. describes his first visit to the Benn family home, Blunt House, in Surrey, for that most popular of all English traditions, the country week-end.

*   *   *

1928 was an idyllic year in England. The Depression had not yet made itself felt, and the "war to end all wars" seemed to have accomplished its objective. The second dramatic transatlantic flight with Amelia Earhart, Louis Gordon, and Wilmer Stultz, took place in June, and the work of the assistant correspondent in the London office of the *Tribune* continued smoothly.

But the idyll was abruptly shattered for P.S. in December of that year, when his beloved younger sister, the "Susie" to whom so many of his letters were addressed, caught a *Streptococcus* infection while working at her first job after graduating from college, and died in a matter of days. P.S.'s parents were visiting him in London at the time, and the agony suffered by the three of them was unspeakable. Early in 1929, P.S. requested a transfer back to the States, and within a few months he returned to America.

P.S. arrived back in the United States in 1929, at the height of the Great Depression. After a brief attempt to settle into the main office of the *Chicago Tribune,* he decided to go east to New York City. Through a friend of Helen Josephy, he heard of a job at International News Photos, a subsidiary of King Features Syndicate. He considered himself fortunate indeed to land it. The salary, although minuscule, would be steady. P.S. somehow was able to burn the candle at both ends, and thus built up his slender finances by moonlighting as a theatre critic and radio broadcaster.

The summer of 1931 found P.S. and Durand Smith traveling back to England together to take part in Glanvill Benn's wedding. P.S. planned to pay for his trip by writing a series of articles for King Features Syndicate.

The wedding festivities were scarcely over when P.S. was struck with a violent attack of appendicitis. He was rushed with blaring sirens through the streets of London to the famous Empire Nursing Home. Thanks to his well-trained journalist's ear, he was able to recall the name of one of London's leading surgeons, and this probably saved his life. He battled peritonitis successfully, but was faced with a long convalescence.

The Benns felt a good deal of responsibility for P.S., since he had come to England especially for Glanvill's wedding, and they invited him to Blunt House to recuperate. The family chauffeur drove him down from London, and the family nanny, a shy old spinster who had never nursed a male surgery case in her long career, took him on as a patient.

It was during this enforced vacation at Blunt House that P.S. had the opportunity to get to know the eldest Benn daughter Betty, who did book reviews for London publications and shared his enthusiasm for writing. To pass the time, they collaborated on an article describing a summer music festival Betty had just attended. To their delight, the piece was accepted by *Etude* magazine.

The hoped-for series of articles for King Features Syndicate was clearly gone by the board, but before returning home at the end of the summer P.S. did manage to achieve one longstanding ambition, which was to get an interview with George Bernard Shaw. The tale of how he chased the playwright all over Malvern during the Shaw Festival, and finally got his story by writing him an insulting letter to which the octogenarian sent a stinging reply, was one that he never tired of telling.

E.B.S.
March 1982

*   *   *

CHAPTER 7

FIRST IMPRESSIONS

One beautiful April morning in 1927 I left my stuffily tidy little Hotel Cecil just off Russell Square in the hope that a morning stroll through Bloomsbury might bring at least a nostalgic pang to the latest American newspaperman to leave Paris behind for London.

This was the Bloomsbury that shared with Chelsea the wistful distinction of being London's "Latin Quarter." Unless those cold rows of identical boxlike facades, distinguished from each other only by the colors of their broad front doors, hid a great deal of burgeoning genius, unexpected humor, and attractive people, there was no spot on earth less like Montmartre and Montparnasse, the twin sentinels of the Paris that I loved.

The *Chicago Tribune,* with an almost frightening prodigality, had given me a choice of two coveted assignments: as assistant correspondent in Berlin under Sigrid Schulz, or in London under the distinguished and fatherly John Steele. It was Steele, striding through the office on his occasional visits to Paris in his voluminous old Burberry, who had given me my first glimpse of the curious aristocracy of shabby English tweeds. I had been equally impressed by Vincent Shecan, who had returned from a brief London assignment in an elegant Bond Street cheviot and tilted bowler. Thus, I picked London, despite three slouchy years on the Left Bank and the warnings of my own café circle.

My first impressions of London were vastly different than those I experienced when arriving in Paris. The grand, gloomy place that we American youngsters were taught to make of it. The Tower! The very word still strikes a certain terror to my heart, unrelieved by any number of memories of "London Bridge Is Falling Down." Yes, it is grand, it is gloomy. But even at this early date, I like the English and what goes with them.

I like their shiny brass plates and doorknobs, their left-hand traffic, their alarming self-possession, their mysterious puddings, their theatre pits, and their magnificent breakfasts.

They have been very kind to me this first week. It is nice to feel that one knows where one stands with them. I was always a bit wary in France, not only because of the language barrier, but because of that tremendous difference in temperament. Though, God knows, the English temperament could hardly be called the same as our own. I have a perpetual terror of scandalizing those around me.

May 4, 1927

Dear Mother and Dad,

Here goes another of those breathless letters dashed off at the office between times. I keep hoping to find a couple of hours to sit down and write you a sane sort of letter, but I'm afraid if I waited for the best moment to come along, the time would fly by without your hearing from me at all.

Things have been going very well so far, and I certainly cannot complain about being overworked. Our chief correspondent Mr. Steele sailed for America Saturday, and now Mr. Darrah is in charge. I'm his assistant. I knew him quite well in Paris, since he used to be managing editor of the *Tribune's* Paris edition. He seems to want to do all he can to make things agreeable.

I came down to the office Sunday because it was May Day, and we were expecting some labor demonstrations which would have been important news. So he told me I could have yesterday off, and I spent the afternoon on a little shopping tour in smart Piccadilly. The clothes proposition here has me worried. A chap can't go around looking like a rag bag as was the case in Paris. The men here are the finest dressed I have ever seen, and a fellow simply must make some effort at keeping up with them.

In Paris, all you needed was an American-cut suit and some clean shirts to look well-dressed. Here, you need half a dozen suits, three or four hats (soft felt, derby, etc.), as well as smart topcoats and shirts. To make it all the harder, the streets are lined with the smartest men's shops in the world with clothes at comparatively reasonable prices. I can imagine now the anguish that less affluent American girls in Paris must suffer. Living in the world's style centers is no cinch.

Anyway, I bought a stunning soft hat yesterday at Joshua Turner's. It's beige, or the new-called "ash" shade, with a turned down brim in front. My old Paris hat was in pretty bad shape. I also invested in a pair of light woolen sox that are a work of art – a beautiful pattern in light brown to go with my brownish-grey suit.

Next comes the terrifying question of evening clothes. In Paris, a dinner jacket was good for anything after six o'clock. But that doesn't go in London! No sir! It's full dress here, unless you want to look like a waiter, and you're expected to have the proper Chesterfield topcoat and a silk or opera hat!

In America we think these things are only for the idle rich. In London they are part of the wardrobe of anybody above a newsboy, as far as I can make out. The clerks in our office make me look like a rummage sale with their smart turn-outs. You must think I've become obsessed with the idea of clothes. I haven't. But I do like to look as well-dressed as the people around me.

May 8, 1927

The biggest news today is that I have taken a new room at 3 Gloucester Terrace, Hyde Park. It's a townhouse in one of the finest residential districts in London, and only a stone's throw from Kensington Gardens. The house is well-kept and there are two maids. My breakfast (the regulation English fare of bacon, eggs, toast, marmalade, and tea) will be brought to me each morning, and I shall take luncheon and dinner outside.

The amazing part is the rental I shall pay – 30 shillings per week, inclusive of service and breakfast – about $7.50. That's frightfully cheap here, and in such a neighborhood, it is unbelievable.

May 22, 1927

We have been fearfully busy the past few days. First we had the police raid on the Bolshevik trade delegation here, and that kept us on the jump shooting the details back to America. The commercial attaché of the Soviet Legation told me confidentially that after such an outrage they "will not be surprised at anything." However, I don't believe there is any question of the fact that there has been a good deal of undercover work going on – stirring up British Labor, and that sort of thing.

Yesterday we were all up in the air over Lindbergh's cross-Atlantic flight, and were here at the office when the exciting news began to come in over our ticker announcing that his plane had been seen off the coast of Ireland, then over Plymouth, then over France! It was very thrilling and was certainly a wonderful achievement, wasn't it!* Such pluck and grit speak well for American youth, which has a reputation over here for synthetic gin and the Charleston...

*Editor's Note: P.S. was soon drawn into the frenzied vortex of Lindbergh's London visit. With his chief away, P.S. covered the hero's program, including a dinner at the Savoy Hotel given for Lindbergh by the Association of American Correspondents in London on May 30th. The colorful menu included Poussin Roosevelt Field, Asperges Le Bourget, and Café à la Croydon.

July 12, 1927

My work continues to be enjoyable; Mr. Steele is now back from his visit to the States. He is a very fine man in his late fifties, I should judge, and most agreeable. He is dean of the *Tribune's* foreign correspondents and is highly respected here.

Last week I had my first taste of sports reporting, covering the last two days of the international tennis tournament at Wimbledon. I saw such great stars as Tilden and Hunter take the men's doubles championship for America. I also saw the women's champion Helen Wills of America. Last Saturday, I covered the great field meet between Oxford and Cambridge on one side, and Harvard and Yale on the other.

A still bolder venture in sports writing was my recent article on American baseball for the *Topical Times,* a weekly sports paper published here. I was paid $10 for it – not bad, considering that I dashed it off in about an hour. The idea was to explain baseball in its relation to cricket, which many people seem to think it will eventually replace.

I'm attending a luncheon this noon to be given by Carl Laemmle's movie outfit, and tonight I'm going to a dinner in honor of the Bishop of New York. Kinda nice, being a newspaperman, isn't it? If I could only make money at the same time!

August 5, 1927

Just returned from a couple of days' vacation in Kent. I lost no time in hiking off to Canterbury, the historic Middle Age cathedral town. I had a wonderful time rambling around by myself among the picturesque ruins, and hated to come back. Sent all the nephews and nieces postcards from there. Also sent a card to Miss Keck, inasmuch as it was she who taught me the poetry of Chaucer, which she made so fascinating in high school that I have always yearned to visit the spot.

Well, Dad and Mother, wait until you see me in my new derby ("bowler" the English call them). I told the salesman that people with noses like mine have to be very careful about derbies, but he insisted that it looked very smart.

August 19, 1927

Was interested to hear about Lindbergh's visit to Grand Rapids, and hope you had a good look at him. According to the *Herald* clipping you sent, they certainly are taking no chances on wearing him out, and I think it is an excellent idea. He seemed to show signs of nervousness coming on before he left Europe – a sort of troubled expression, although he really is a fine-looking chap.

170

Life has taken on an even rosier hue for me lately. I have taken to horseback riding, and you should see me trotting through Hyde Park! I simply had to have some sort of exercise, and since the park is so near and I have always yearned to ride, it seemed an excellent opportunity.

Am just beginning to get on my feet financially, and am trying to put a bit in the bank each week. Wish my job paid more, but I guess I can't complain. Other chaps seem to be dying for a similar chance at practically no salary at all.

August 21, 1927

Not long ago I was sampling the punch between dances with an unusually attractive English girl at Lady Beecham's party. We were speculating upon the significance of a startling blazer which the young Englishman beside me was wearing with his dinner clothes. She said, "I say, you ask him what he represents! You Americans can get away with anything over here!"

Think of it! We Americans can "get by" with *anything* over here! Needless to say, I was overwhelmed by this cool announcement of powers that I never dreamed of possessing. And soon we learned that the young man had come up that afternoon with the Cambridge swimming team.

*   *   *

I have no murders to my credit as yet, though I have come dangerously close to the deed on several occasions. To which observation, if I were addressing an Englishman, I should expect the obvious rejoinder: "But, my dear fellow, you Americans murder the English language every day of your lives!"

And to which, if I wished to be Maughamish, I should issue a sparkling reply: "Too true. Too true. It *has* been dead a long time, hasn't it? Now what do you think of the American language?"

Which is a question I should much rather ask than answer.

*   *   *

Quite frankly, I think I prefer the sound of "re-ally" to "reely" and "Frahnce" to "Frannce," though I can't for the life of me see why they say "shedule" for "skedule" and then agree with us in the pronunciation of "school."

*   *   *

But all this is beside the point. What I started out to say is this: Now that I am more or less permanently established in London for the rest of the year, and having been informed that I can "get by with anything," it seems feasible to attempt giving you my impressions of "these charming people" from the point of view, not of the eternal tourist, but of one who lives among them.

To be sure, I make no claim to a complete understanding of our English cousins. They are a far too complicated subject to master in such a short time. The job of mutual understanding, I am convinced, is much more difficult for us than it is for them ... which is no tribute to our ingenious selves, is it?

I don't suppose there is a more decisive boundary in the world than that narrow strip of water between Dover and Calais. The abrupt change from France to England left me almost suspended in mid-air. Three years among the French is a long time, isn't it? And it doesn't contribute one iota to an understanding of the English. *Au contraire!*

*   *   *

I find there are not so many crossword puzzles to be solved here. And when one does come along, the answer is generally in the back of the book. Their superb self-composure is alarming at times, but I miss the street corner altercations. But there is a pleasant air of "substantiality" about these people. I suppose the English, above everything else, are substantial. Even too substantial at times ...

*   *   *

My sole recreation thus far has been the theatre. But the theatre is at its zero hour in August, and there is nothing new to report, though I dropped in to see Mr. Cochran's review *One Damn Thing After Another* for the second time the other evening and am now convinced that it is the best I have seen ... anywhere. And that makes no exceptions for Ziegfeld's *Follies,* George White's *Scandals,* the Moulin Rouge, Casino de Paris, or Folies Bergère.

I am glad that two Americans helped tremendously to put it across, though by no means dominated the show. They are Edythe Baker and Art Fowler. I saw the former in the States several years ago and she is vastly improved. She and Jessie Matthews, the English star, make a stunning pair. And Fowler's "uke" helps him sing several naughty songs in a nice way....

Take it back – I have one other recreation – my riding. My riding master tells me the King rides at the same hour as I. Which rather frightens me. Molly is inclined to be temperamental. I should hate to have her suddenly decide to open with a "pawn to King's fourth." The man who rides with me was riding master for six years to our own late Joseph Pulitzer, founder of New York *World.* He has tons of amusing yarns about painted ladies who take riding lessons in the rain, gentlemen who ride because their wives make them, etc....

You seem to hear quite a bit of English music, according to your letter, and I'm sorry I can't tell you more about it. I haven't the same enthusiasm for music in London that I had in Paris, but there are some very good things here. Are you familiar with Sir Thomas Beecham's orchestra? It seems to be the best, although I haven't heard it. The brief annual season of opera is now running at Covent Garden, and I heard *Tannhaüser* sung very well the other evening. The season is divided into three sections of German, French, and Italian operas, with native singers. But most of my diversion is in the theatre, and in short trips into the English countryside, which, to me, is in many ways the most beautiful in the world.

September 10, 1927

So our friend the Countess de Caen really did get to Grand Rapids! It must have brought pleasant memories of Paris to you both. Do you remember our tea party at the Pavillon D'Armenonville in the Bois de Boulogne? I must imagine the Countess was quite a sensation in Grand Rapids! Did you know she had been decorated by the French Government?

I was much pleased yesterday when Mr. Steele told me he liked my work and was writing to Colonel McCormick (owner of the *Chicago Tribune)* suggesting that I be permanently attached to the London bureau as assistant correspondent. You see, I was really transferred from Paris only temporarily. Col. McCormick is rather erratic, however, and might not favor the suggestion. But that won't bother me, as I'm not sure that I care to stay here "permanently." It's a fine opening and might lead to good things and a fair amount of fame, but I get lonesome for home. ...

*   *   *

The moment finds me living in a vast, rather barren, fourth floor room of a spacious old townhouse converted into a residential club for men. I have just been sitting for several minutes at one of my windows overlooking Kensington Gardens – really beautiful during a late summer's afternoon.

Yes, it is a barren room – two iron cots, four strips of red carpet, two dressers, two straight chairs, two wicker arm chairs, a gilded waste basket on either side of the white marble fireplace. In the center of the room, a crude table, covered with a red spread, and my silk-shaded lamp – the room's single claim to elegance. (It is responsible for Secretary Staines' description of my room as "posh.")

My books stretched along the mantle, my typewriter on the table, and one picture on the wall – the etching which Gremillet gave me in the Place du Tertre. The room *is* barren, but "it's a good address," as Hayden said, and it is not lonely. In fact, I find certain pleasure in the mere reflection that my fellow lodgers in Devonia House are some 35 to 40 British chaps. They seem a decent sort, but cold. Nobody seems to know anybody. Each appears to be a perfect stranger, perhaps just arrived. A queer people, these English.

The lounge with its good radio, gramophone, and adjoining garden, is not half bad. But it, too, is cold. How I should like just a few degrees of warmth! ...

173

November 1, 1927

Streams of visitors from America have supplied me with a little American Legion convention all my own. It is nice to have them, but a bit strenuous at times. The poisonous English coffee must be explained, meetings with the Royal Family must (or at least should) be arranged, Limehouse must be disclosed in its true colors, all barriers to Chelsea studios, Noel Coward drawing rooms, night life, and the Mayfair whirl, should vanish at a signal. Otherwise, what's the use of being a journalist in London for six months?

I think you see my point.

*   *   *

It looked very much as though I should be sailing westward this fall, and I may yet. My temporary appointment in London expired, and I was slated to return to Paris. That, I decided not to do. The Paris chapter was perfect, but it is closed. I detest the anti-climax. The only possible alternative seemed to be Berlin, but they seem to have decided to keep me here as assistant London correspondent permanently, which, of course, means anything but permanently to me.

Perhaps, however, I am getting to know the English. My first few months here were spent in glaring evilly at those about me from my hermit corner. I was nauseated by what appeared to be the perfect in affectation – the drawing room manner, tea cup epigrams, a monumental self-consciousness, and the "sporting thing to do."

The theatre suffocated me (much of it still does, viz. Somerset Maugham, Frederick Lonsdale, and that precocious fool Noel Coward); the press drove me into frenzies of rage; and the food annihilated me.

Well, I still tear my hair out and gnash my teeth, but the intervals in between are longer. Then too, I discovered Workshop VI, in the heart of Soho! An amazing little theatre tucked away in a back room on the second floor where the spirit is so perfect, that I rushed back the next day and subscribed to the extent of a membership. I am taking no active part, only as audience. But it was a revelation to find such a place in the heart of London. Across the street is Genarro's, an Italian restaurant that brings recollective tears to my eyes. You shall see it all, if you will only come over while I am still here.

Armistice Day
November 11, 1927

Since that first Armistice Day, I have never seen one that seemed to approach, in spirit, those Two Minutes from 11:00 to 11:02 a.m. at Marble Arch today.

I had settled comfortably in the sunshine at a table in the Express Lunch Room overlooking, from a first floor window, Marble Arch and the busy corner. A trifle sentimental, perhaps, but not too sentimental for several slices of toast, jam, and coffee (late breakfast). Shortly before 11:00, I asked for more toast. The sweet-faced young waitress glanced apprehensively through the window at the clock outside and hesitated, Then she said I should only be kept waiting a minute.

I knew what she meant and was rather ashamed of myself. As 11:00 approached I noticed a considerable number of people had collected on the curb below. There was a strange tension in the air that reached me through the window. People seemed a bit nervous, agitated.

The crowd became larger, and traffic seemed slightly jammed, despite the calm policemen who directed it from the center of the pavement. A handful of waitresses and kitchen-maids in somber dark blue dresses and white caps silently marched to the window next to mine and stood huddled together looking out upon the square.

I rose to my feet and watched the clock below. It seemed to indicate 11:00, but traffic continued to swirl around the great Marble Arch, and there were no signs of a literal observation of the Silence, though the crowd was motionless. I was slightly disappointed. I wanted to ask one of those drivers where he was going, that it was too important a mission to interrupt for two minutes.

Then several motorbuses, each filled inside and on top, were momentarily halted beneath my window. More traffic congestion.

As I stood a trifle unhappily watching the scene, something happened. I had heard no unusual sound, but people began rising to their feet on the bus tops below. Without warning, I discovered that everything and everybody was motionless. Men's hats were quietly removed – almost in unison. Heads were bowed, the last faint sound was hushed. A deadly silence. It was the Silence!

I have never heard Silence before, but I heard it at that moment. It was the Silence of a great cathedral, a hill-top at midnight, the heart of a forest, but much deeper than any of these. Hundreds of people, surrounded by swirling traffic, stilled as though by a terrible magic wand. It was the Silence of eternity.

Then, from far off came the faint sound of muffled drums – scarcely audible from where I stood – but low, throbbing drums, with a soul-scraping rumble. It was as though a phantom legion marched somewhere, far, far off, nobody knew where – but far in the distance.

The faint echo seemed to pass dully down a great endless corridor – through the ages – back to the beginning of time. There was one more silence. I spoke a few words inside myself. A fractional pause from the deepest sleep. Then it was over.

The Silence had passed.

*   *   *

November 28, 1927

In regard to coming home, I have carefully thought over your advice and about decided that maybe it would be best to stay on. Mr. Steele has been very nice to me, and the way seems to be clear for some excellent openings with the *Tribune* in Europe. Perhaps ultimately I can become a full-fledged correspondent in one of the capitals.

Tonight I am going to the theatre with a chap named Durand Smith, who comes from a prominent Chicago family, and whom I met a short time ago. Seems to be an unusually fine sort, who was very popular at Cambridge, winning his "blue" on both the hockey and tennis teams there. Since "coming down" from Cambridge, he has been with the *London Daily News*.

December 7, 1927

We are in the midst of the typically delightful London winter – fogs, grey skies, damp, raw atmosphere, with occasional rain. However, it is not as depressing as you might think, and I am feeling fine.

The Berkowitz family have invited me and a very nice English chap, Winter Stanley, to spend Christmas with them in Paris. *And* Mr. Steele has very decently let me off for three or four days. I also had a letter from Wanda quite recently, and she invited me to spend Christmas with them if I managed to get over to Paris. There are only one or two other friends that I shall have time to see – the Allens, Rita Keating, and perhaps the Griggs and the Smysers. It's almost like getting home again for me to return to Paris.

There is so much unemployment in England as to be positively depressing. I have had English chaps ask me (a foreigner) if I could possibly help them. Naturally, they would all like to go to America – the land of gold.

Yes, Grandma's death was a great shock to me. She never seemed to grow a day older, but remained exactly the same. My last memories of her are fine ones. She clung to me, smiling through her tears, and I went back a second time to kiss her good-bye. She was the only grandparent I ever really knew, and I did love her.

Did Miss Allen tell you how we drank beer and ate potato chips between acts of *The Gondoliers?*

December 28, 1927

Well, another Christmas away from home has just come and gone. As I told you, Win Stanley and I were both invited to be houseguests of the Berkowitz family in Paris, where they have a beautiful new apartment. I got away Friday night along with Durand Smith (who was also spending Christmas in Paris) and arrived there on Saturday morning.

It was an endless round of festivities. A dancing party at the Berkowitz apartment for Saturday night, and we danced until 3:30 Christmas morning!

Christmas morning we all slept late, but I did manage to get around to Notre Dame and also stopped in at the old, dilapidated *maison des étudiants* where Cecil and I shared rooms more than two years ago. The old concierge remembered me at once and was delighted to see me.

The Christmas dinner was a marvel – turkey and all the trimmings, including a real English plum pudding that Win's mother had made.

Win and Harriette wanted to see the new movie theatre, the Paramount, in the afternoon, but I preferred to slip off to the American Hospital where Ruth Allen has been since her baby was born two and a half months ago. The baby is strong and healthy, but Ruth has been seriously ill. She is better now, and Jay hopes to have her home on New Year's Day. I saw the baby, who is christened Jay Cooke Allen III (as Jay says, "for financial reasons").

Christmas night, Harriette, a sculptress friend of hers from Chicago, Win, and I all went to the Casino de Paris to see a first class review, and then went on to the Florida Club next door, which is one of the swanky places to dance. Harriette is superb on the dance floor, and she was a picture in a lemon-colored evening gown with Spanish shawl of the same color, shingled hair, and flashing dark eyes. It is a marvelous place to dance, and we didn't leave until nearly 3:30 a.m.

Next day I went out to Colombes to take luncheon with the Krzyanowskas. I brought Wanda back to town in the afternoon, and we met Win and Harriette at the new Blue Room for tea dancing. Wanda was the picture of French chic – a stunning black lace frock with a narrow belt of crimson velvet, a string of pearls, and a swagger little black hat hanging over one eye! Fortunately, I had a new suit made before leaving London, and so managed to hold my own. Win, of course, is always the smartly dressed Englishman. We had the time of our lives.

I returned to London Monday night and reached here five hours later after one of the wildest Channel crossings on record. They said ours was the only boat that didn't cancel its crossing, and I can believe it. There were only twenty people on board, and Durand and I wisely decided to go to bed as soon as we got underway. I got practically no sleep, but at least I didn't get sick. Just before we cast off, one of the French stewards cheerfully remarked, "On va danser ce soir!" Another said that everybody better say his prayers! At any rate, it was one of the most enjoyable Christmas holidays I have had since my last Christmas at home, which was 1923 – think of it!

February 3, 1928

Mr. Steele has been gone since January 11, leaving me in charge, with the result that I have not only been doing my own work as usual, but have had to take the responsibility of acting as chief correspondent as well. It's kept me on the jump.

We have had several important stories to cover during his absence, including the death of Field Marshall Haig, the British Foreign Office scandal, the British note to Geneva, and the floods. However, there have been no complaints from Chicago, which is generally considered as the equivalent of satisfaction. They're not at all slow to spend cable tolls on sharp criticisms of the way the work's done.

*   *   *

The biggest news is concerning the new lodgings which I have taken with Durand Smith. The rooms are in Clifford's Inn, one of the most historic spots in London, and two minutes from our offices in Fleet Street! We have a woman come in for an hour to wash up the breakfast dishes, make the beds, and clean a bit, for a shilling per morning. Total expenses will be about the same as I have been paying for a room with breakfast. She keeps the place spotless and is in and out before we know it.

My one hope now is that you both will be able to come to London while I am still here.

*   *   *

CHAPTER 8

HISTORIC CLIFFORD'S INN

February 13, 1928

Two weeks ago tonight this new London Chapter began, and I came to share "digs" with.Durand Smith in this enchanting eighteenth century corner of ancient London – Clifford's Inn.

If it were in America, the place would be put in a glass case and exhibited in a museum. But to actually *live* in such a place! To call it home! It doesn't seem possible.

Almost opposite that hideous monument known as Temple Bar, which stands at the juncture of Fleet Street and the Strand and which marks off the proud City of London from its less distinguished neighbors (also known as London), is a narrow passageway leading between two buildings to the ancient stone doorway. Above it, the name "Clifford's Inn" has almost fallen away in ruins. A porter's lodge beside it sanctions admittance to the quaint old stone-paved Inn, enclosed by the irregular, dingy, old brick buildings with small-paned windows and a series of entries, above each of which the keystone is marked with a number.

To one side, and projecting from one of the main buildings into the courtyard, are the remains of an old chapel, its dull grey walls and old Gothic windows offering mute protest to the ironic signboard of the present occupant of the premises – Opticians. Around the corner are the colorfully draped windows of the Clifford's Inn tea room, where one lunches respectably and cheaply for a shilling or so.

At night, the scene is irresistible. A gentle tap at the Inn's heavy oak door will give a glimpse of the bedraggled old self-appointed porter behind the two-inch square peep-hole. As he rattles the bolts and swings the door open with a solicitous nod, the porter touches his old hat. But generally, it is unnecessary to tap. The sound of approaching footsteps in the passageway alone is sufficient to arouse him to a scrutiny of the caller and the ultimate endorsement.

Inside the dimly lighted enclosure, one stares up at ghostly shadows of old buildings, romantically limned by three or four old gas lamps. Around the corner and past two entries is No. 17. Just inside are painted in neat black letters the names of the occupants. At the top under "3rd Floor" appears "Mr. Paul A. Shinkman" and "Mr. Durand Smith."

One mounts the winding wooden stairs past heavy iron barred doors swung open, to a final closed door. It is the barrier to our "digs," and the Heaven which hovers above. . . .

A small carpeted entry furnished with a handsome old grandfather clock (which ceased operating years ago), a prepossessing old high-backed, rush-seated chair, and a small table. A door gives access to the little low-ceilinged beamed living room with a gas fire at one end and two sets of casement windows at the other. These last overlook the grey towers of the picturesque Public Records Office (where the *Domesday Book* is kept), as well as a charming expanse of green. A soft yellow-shaded lamp casts a warm glow over the quaint old pieces of furniture, including a gateleg table, towering chest of drawers, well-worn rugs, concave floor, and a ceiling apparently on the verge of giving way after centuries of strain.

At one end two doors lead to a cheery little bedroom with twin beds and an adjoining lavatory, and to a tiny kitchen, complete with gas grill, geyser water heater, and bath tub!

*   *   *

Yesterday I was host for the first time since long before crossing the Atlantic. My first party *chez moi* in Europe! And it apparently was an unqualified success.

Guests were invited for tea. The place looked charming, with a bunch of bright yellow jonquils and another of fragrant violets. Howard Lund, of Whitby, Yorkshire, was the first arrival. He is "down" from Cambridge for a few years and has visited almost all of America. Dear little Boom Cannon came next, and we had a rousing reunion at the bottom of the stairs. Our first meeting in London, though we both came over from Paris months ago. Next came Molly Sinclair, a stunning young English girl, and her friend Betty Lee. Then Joan Neville, who now writes occasionally for London publications. Then Durand breezed in, wearing plus fours, for a sip of tea, though still on duty at the *Daily News* down the street. Finally, Win Stanley, from Purley, Surrey, my fellow houseguest at the Berkowitz's in Paris at Christmas.

A jolly party around the fire, with port, sherry, tea, and cakes. The last guest left well after seven, Win remained for a quiet chat before the fire, until Durand returned with his friends Jane Scriven, young Chicago heiress, and Dr. Blitzsten, his psychoanalyst, now of Berlin. More chatting, then I took Win out to his bus and picked up some sandwiches at Sandy's. Chicago filled the air until about 11:30 p.m., when I was left alone while Durand saw them home. It was a strenuous but great day!

D. is now "sorting" or something of the sort. It is time for our financial session – sinking fund, ways and means.

February 15, 1928

Mr. Steele says I am second in line for an appointment to an independent post in Europe. The *Tribune* may re-open a permanent correspondents' bureau in Moscow, which would mean shifting the men around, and I could be given a chance in Central Europe, perhaps Vienna, Budapest, or Belgrade. However, this is the merest speculation, and besides I think I shall want to be coming home before long.

Durand spent last week-end at the country place of Sir Ernest and Lady Benn, who have a son who went to Princeton and whose book on the subject has just been published. It is called *Columbus Undergraduate* and has caused quite a stir here. D. is considering writing a similar book from an opposite point of view – an American at Cambridge.

Meyrick Mansion
Bournemouth
February 25, 1928

Had a very quiet time, and thoroughly enjoyed it. Did a little dancing, and some horseback riding along the beach. The continuous rain and dreary weather in London got on my nerves at times, but we've had sunshine every day here.

The first dinner gong has just sounded, and I must rush off and dress for dinner. Yes, that's how English your wandering boy has become!

April 15, 1928

Attended an interesting dinner in honor of Mr. and Mrs. Henry Ford the other night. It was quite amusing. Ford practically never attends banquets, I understand, and the poor fellow had to listen to a lot of Ford jokes and "kidding" by the speakers. He only spoke a dozen words himself. He looked ready to pass out, but of course was helpless and had to remain. There are some things that even the richest man in the world can't avoid!

181

P.S. at Bournemouth, 1928

May 11, 1928

Had quite a fling last night. Durand had been invited to a gay dinner and theatre party in honor of Betty Benn, the daughter of Sir Ernest and Lady Benn. It was quite a large party and yesterday, at the last moment, they found that one of the fellows wouldn't be able to come. Although I had never met any of the Benns excepting one of the boys, they asked Durand if I would fill in, and I was delighted.

The Benns are very good friends of Durand and are quite a distinguished

English family. Sir Ernest is the head of Ernest Benn, Ltd., one of the foremost British publishing houses. His two sons John and Glanvill were classmates of Durand at Cambridge. Since the father is a baronet and not a mere knight, John will someday inherit the title and be Sir John Benn.

They are a nice, homey sort of family, very much attached to one another. The party last night began with dinner at the Café Royal, after which we were taken to see one of the smartest London reviews, *This Year of Grace.* Then we all went to the Benns' town flat for supper, amateur theatricals, charades, and dancing. Durand and I didn't leave until 2:00 a.m., and we were the first to go. So, you see, it was quite a success.

Please don't think I am being spoiled. I heartily enjoy these things, but I am not swept away by them and will never be a social butterfly. In the first place, I can't afford it, and in the second place, I am too interested in my work. But it's rather nice to know representatives of English families from the inside. The Benns' guests, mostly young people, included some distinguished names – the daughter of Sir John Simon, who just returned from heading an important government mission to India, the daughter of the Runcimans, both of whom are prominent members of Parliament, the daughter of an admiral, etc.

Durand doesn't put on any swank, or "side" as the English call it, and we get along well together. You should see us figuring up household budgets. D. is far more practical about managing housekeeping detail than I, and he takes complete charge of George VI, our cleaning woman. He's very thrifty and also looks after most of the food, although we only eat breakfasts and occasionally tea in our rooms. He looks after the weekly change of linen, and all I do is take charge of paying the rent ($60 a month for our furnished flat.)

May 18, 1928

I must tell you about our last "tea." It was quite a success. It happened that Tito Scipa, the great Chicago Opera tenor, gave a return concert in London last Sunday. I had previously met his publicity manager, who was so delighted with the story I sent back to Chicago about him a few weeks ago that he insisted on presenting me with about fifteen seats for the concert, including a box for eight!*

Editor's Note: The reason Mr. Scipa's press representative was so attentive was due to his gratitude for P.S.'s help in a moment of crisis.

The famous singer had a pet monkey, a marmoset, which traveled with him. Scipa insisted that the pet be with him in the dressing room before every concert. Shortly before Scipa was to appear at the Albert Hall, the monkey was nowhere to be found. What to do? An advertisement in the paper requesting the loan of a monkey for the occasion. The pandemonium caused by the response to this ad was at its height when P.S. appeared on the scene. He somehow was able to select the most suitable replacement, appease the disappointed owners of all the other chattering monkeys, and thus earn the good favor of Mr. Scipa's entourage.

So Durand and I got busy and arranged to throw a little box party, bringing our guests back here for tea afterwards, including Waverly Root, my new assistant (during Mr. Steele's absence) from Paris.

The concert was beautiful. We all came back here afterwards, and everybody seemed to have such a good time that our last guest wasn't gone until nearly 11:00 p. m. There was quite a dramatic scene while the party was at its height. Our bell rang, and when I went down to the door I was rather startled to find a gigantic London cop, in his funny helmet, fiercely inquiring for the owner of a car that had been left parked outside – illegally and without lights – for about five hours.

It was Carolyn Cannon's car, and he growled that it could mean a couple of stiff summonses. Everyone got rather excited until Lund, with his perfect English composure, took the matter in hand. It took him about half an hour, but he finally got things patched up, and even got the bobby to keep an eye on his own car while he came back for another cup of tea!

Don't worry about my drinking too much tea, Mother. We have it every afternoon at 4:00 in the office, but I generally prefer coffee with my meals. In between times, I like a good old English whisky and soda.

I attended quite a brilliant luncheon yesterday at which Sir Thomas Lipton, the great tea king, sat almost in front of me. In the evening, I went to a dinner in honor of the Honorable Timothy Healy, one of the founders of the Irish Free State. The guests included the Archbishop of Canterbury, Cardinal Bourne (the English Roman Catholic Cardinal), and the Earl of Birkenhead (Secretary of State for India), as well as other cabinet officials.

June 17, 1928

I had a most enjoyable trip to the ancient town of Rochester in Kent last week.

A party of London journalists was taken down in luxurious Pullmans as guests of the city of Rochester and the Rolls-Royce Corporation, in order to be present at the reception in honor of Sir Alan and Lady Cobham, the former being the great British ace who has just completed a long flight around Africa in a plane with Rolls-Royce engines.

We arrived in grand style, and were rushed to the city's harbor, where the frenzied city fathers, including the mayor, had assembled in their state robes and gold chains for the reception. As soon as they had arrived, we climbed back into our Rolls-Royce charabancs and were rushed to the guildhall where the ceremony of welcoming and presentation of trophies took place.

After the ceremony there was a swell feed. All kinds of champagne, whisky and soda, wines, sandwiches, caviar, tons of cake, etc. Everybody got just nicely oiled – just enough to forget the scarlet robes and gold chains and have a good time. One old alderman in his flowing crimson gown insisted on taking me under his wing

184

and giving me the time of my life. (I was the only American present.) Throwing a fraternal arm about my shoulders, he begged me to sample the champagne freely, and presented me with much *éclat* to the other city fathers. I later discovered that he was not only the respected patriarch of Rochester, but had served twice as mayor.

In the midst of the excitement he became so enthusiastic that he insisted upon personally calling for the city's Great Book, in which distinguished visitors are registered as far back as the fifteenth century, and calmly turned the pages for me much as anyone might turn the pages of a new catalogue. All this time, the distraught official keeper of the book was tearing his hair in a frenzy of anguish at the book's being out of his hands.

It then appeared that my friend had just published a huge book, the first complete history of Rochester, and had sent copies to Rochester, New York, and Rochester, Michigan, the mayor of the former having visited Rochester, England a year or so ago. He called loudly for a copy of the book and insisted upon presenting it to me, inscribed by himself. All very lovely as you see.

*   *   *

Life flows along at a staggering rate – and almost too colorfully. I haven't yet been able to harden myself to Old World impressions and sometimes think that the succession of "high strung" experiences should not be carried beyond a certain point. That's why I think I shall be ready to return to America soon. My three years in Paris and one in London seem to have about reached their logical close.

I think I have come dangerously close to settling down over here once or twice, but I've stoutly fought the Benedicts and emerged with my celibacy intact.

June 28, 1928

We've been having some rather distinguished visitors lately. Day before yesterday D. had Professor Henderson of Yale and his son and daughter to lunch. Yesterday he had Captain McLeod, a rugged old Scotch gentleman with his American wife, and Bernard Babington-Smith, the famous Cambridge pole-vaulter, whose grandfather, the Earl of Elgin, was Viceroy of India from 1894-1899. (I'm afraid I'm beginning to fuss about *family* the same as the English do. Don't worry. I don't take it too seriously.)

Glad Aunt Abbie was proud of my picture in the Sunday *Tribune,* but I assure you *I* wasn't. It looked simply hideous to me, and I never dreamed it was going to be used in the Chicago edition as well as in the *Tribune's* staff magazine. I hope you won't think I actually look as sullen and dissipated as I appear in that picture.

*   *   *

185

Music in London cannot compare with that of Paris. Still, there is a very good symphony orchestra conducted by Sir Henry Wood which is now giving a series of promenade concerts for broadcasting. One can stroll about the ground floor of the concert hall, where there are seats for just two shillings.

London is having an exceptional summer. The weather has been beautiful – the finest in years – and since the first of June we have had a succession of priceless sunny days. I'm fairly aching to go for a stroll through Hyde Park and Kensington Gardens.

Who are you boosting for President? I believe Hoover is the general favorite over here because he is better known, but it is surprising to see such a strong element for Smith also. He appears to be a very vigorous type, quite capable of acting for himself.

Gene Tunney, of course, swept the town by storm and was received by the Prince of Wales. The English could scarcely believe that such a character as Tunney could actually exist. A combination of the high-brow and the scrapper.

Wish you could see your handsome son in his new silk topper. It's a concession to London life, where top hats for the theatre and dancing are almost a necessity.

July 10, 1928

Great excitement – horrible odors reaching a climax this morning in a joint call upon our landlords the Gades, an insistent telephone call to the Works Office, and the arrival of experts to sniff and try doors below.

All sorts of bloodcurdling conjectures. (I had fashioned the suicide one while tossing at 4:00 this morning.) The arrival of a carpenter, who took up one board at the most odoriferous spot ... gropings ... and the arrival of another joiner. A slight "Ahem, ahaw," and I was shocked to see that they had quietly dug out a huge dead rat – quite the largest I had ever seen.

A certain repressed, but nevertheless unmistakable excitement. Another gentleman had arrived. I frienziedly tore out pages of the *Chicago Tribune* for the body to be wrapped in. "Don't touch it with your hand!" – friendly admonition from boss to laborer – and away it went to the flames.

Creosol as disinfectant, which one scattered about while another put in a new board between the rooms, and still another looked on as though envying them their work. "Blimme, it's nearly tea time," which I thought sounded very elegant coming from a horny handed odd-jobber.

August 26, 1928

This garret window in Clifford's Inn is an entrancing nook (I hate the word)

186

with a cool August Sunday afternoon rain rustling the leaves outside. There is a delightful quality about the domestic-looking dish of fruit (the gift of "Cambie," our cordial neighbor) on the gateleg table, beside it a stack of letters from Susie, J.J., Wanda, Durand, and home, and behind me – a row of books – Melville, Joyce, Carl Van Vechten, O. Henry, Flaubert, and Shakespeare. Yes, *Peter Whiffle* is still with me.

It was Henri Murger's *Bohème* and George Moore's *Confessions of a Young Man* that drove Carl to Europe. And it was Carl's *Peter Whiffle* that drove *me* to Europe, assisted by the *Confessions.* Certainly no book has ever exerted a more overwhelming influence upon a young man that has *Peter Whiffle* upon myself. It is perhaps superficial, and smacks more than a little of the dilettante. But it came along in my own life at a great moment when it not only struck fire within me, but actually changed the course of my life. For some reason, Carl reaches out and grasps me, even when I am most conscious of his faults. I think it is his tremendous love of life that does it.

I glanced through a copy of Katherine Mansfield's journal at C.M.'s the other evening, and was caught by her terror at the prospect of leaving only "scraps" and "bits" of writing behind her – nothing complete, entire. Yet it seems to me that these "scraps" and "bits" might easily represent the pinnacles and highlights of a great life. Certainly they are often the least conscious of one's writings. And most writing is far too conscious.

*　*　*

I dined with Paul Robeson, that great Negro singer and actor, at a little French restaurant in Bloomsbury last night. What a magnificent figure! In the afternoon, I had taken C.M. to see and hear him in that great spectacle *Show Boat* at the Drury Lane, and we experienced that wonderful satisfaction of extracting enjoyment from every moment of the performance.

Robeson's singing of beautiful "Ole Man River" had left us tense, unable to applaud. Charlotte actually wept. There are two words to describe Robeson and his singing – heroic and eloquent. A heroic figure. And with eloquence in his deep, resonant, soul-stirring voice.

The prospect of sitting with him at dinner almost frightened me. I'm afraid I was a bit inarticulate. It was so difficult to say what I wished to without appearing extravagant, gushing or hero-worshipping. I asked him why he electrified his audience into watching him breathlessly every moment he was on the stage, no matter what else was going on. Of course, he could not answer. But he said Edith Day and the producer had been extraordinarily generous giving him opportunity to "shine."

He admitted the performance yesterday afternoon had been one of his finest. He knew a particular friend was in the audience listening to him. A sincerely

187

admiring note, a tribute of any kind, makes the difference, he said. I told him that his singing, particularly in the fifth scene of the second act, actually seemed inspired. Much more affecting than the first time I saw the performance. Perhaps C. M. was largely responsible. She flattered me outrageously by telling me there are, for her, four Pauls: her father, the apostle, Paul Robeson, and ...

There is a naive simplicity about Paul Robeson that is a pure racial heritage. Yet he has avoided the pitfalls that invariably snare his successful brethren, without appearing in the least down-trodden, martyred, or glorified by the sentimental into a sort of angelic child. He told me that he had sung privately for the Prince of Wales, the Duke of York, and the King of Spain, a few weeks ago – quite modestly, as we shook hands at the stage door of the Drury Lane.

*   *   *

It struck me while lunching ignominiously at Lyon's in Ludgate Circus today that I do not know the Big City of my own country. It is an odd circumstance that I should know life in Paris and London so intimately, and yet be a total stranger in New York. The British foreign minister said the other day that one loves Paris as one loves a woman. How does one love London ... and New York? Certainly Paris is feminine, London is masculine, and New York is ... hermaphrodite?

Old George Hotel
Salisbury
September 27, 1928

After a rest of eight days at Bournemouth, I got in my plus fours yesterday morning, put a toothbrush in one pocket and a razor in the other, hired a bicycle, and started out on my jaunt through Hampshire, Wiltshire, and Dorset.

The weather has been perfect. Just a bracing autumn tang in the air, and there is no other way of getting so close to the very soil of a country. I passed through the ancient town of Christchurch, then up the Avon River valley through Ringwood to the little old town of Fordingbridge, where I stopped for tea in a charming hotel garden beside the river and decided to spend the night there.

Before dinner I went for a row on the river, which is one of the most picturesque I have seen. At dinner I met a fine young English chap who lives in the hotel, and we sat before the fire in the little parlor until midnight, sipping beer and chatting.

He promptly asked me if he might refill my tankard, and then proceeded to stir up the fire before which we sat in the little parlor of the inn.

I know no person who can make better use of a fireside than an Englishman. Steam heat has made such a slow and very painful progress into England, that a fireplace is still a fireplace, and not an ornament. It is only when such is the case, that an open fire assumes its true aspect and function of spreading warmth throughout a room and through the people assembled before it. It is the difference between candles used as ornaments and those used to light rooms.

It is somehow easier to speak truth before a fire. The warm glow that comes from such earthy materials as burning wood or coal is as completely disarming as twilight on a hilltop. Gilt radiators and electric heaters were meant for solicitors' offices, and conference rooms for boards of directors.

*   *   *

This morning I came into Salisbury to see one of the most famous cathedrals in the world, and am stopping at this old inn where Samuel Pepys once spent the night. After having had more than four years of the Old World, I still find myself thrilling just as kiddishly over those things as I ever did – if not more so. These people have something back of them that we shall never know. Call it tradition or anything else, but it's there.

*   *   *

Tomorrow I'm heading back to Bournemouth, where I left all my luggage. Then to London and work on Sunday. One of the most delightful holidays I have ever had – jogging along without any worries.

October 8, 1928

I've been going to the theatre quite a bit lately. I arranged to write a regular column called "Drama Notes from London" for our Paris edition, and this gives me access to almost all of the shows here. It's an inexpensive way of entertaining, and I enjoy it hugely, although the London stage is none too good at the present time.

I had a very interesting day yesterday at Hounslow, a suburb of London, to attend the opening of the huge new British factory that the Firestone Tire Company has just opened. We were driven down in motorbuses and entertained with a fine luncheon after being shown over the place.

I'm having a quiet day at home and getting a good rest, having just returned last night from a strenuous trip to Leeds and Hull in the north of England to interview Aimee Semple McPherson, the famous American evangelist who is taking a tour over here.* Have you read any accounts about her? I'm afraid I was a bit disappointed, although she is obviously an extremely kind woman with much personality. Many people think she is a mere grafter. I'm not so sure of that, but she is not my idea of a great evangelist. She is a bit too conscious of the impression she is making.

October 26, 1928

I'm beginning to realize how many fine English friends I have made through Durand. Tuesday Glanvill Benn invited me to lunch. He and Durand were at Cambridge together, and he has been up here several times. He spent four months after graduating getting experience on the *New York Times* in New York. We had a pleasant chat, and he invited me to a week-end party at their place in Surrey on November 16.

By the bye, Mother, if you want to show people that you know England, you must refer to Sir Ernest Benn never as "Sir Benn," but as "Sir Ernest Benn," or (if it is clear to whom you are referring) as "Sir Ernest." It's just one of those things one learns by living in England.

I also like very much another of D.'s English friends named Irene Matthews, who teaches at Cambridge and will come to London after Christmas to become a speaker for the Women's Conservative Party. She is a charming girl.

Still another of my newer friends for whom I must thank Durand, is Bernard Babington-Smith. He is a fine English chap, and his mother is the daughter of the late Earl of Elgin. Her late husband was one of the finest ambassadors England ever sent to America and was a member of the British mission to Washington, D. C. during the war. Bernard has now taken a position in the City and drops in at Clifford's Inn quite often.

It's true the English are extremely reserved, and I was inclined to resent it at first. But I'm beginning to think there is something to be said for their apparent "coldness." When you *do* know them, you find you have friends worth knowing.

Editor's Note: When P.S. took the midnight train to Leeds to keep his appointment with Aimee Semple McPherson, the blonde evangelist from Los Angeles was at the peak of her spectacular career. His objective was to find out how much interest the beautiful preacher, with a strong sense of the theatre, had managed to stir up among the staid populace of the British midlands.

Always dressed in white, she made a well-staged appearance and created a sensation wherever she went. Her Leeds-Hull crusade was no exception. P.S. records that as she stepped onto the platform of the vast, dreary railway terminal to face the waiting crowds, a shaft of sunlight coming through a broken pane in the dirty glass roof of the station lit up her dramatic appearance with the precision of a well-directed floodlight.

One of the few skeptics present was the sleepless, exhausted correspondent of the *Chicago Tribune.*

November 18, 1928

After living in England for a year and a half, I am more than ever convinced that the visitor cannot hope to know this country or its people, until he has been invited to be one of a week-end party, a *semaine anglaise*, at a typically English country house. I have just enjoyed that experience and I actually feel that the past forty-eight hours have taught me as much about the English as I had gathered in the preceding year. It is as significant a custom as four o'clock tea.

Blunt House, the country home of Sir Ernest and Lady Benn situated near Oxted in south Surrey, will always typify for me what is known to be English hospitality, and I hope I shall always consider the Benns as the typical English family.

A nasty rain made the dickey seat of my friend Glanvill Benn's car undesirable, so I journeyed down to Oxted by rail on the 5:50 p.m. Friday. Glan was on the platform to meet me and another guest from London, Claud Simmons. Horne, the Benn chauffeur, was in attendance with the family car, and took our bags along with his passengers to Blunt House, while Claud and I drove back with Glan in his own roadster.

Briskly along narrow, winding country roads, then between two brick pillars and up a curving drive between two more pillars, and to the entrance of Blunt House, cheerily lighted at either side of the entrance. Into the wide hall, off with our coats, and then Lady Benn appeared to welcome us before the cheery fire. It was already late, and there was barely time to change for dinner, so we were shown to our rooms. Mine was a cozy chintz-hung affair with every detail a guest could dream of wanting. Such things as a reading lamp beside the bed, a writing desk with plenty of crested stationery, and a well-supplied pin cushion on the dressing table.

A smiling, elderly maid bustled quietly about the room. She had already laid out my evening clothes, brought hot water, and awaited orders. In another moment, she had gone to prepare a bath for me. Dinner was at 7:45 p.m., and I came down to the drawing room to meet Sir Ernest, John, and Betty Benn, and the other guests, Katharine Hewart (the beautiful daughter of the Lord Chief Justice of England), her friend, a decent chap whose name I've forgotten, Ruth Runciman, whose parents are both distinguished members of Parliament, and Patrick Devlin and Claud Simmons, Cambridge friends of Glan.

It was a delicious dinner in the pale green paneled dining room, softly lighted with a few dim wall lights and candles. The ladies withdrew afterwards, and we remained for cigars, cigarettes, and chats, and then met in the drawing room to receive the guests who had come from the houses nearby for dancing – alternating gramophone and radio, with occasional piano. It was most enjoyable. The standard of feminine dancing was far above the average!

There was a delicious buffet supper in the dining room. I enjoyed ices and punch (non-alcoholic) with Ruth Runciman. About 1:00 a.m. the last guests had left and everybody was so tired that a few brief chats were enough before toddling off to our rooms.

Hot water at 8:30 a.m. with breakfast gong at 9:00. I tarried, and Glan burst to rout me out with such success that I was third down to breakfast – serve-self at the well-stocked grill on the sideboard. Plans during breakfast, and I cast my lot with the party who were off to see the Old Surrey Hunt.

It was a thrilling spectacle – the scarlet-jacketed men and bowlered women on handsome horses, the pack of hounds, and the Master in his long-visored, velvet cap! We drove back (Glan, Patrick, and I) while the others took Claud to his London train.

The library of Blunt House drew me, and I found a fascinating little anthology, together with a soft chair beside the fire, where Sir Ernest joined me to go through his morning mail. Luncheon at one, and a tennis party in the afternoon. They all played until tea time, while I cheered from the bench, and then there was tea, with guests in the cheery drawing room, followed by ping-pong in the hall.

Off to dress for dinner, and bridge in the evening with Glan and me versus Sir Ernest and Patrick, who overwhelmed us. The others were off to the town to hear Harold Samuels, the pianist, but returned at about 10:15 p.m. for refreshments and early bed. We were all tired, but my bedside lamp and anthology supplied the perfect nightcap to the perfect day.

Up at 9:15 for a quick tub, and down to breakfast to find Lady Benn, John, and Patrick ahead of me. The others had all breakfasted very early and driven off to Brighton. Glan joined us, and Lady Benn left us to enjoy a pleasant college-boy chat over coffee and pipes until Sir Ernest came down and brought the discussion up several notches. It was resolved to leave for town in an hour, so I went off to pack by eleven, and then down for a delightful farewell chat around the hall fire with Sir Ernest, Patrick, and Glan before bundling into the car and back to London. Lady Benn had left earlier for a walk, and Sir Ernest, who saw us off from the door, expressed their pleasure at our visit and hoped we would come again. Back in town slightly before 1:00 p.m. and to Clifford's Inn for an afternoon of work.

I can't tell you how much I enjoyed the week-end and what a real privilege it was to be a guest in a fine English home. Such hospitality! No gush or effervescence, but when you are calmly told you are welcome, you know it's really meant. How I should like to have you meet Sir Ernest and Lady Benn. I believe I learned as much about the English temperament during that week-end as I have during the whole year I've been here.

* * *

CHAPTER 9

LINDBERGH AND EARHART

Introduction

When P.S. returned from Europe and settled in New York in the early 1930s he began an eight-year period as an editor for King Features Syndicate. He also felt the urge to do some creative writing of his own, and the opportunity presented itself in the form of a Sunday afternoon radio broadcast over station WINS, to be entitled "Headline Flashbacks." The fifteen-minute program comprised items from news of the preceding week that led into a "flashback" that used material from P.S.'s own experiences in Europe.

An obvious example was the story of the Lindbergh baby's kidnapping, which gave him the opportunity to retell the story of his encounter with the hero of the first transatlantic flight, at the officers' mess of a small aerodrome on a hilltop in June of 1927. Similarly, when Amelia Earhart made the first solo flight from Hawaii to California in January of 1935, P.S. was able to tie this news item with the story of how he met the boyish girl-flyer at Southampton on her own transatlantic flight in June 1928.

P.S.'s original front-page stories from the *Chicago Tribune* are reproduced here, together with the later "flashback" accounts.

E.B.S.

*   *   *

Fog Downs Lindy: Off Again
Flies To Paris After Landing Near The Coast
Determined to Make Channel Hop

Bulletin

LYMPNE, England.* June 3, 1927 (UP) – Captain Lindbergh resumed his interrupted flight to Paris at 8:13 a.m, today.

Bulletin

LYMPNE, England. June 3, 1927 (AP) – After flying 38 minutes from Kenley, Captain Lindbergh landed here at 6:50 a.m. today, deciding to postpone his crossing of the English channel and his return to Paris until more favorable weather conditions. There was fog in the channel.

Bulletin

KENLEY, England. June 3, 1927 (AP) – Captain Charles A. Lindbergh hopped off for Paris at 6:20 a.m. today.

WHITEFIELD, England. June 2, 1927 – On a deserted hilltop two miles southeast of this sleepy little Surrey village, the youth who for twelve days had swept nations off their feet and has been feted by kings and queens is spending the night almost alone.

For the first time since the memorable May 21, Capt. Charles A. Lindbergh has escaped the adulation of Europe and is quietly resting without pomp in the lonely buildings of the officers' mess at Kenley Aerodrome, thanks to fogs of this afternoon, which upset his departure for France.

Capt. Lindbergh's disappointment over the unfavorable weather was obvious in the club room of the building where he sat with a handful of officers.

Steward is Upset

"I was totally unprepared for this occasion," the officers' steward said to the

---

* *Editor's Note:* Lympne is about 70 miles southeast of Kenley and about 5 miles from the Kentish shore of the English Channel.

Tribune correspondent. The steward was flabbergasted by the sudden honor of catering to the Atlantic hero.

"I had only the regular officers' mess fare tonight – soup, cold joint, and tea. What does he like for breakfast?" asked the butler, who proudly announced his American ancestry.

The little village at the foot of the hill was serenely ignorant of the celebrated guest. The village loungers at the town "pub," the Whitefield Tavern, are discussing over their beer the wonderful Yankee chap who will leave early in the morning. Even as they talked in the twilight the rain began pattering drearily on the windowpanes, indicating that it may not be necessary for the steward to call Capt. Lindbergh at 4 a.m. as planned.

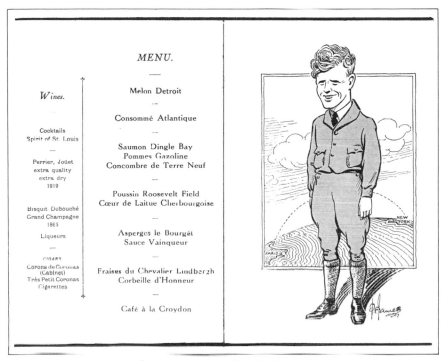

Menu from dinner given for Charles Lindbergh
by the Anglo-American Press Association of London, 1927

"Headline Flashbacks"
Station WINS
January 13, 1935

The great drama of Flemington, New Jersey rushes on towards the big climax. The eyes of the entire world are glued upon that little courthouse which has become the stage for the most nerve-wracking tragedy in the history of American law. Already enough words have been written about the trial to fill eighty-five full-length novels, according to telegraph officials. Twentieth century Barnums have already got the wires humming with offers to headline the principal figures in the trial behind the footlights at fabulous salaries. Dr. Condon, Betty Gow, even the members of the jury have received tempting offers, they tell us. And still the two principal figures have yet to face the world from that sturdy, old-fashioned witness chair – Colonel Charles A. Lindbergh and Bruno Richard Hauptmann himself.

In the midst of all the wild speculations, grim accusations, and recriminations that fill the air, let me take you back nearly eight years to my own last meeting with Charles Lindbergh, when I managed to score one of the best beats of my London newspaper days. It was quite a different chapter in the epic life of the modest American youth who couldn't stop the world when it first decided that he was a real hero.

The Colonel (he was a captain then) had just completed his spectacular visit to London following his now historic transatlantic flight of May 1927, and was expected back in Paris June 3 to prepare for his triumphal return to the United States aboard a battleship. The police remembered those wild crowds that greeted Lindbergh when he had arrived at Croydon airport a few days before, and had actually come close to mobbing him to death, to say nothing of ruining his plane. He had already landed and was taxiing across the field, when he saw the mob break through the barriers and come surging towards him. Without ever coming to a stop, Lindy sped his plane forward, took to the air once more, and then circled over the field until the police had succeeded in getting the hysterical crowd in hand.

In view of all this, it was decided that it would be safest for the flyer to leave England from the obscure little military airport of Kenley, near London, instead of from Croydon where the monster crowd would be waiting to see him off.

The news leaked out, but not until he was thought to be safely on his way back to Paris. Then, by one of those strange tricks of fate that give newspaper work its glamour, a vague report trickled into the London office of my newspaper to the effect that Lindbergh had been prevailed upon at the last moment to cancel all his plans for flying across the Channel that afternoon because fog and rain had swept through the south of England, making flying extremely dangerous. Would he spend the night in little Kenley while all of Paris waited and the whole world watched? Here was drama: Lindbergh, the idol of the world at that moment, the youth who had been wined and dined by kings, queens, prime ministers, and ambassadors, sleeping each night in a palace or a mansion under special armed guard. This fabulous hero was going to spend the night in a lonely little officers' barracks on a deserted, rain-swept hill top down in rural Surrey! It was worth going after.

Feeling a little like Sherlock Holmes, I was whisked to Victoria Station in a creaky London taxicab and there found the fates had been kind to me. A train was leaving shortly for Kenley. It didn't take long to buy my ticket and find an unoccupied compartment that would give me a chance to consult my maps and plan my campaign in silence. The first blow came at Kenley. The Kenley aerodrome, it seemed, was several miles from town and couldn't be reached direct. A few hasty enquiries among the villagers, and I found that I could travel by bus to a neighboring hamlet that nestled at the foot of the hill on which the aerodrome was situated. Another bumpy trip through the dismal grey twilight brought me to the village. The long winding road up the hill was too uncertain to risk on foot in the rain and the darkness. It began to look like a wild goose chase, but I commandeered what must have been the only available vehicle in the village, a shaky automobile driven by a garage hand anxious to earn a few extra shillings. I took him into my confidence, and he entered into the spirit of the chase. For we were hot on the trail of Charles Lindbergh, the world's greatest man at that moment! In a few seconds we were rattling up and around the hill. After all this breathless scheming, I didn't dare let myself think that maybe the whole thing was a false alarm, after all! Perhaps Charles Lindbergh was at that very moment being cheered in Paris. Now we were driving boldly into the grounds and up to the door of the lonely barracks. There was no need to guard the flyer in this lonely corner of the world. I told my companion, now as excited as I was, to wait for me and to be ready to leave at a moment's notice. Then I walked boldly up to the door.

I'll admit my heart was pounding like the engine of a transatlantic liner but I tried calmness. Newspapermen were already off the Lindbergh receiving list, so it would be fatal to reveal my business at the start, or even to show any doubt as to the flyer's being here. I told the butler who opened the door to inform Captain Lindbergh that I was waiting to see him. My American accent saved me. I could have wept for joy when the flunky nodded respectfully, asked me to enter, and then disappeared. I had guessed right! I could hear voices. The great American was at dinner with his admiring hosts – a handful of officers of the Royal Air Force.

In a few moments the familiar boyish figure was striding towards me, There was a puzzled look on Lindy's face. Of course he didn't remember me, although I had met him at luncheon a day or two before. I couldn't keep up the game any longer. I had to admit that I was just another newspaper reporter who had dashed down here through rain and fog to get a few precious words from him.

He refused to be interviewed because his own newspaper contracts now made that impossible. But I had seen him, and did manage to worm a few "yesses" and "nos" from him. That was all I needed. In another second he was gone, and the butler was beside me once more. A gentle reminder that it was time to leave.

My head was whirling. I had my story, and not another newspaperman within miles of the place. One last touch for my big story – the human interest touch. I smiled at the man. "I'll bet you never dreamed you were going to have such a famous guest to look after tonight, did you?" I asked him. It was all he needed to express his feelings. His voice trembled. "Oh no sir. If I had thought, sir, that Captain Lindbergh would be spending the night with us!" His profession came to the fore. "Please, sir, what do you think I should give the Captain for breakfast, sir? I don't know what you Americans like, sir, for breakfast. And I do so want to please him." It was my chance to return a favor. "Don't worry," I said, "he'll like whatever you give him. I'd suggest some fresh fruit, bacon and eggs, coffee, and plenty of crisp toast." He looked relieved, murmured his deepest gratitude, protested at the bank note I pressed into his hand, and then was staring after me as I leaped into my waiting car, and was whirled back to the village. Well, in less than an hour my story was humming over the cables under the Atlantic. I made the last edition of my paper. It gave me one of those glows that only a newspaperman who has got his story can experience.

*   *   *

Southampton Goes Wild Over Earhart
Lady Mayor Greets First Woman To Fly Ocean:
Touching Scene As Mrs. Guest Embraces Protégée

SOUTHAMPTON, June 19, 1928 – A slender, grey-eyed girl with lips twitching nervously in a wistful smile faltered up the treacherous runway at the Woolston docks at Southampton at 1:45 this afternoon, and a frenzied mob of men, women, and children broke out into piercing screams of "Earhart! Earhart!"

As the first woman to fly the Atlantic crossed the boundary of the city which was her original goal, she seemed to breathe a sigh of happiness which was interpreted by many as a sign of terrible strain. But when Southampton's mayor, the Honorable Mistress Foster Welch, wearing the historic heavy gold necklet which is the insignia of her office, stepped forward with the American Consul, Mr. John M. Savage, Miss Amelia Earhart showed the first signs of relaxation. The crowd went wild as she stepped forward with a sunny smile and outstretched hand.

Twenty minutes before there was a preliminary roar of excitement as the immortalized golden brown plane appeared as a speck on the southern horizon rapidly growing larger and finally circling over the crowd. Immediately, Woolston became a distraught village. White-aproned shopkeepers, hysterical barmaids, beaming housewives, and yelling errand boys, all rushed out of houses and raced towards the docks.

Just as the *Friendship* finally decided to settle gently on the open water at Southampton Harbor at 1:27 p.m. there burst forth an earsplitting blast of dozens of factory and steamer whistles.

Another second, and the American air queen was smiling embarrassedly through the tiny cabin window of the cockpit as a fleet of speedboats raced out to meet her.

Faces Battery Of Cameras

The *Friendship* slowly made its way between gigantic hulks of transatlantic liners towards the landing buoy. A launch took the three flyers from the plane and carried them to the wharf.

There was a touching moment when the slim girl rushed to embrace Mrs. F.E. Guest, the American wife of Captain Guest, former Air Minister, who financed the flight. She then embraced Mrs. Scott Payne, wife of the Imperial Airways director, and then turned to face a battery of cameras.

While the sweating bobbies heaved back at the struggling crowd, Miss Earhart, Pilot Wilmer Stultz, and Navigator Louis Gordon passed beneath the huge American flag through a narrow lane to waiting limousines.

Woolston refused to believe that Miss Earhart was leaving at once to cross to the swankier metropolis across the river and formed a solid mass around the town and refused to budge. Military police cleared a way for the cars which proceeded to the Southwestern Hotel at Southampton. Another mass of cheering people greeted the party, and Miss Earhart was at once taken to a quiet suite for absolute seclusion and rest. Mrs. Guest was the only one to accompany her.

Stultz Gives Interview

In the meantime Captain Stultz and "Slim" Gordon ducked through the crowds and retired to the modest bedrooms where the *Tribune* representative found them washing up in preparation for lunch.

"I have no suggestions for future transatlantic flights, but I am mostly interested in commercial flying," said the firm-jawed pilot. "It is unquestionably one of the most important fields of development in America, and I would like to take part. At any rate, I am not considering offers to fly back over the Atlantic As regards the absence of landmarks and the lack of indicators on this side in order to give flyers their direction, we had no trouble of any kind, and it is untrue that we were lost. Our attempt to get location from the liner *America* was made in an effort to check up on our course. Naturally we were not particularly interested in landmarks since practically our entire flight was over water.

Miss Earhart Had His Razor

However, the question of inadequate maps and charts which was mentioned, is absurd. Our maps, issued by the government, were entirely satisfactory."

The pilot and mechanic-navigator admitted that they did not carry mascots, but Slim Gordon confided with a chuckle that he was astonished to find the razor which he had bought during his last day at Trepassey Bay and which he believed to have left behind, turned up in Miss Earhart's handbag aboard the *Friendship* just before they landed.

"We did not do much shaving or dressing for dinner en route," grinned Gordon. "Our dinner consisted of a sandwich and several cups of coffee."

After a short rest Miss Earhart agreed to face newspapermen for a few minutes and told them with smiles that she was never once afraid during the crossing and would like to do it all over again.

Felt Cold At Times

"There was nothing that I could call a physical thrill, but there was mental exhilaration which was overpowering. We couldn't see the ocean. That made it more impressive. I felt cold and uncomfortable at times and climbed into the cockpit in order to get a little warmed and then I returned to the fuselage and sat on the floor trying to write in my diary."

Miss Earhart carried no luggage, merely wearing an airman's leather suit and helmet which she admitted having borrowed. She bought nothing for the trip because "you never know what might have happened."

At three o'clock, closed cars were drawn up at the entrance to the hotel and mobs collected to cheer the flyers. Scurrying nervously through a side door they hoped to evade the crowds but were seen just as they climbed into the cars and were able to escape only by a sudden burst of speed on the part of the drivers.

A fleet of cars took up the chase through the charming Hampshire country-side toward London. The party arrived at 5:30 p.m. at the fashionable Hyde Park Hotel, which will be the flyers' home at least during the early part of the proposed ten-day visit.

It is considered possible that Miss Earhart will be the guest of Mrs. Frederick Guest at her beautiful town house in Park Lane.

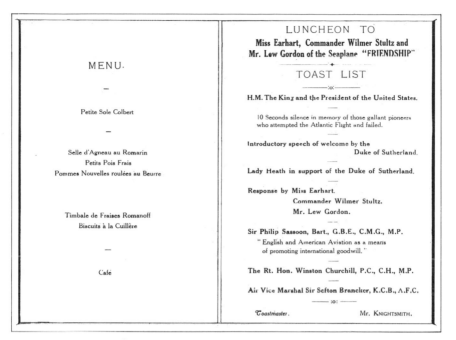

MENU.

—

Petite Sole Colbert

Selle d'Agneau au Romarin
Petits Pois Frais
Pommes Nouvelles roulées au Beurre

Timbale de Fraises Romanoff
Biscuits à la Cuillère

—

Café

LUNCHEON TO

Miss Earhart, Commander Wilmer Stultz and
Mr. Lew Gordon of the Seaplane "FRIENDSHIP"

—♦—

TOAST LIST

————:o:————

H.M. The King and the President of the United States.

—

10 Seconds silence in memory of those gallant pioneers
who attempted the Atlantic Flight and failed.

—

Introductory speech of welcome by the
Duke of Sutherland.

—

Lady Heath in support of the Duke of Sutherland.

Response by Miss Earhart.
Commander Wilmer Stultz.
Mr. Lew Gordon.

Sir Philip Sassoon, Bart., G.B.E., C.M.G., M.P.
" English and American Aviation as a means
of promoting international goodwill. "

—

The Rt. Hon. Winston Churchill, P.C., C.H., M.P.

—

Air Vice Marshal Sir Sefton Brancker, K.C.B., A.F.C.

———— :o: ————

Toastmaster. Mr. KNIGHTSMITH.

Menu from luncheon given in honor of Amelia Earhart,
Wilmer Stultz, and Lou Gordon, 1928

June 28, 1928

Dear Family,

I guess I told you about my midnight dash by motorcar down to Southampton to meet the three Atlantic flyers, Earhart, Stultz, and Gordon. One of our photographers and myself left London at 3 a.m. and arrived there about 5:30 a.m., just in time for breakfast and to dash off to the docks where they were expected to arrive in their seaplane.

It was nerve-wracking waiting for them, with reporters representing newspapers all over the world pacing nervously about, hoping to get off the news to their papers before anybody else had done so. Shortly after noon, the word went around that they had been sighted over the harbor, and everybody went mad with excitement. Some other newspapermen and myself had chartered a motorboat to take us out to meet them, and we tore off at great speed while crowds gathered in great excitement, and welcoming aeroplanes circled over the harbor.

In another few minutes, a powerful speedboat drew along beside us, and a man shouted to us that it was a false alarm. The flyers had been obliged to make a forced landing at Burry Port, Wales! You can imagine our disappointment as we had to turn around and rush back to shore, so that I could dispatch an immediate rush cable to the *Tribune* in Chicago, telling them what had happened.

Then the rush began to get aeroplanes for the trip to Burry Port. Several of the newspapermen, including myself, were after the "story" in dead earnest, and felt that we simply had to be on the scene as soon as anybody else. There wasn't a plane to be had in Southampton, not even a seat in a plane. We had to stand helplessly by while a single Imperial Airways machine took off for Wales with only the flyers' personal representative and a single reporter in it. I at once got in touch with our office in London and had one of the chaps who is helping me, charter a plane immediately from London and fly direct to Wales, where he saw the flyers and got an excellent story. He followed them by air to Southampton next day, and joined me there. Meanwhile, I wrote the entire story from the Southampton angle and then drove back to London behind the flyers in their high-powered Rolls-Royce.

I had just three hours' sleep in forty-eight hours, with meals on the run, so you can imagine how I looked upon my return to London – simply exhausted. However, a hot bath and a good night's sleep put me back in good shape, and the Chicago office seems to be fairly well satisfied with our efforts.

Miss Earhart resembles Lindbergh in appearance to an amazing degree, but she of course is not the spectacular figure that he was. However, it was an interesting, if strenuous, assignment.

*   *   *

CHAPTER 10

STORY BEHIND THE NEWS

Introduction

I n contrast to the three years in Paris, where P. S. had confined his activities mainly to the close-knit, parochial world of the writers and artists in the Latin Quarter on the Left Bank, his two years in London gave him much wider scope in his work.

As assistant correspondent for the London bureau of the *Chicago Tribune,* he covered stories of international importance, and met with a wide variety of celebrities. Later, these experiences provided him with colorful material for "Story Behind the News," his weekly radio program on WINS in New York. His listeners were regaled with fascinating accounts of the background to his news stories. He also used the program for live interviews.

Also reprinted here are stories from the *Tribune* on Thomas Hardy's funeral, on Joe Kennedy's crackdown on Court presentations of American debutantes, and on a surprising speech by Sir Austen Chamberlain in the House of Commons. All are examples of P. S.'s vivid reporting of the "story behind the news," both in broadcasting and in newsprint.

E.B.S.

*　　*　　*

King Carol II of Rumania

November 2, 1933 – At the far end of the Mediterranean, that dashing comic opera hero, King Carol II of Rumania, once more has stepped into the limelight. And, as on practically every other occasion when the handsome Carol has taken center stage, there is a new love interest.

In 1921, Carol was married to Princess Helen of Greece. All went well until the beautiful Magda Lupescu, flaming-haired former wife of a Rumanian army officer, appeared on the scene. She was too much for the susceptible Carol, and poor Princess Helen was practically forgotten in the Crown Prince's mad dash after his new inamorata.

Carol's father, the aged King Ferdinand, ordered the young woman to leave the country in November 1925, but Carol, returning from the funeral of the dowager Queen Alexandra in London, met his beloved in Paris, and they fled to Venice together. King Ferdinand, bedridden and dying, sent a close friend to beg his son to return home.

Carol replied by renouncing not only the throne but all his rights under Rumanian law, including those over his child and over his estates. The princely exile and his red-headed companion became familiar figures in the fashionable corners of Europe – Deauville and on the Paris boulevards.*

Death finally came to the stricken sovereign and little Prince Michael, barely six years old, ascended the throne on July 20, 1927, as King under a regency.

This was the signal for the boy's father, Carol, to get busy. From his headquarters in Paris he let it be known that he might be persuaded to reconsider his renunciation of his rights to the throne if enough of his countrymen expressed a desire to have him back. Trouble was brewing. Carol and Lupescu suddenly disappeared from Paris and turned up at the palatial country estate in England of a wealthy Rumanian named Jonescu.

Government in England and Rumania was thrown into a turmoil by the reports that the quixotic prince actually was planning a daring *coup d'état* to place himself on the throne he previously had scorned. Rumanian authorities who were hostile to Carol called upon Scotland Yard, Britain's world-famed criminal investigation bureau, to watch the fugitive prince and his titian-haired mistress.

The sleepy countryside round about the Jonescu estate near Godstone to the south of London suddenly became alive with newspapermen, photographers, secret service men, and spies. This dramatic chapter in the bewildering career of the Graustarkian Carol was the only one in which I personally was involved.

As a correspondent in London for an American newspaper at the time, I took my place in the small army of newspapermen from all corners of the world who

---

Editor's Note: The story of Prince Carol and his red-headed Rumanian mistress, Magda Lupescu, might have been regarded as a dress rehearsal for the drama enacted ten years later by his young relative, the Prince of Wales.

The latter, like Carol, gave up his throne for his mistress – in this case, an American divorcee. The two renunciations were identical in almost every respect, except that Carol was a married man and handed his throne to his son Michael. The Prince of Wales, unmarried, abdicated in favor of his brother the Duke of York.

Perhaps the most striking difference between the two young princes and their mistresses was in their appearance. Prince Carol's manner of dress gave no hint of his exalted status, while Magda, in spite of the famous flaming red hair, was positively dowdy. Both contrasted sharply with the sartorial excellence of the Duke and Duchess of Windsor.

maintained a day and night vigil around the Jonescu mansion to keep close track of the movements of the runaway prince who wanted to reclaim his throne.

We received a grim warning to keep off the premises. As an occasional closed car would speed in or out of the closely guarded gate, the nervous tension among the newspapermen increased. Who was calling on Carol? Was the wily prince himself, perhaps in disguise, being whisked away in one of those outgoing cars? There were wild rumors that an airplane was ready to carry Carol and Lupescu straight back to Bucharest for a triumphal return to the throne.

It was known that sympathy for Carol was spreading in Rumania, particularly among the powerful army officers. Several days and nights of watching followed. The thickets and underbrush surrounding the house were swarming with newspaper sleuths, many of them crawling on their stomachs to work their way nearer to the quarry without being seen. There were tense, whispered challenges: "Qui est là?" And the hissing answer: *"Die Frankfurter Zeitung!"* or *"International News!"* *

After a few days came the humiliating British government orders expelling the royal exile from England. The story, at least from a journalistic point of view, was killed. Instead of the expected and, it must be admitted, hoped-for dramatic flight back to Rumania to claim the crown, Carol's departure was merely that of a humble commoner, crestfallen and in disgrace.

But the humiliation was comparatively short-lived. Today, barely five years later, this Don Quixote of European royalty is on the throne which he once disdained. He is now King Carol II – forty years old and unmarried, having been divorced by Helen in 1928. Will the Princess Eudoxia of Bulgaria be the next royal personage to play a star role in Carol's comic soap opera? That remains to be seen.

Opening of Parliament

November 23, 1933 – Newspapermen will tell you that there's more color and drama behind the world's news today than there has been at any other time, excepting the desperate years of the World War. Sometimes the thrills are on the surface of the news. Sometimes you have to dig down deep to find them. But they're always there. Imagine that dramatic moment in Britain's stately House of Lords the other day when a former plumber from Glasgow leaped to his feet, just

---

* *Editor's Note:* One of the bolder members of the press corps, herself a redhead, left her male colleagues flabbergasted and frustrated when she brazenly walked up to the gates, continued on up the driveway, and managed to get a glimpse inside the house before she was finally ejected by the guards. She became very popular, however, with the bedraggled, ditch-crawling members of the night vigil when her mother arrived by car from London the next morning bringing hot coffee and doughnuts for the whole press corps.

after King George solemnly opened Parliament, and shouted his fierce contempt into the faces of the sovereign and the assembled lords and ladies. Only one who has sat in the presence of the King and Queen on that impressive occasion can realize the almost terrifying drama of the scene. Let me reconstruct the magnificent picture for you as I watched it from the front row of the press gallery during my own newspaper days in London.

It is 11:00 a. m., and the dim, gothic hall of the ancient House of Lords is filled with the low hum of suppressed excitement. The small spectators' gallery is already packed with accredited newspaper correspondents from every corner of the world. Down below, the noble lords and ladies, bearers of the great titles of England, are filing slowly to their benches, facing two thrones at the end of the room, each on a dais, but one a little lower than the other. All are in full court dress, the dukes and earls in flashing gold braids, swords, and all the trappings of nobility; their wives resplendent in blazing jeweled tiaras, brocaded low-cut court gowns, and long white gloves. A strange spectacle at eleven o'clock in the morning. Big Ben booms the hour from its tower high above. Suddenly the myriad lights in the blazing chandeliers grow dim. A death-like hush falls over the gathering, as the lords and ladies silently rise to their feet. Then, as the lights gradually flare up to their full brilliance once more, their Britannic Majesties King George and Queen Mary, in jeweled crowns and regal ermine robes, are escorted silently into the room and led to their thrones.

In 1928, when I covered the Opening of Parliament, Queen Mary was too ill to be present. Her place was taken by the heir to the throne, the ever-popular Prince of Wales. On that occasion, the Prince was escorted to his throne just before his father. He looked uncomfortable and not at all pleased in his flowing scarlet robes trimmed with ermine, the fur of royalty. Striding to his throne with a careless, swinging gait, he seated himself perfunctorily. Then, quite unconsciously, he indulged in a boyish show of impatience that made him seem all the more human to those of us who noticed it. Eager to get the whole thing over with (so that he might return to his golf or squash racquets perhaps), the heir to the throne gave vent to his restlessness exactly as an audience of American college students would do. Beneath his scarlet robes, his foot began to beat impatiently, tap . . . tap . . . tap . . . tap . . . tap. We liked him all the more for it. But it must have shocked the older lords and ladies who noticed it. The King soon arrived. Within half an hour, he had read his speech in a firm, even voice, standing before his throne. The British Parliament had once more been formally opened by George the Fifth, "by the Grace of God of Great Britain and Ireland and of the British Dominions Beyond the Seas, King, Defender of the Faith, Emperor of India."

In the midst of this magnificent display of royal pomp and color, there is always a somber and almost incongruous touch. That is provided by the American ambassador, in conventional black dress clothes, seated among the brilliantly gold-braided diplomats from foreign countries in their enclosure just to the left of the throne. Only the Soviet envoy and one or two others, besides the American ambassador, scorn the colorful trappings of court splendor. Members of the House of Commons, of course, also appear in conventional black. But, in accordance with ancient tradition, they are not allowed to penetrate beyond the far end of the hall. For this is territory sacred to the peers of England. It is their day. For this once, at least, the House of Lords each year loftily scorns the lower House, which has played such havoc with its ancient rights and privileges.

"One dollar per word, Sir!"
George Bernard Shaw

Kenneth MacDonald of Detroit has hit upon a new way of getting the autographs of the world's celebrities. Close followers of the news are chuckling at the way he twisted an autograph out of the great Bernard Shaw. Shaw has an evil reputation among newspapermen as the hardest man in the world to interview; that is, unless you are prepared to tickle his palm with a silver dollar for every word he utters. He is said to charge the same fee, $1, for every letter of his autograph, or a total of $12. Figure it out for yourself. He now signs his name "G. Bernard Shaw," but, at the dollar-a-letter rate, it is suggested that he may soon change the signature to "George Bernard Shaw," which would add $5 per autograph. Mr. MacDonald, however, got his autograph for nothing by writing a letter to the 77-year-old playwright saying that unless he received a reply to the contrary, he would feel free to use Shaw's name in marketing a certain new vegetable compound. A fiery letter denying permission to use the name was promptly received, and MacDonald had succeeded in obtaining the coveted signature of G. Bernard Shaw.

As a newspaper reporter, I myself had two opportunities to ensnare the elusive Mr. Shaw. One involved a personal interview; the other, as in MacDonald's case, an exchange of letters.

In the summer of 1931 I had written to Shaw to request a personal interview with him at the annual Malvern Festival, where his new play *Too True To Be Good* was to have its first performance.

I received in response a printed message that read as follows: "Mr. Bernard Shaw is obliged to remind correspondents who seek to interview him for publication that as he is himself a professional journalist, he naturally prefers to communicate with the public through the Press at first hand. He is willing, when time permits, to answer written questions on points of fact when they happen to be interesting as current news; but he receives personal visits only on the understanding that his conversation is not to be reported."

Mr. Bernard Shaw is obliged to remind correspondents who seek to interview him for publication that as he is himself a professional journalist, he naturally prefers to communicate with the public through the Press at first hand. He is willing, when time permits, to answer written questions on points of fact when they happen to be interesting as current news ; but he receives personal visits only on the understanding that his conversation is not to be reported.

This is pointedly relevant to my Russian visit, - and to the American press

(4 Whitehall Court (130)
London S.W.1.)

The Malvern Hotel. Great Malvern. Worcs.
11/8/31

TELEGRAMS,"SOCIALIST, PARL-LONDON".
TELEPHONE,WHITEHALL 3160.

4, WHITEHALL COURT, LONDON, S.W.I.

4th May 1932.

Dear Mr Shinkman,

    Please do not join the idiots who are identifying me with the young rascal in my play and imagining that his piteous cry for affirmations is my "poignant cry of defeat". I have supplied affirmations enough to keep America busy for th next hundred years, and am quite cheerful about them, thank you.

    You must not imagine that you can get away with any maudlin sentiment about me: it is hopeless.

    Shall we have the pleasure of seeing you at Malvern agai this year to compare the English production with the American one?

             Faithfully

             G. Bernard Shaw

Paul Shinkman Esq
107 East 39th Street,
New York City
U.S.America.

Shaw's indignant letter to P.S.

Just below, in the tightly-curled writing of Shaw appeared this postscript: "This is pointedly relevant to my Russian visit, and to the American press. GBS. The Malvern Hotel, Great Malvern, Worc. 11/8/31."

Whether or not it was so intended, and knowing full well that this was his customary way of responding to eager journalists, I chose to read a challenge into the disclosure of my quarry's fumed-oak retreat among the hills of Worcestershire. Within thirty-six hours I was domiciled under the same roof and on the same floor as Mr. and Mrs. Shaw. And when a series of polite notes left with the hotel manageress for the distinguished fellow-guest brought no response, it was time for the direct attack to be launched.

The solemn after-dinner retreat from the small dining room next evening found me squeezed into the Great Malvern's three-passenger automatic lift with the Shaws. Two piercing grey eyes drilled me questioningly from beneath billowing white eyebrows. I replied in an unmistakable American accent that I would have to leave it to my fellow-guests to operate this strange English mechanism in heading towards my floor, the third.

Once we were caged and in full but barely perceptible motion as charges of G.B.S., I quickly identified myself and asked our operator when he would make his first visit to the U.S. He bristled, shook his head and grated: "Why should I, a journalist like yourself, give you a free interview? My fee is one dollar per word."

I pleaded that, like himself during his early Fleet Street days, I had no expense allowance which would remotely approach meeting such a contingency. And what did he think of America and the American people these days? We reached our floor and strode down the broad corridor, he chanting the refrain "One dollar per word!" and I carefully maintaining my position between the Shaws and the side of the hallway on which I knew their room would be located.

Suddenly both swerved away from me and were disappearing through a doorway exactly opposite the one which I knew to be their own. As the door slowly closed, a saturnine head, still shaking a refusal to speak at less than one dollar per word, gradually vanished. Mr. Shaw had cunningly engaged rooms on *both* sides of the corridor.

Six months later I had my revenge and my reward. The new play *Too True To Be Good,* coolly received by the critics both in Malvern and in London, aroused even less enthusiasm in New York. It was a moment for testing the mettle of a 75-year-old man in the face of unusual defeat.

Just returned from a performance of the play at the old Guild Theatre in New York, I typed a profusely sympathetic note to the author, delicately suggesting that perhaps his play writing days were over. In any event, I added, I was sorry for my rudeness at Malvern.

Back came a fiery bolt from the ramparts of Whitehall Court, high above the Horse Guards' Parade and Downing Street: "Dear Mr. Shinkman: Please do not join the idiots who are identifying me with the young rascal in my play and imagining that his piteous cry for affirmations is my 'poignant cry of defeat.' I have supplied affirmations enough to keep America busy for the next hundred years, and am quite cheerful about them, thank you. You must not imagine that you can get away with any maudlin sentiment about me: it is hopeless. Shall we have the pleasure of seeing you at Malvern again this year to compare the English production with the American one? – Faithfully, (Signed) G. Bernard Shaw."

Two years later, G.B.S., well-armed with new affirmations at the age of seventy-seven, was paying his first visit to America. An audience, which packed New York's Metropolitan Opera House to the roof, sat entranced as he gravely addressed them on the subject "American Boobs."

I had my story.

Opening of the Royal Court

May 10, 1934 – If you happen to be strolling in London next Tuesday evening, turn your steps to the southwest from Trafalgar Square, pass under Admiralty Arch, and – then stop to stare! You will see one of those strangely impressive spectacles that is such an important part of British tradition and that contributes so much to the passing picture of life in stately London. Stretched along the entire length of the Mall, that beautiful avenue which is the formal approach to Buckingham Palace, there stands a motionless line of glistening limousines, many with the crest of nobility emblazoned on their doors. In the driver's seat of each sit a smartly uniformed chauffeur and a footman, staring straight ahead. Crowded tightly around each luxurious car is an admiring throng of breathless men, women, and children from England's great and good-natured middle class, staring unashamedly at the imposing figures seated inside.

And who are the objects of all this attention? Britain's aristocracy and its guests from abroad are on parade! The glittering procession creeps at snail's pace towards the massive wrought iron gates and then circles up the imposing entrance to Buckingham Palace. England's King and Queen are holding their first royal court of the 1934 season, and the brilliant occasion has drawn thousands of the social-elect from all corners of the world. In the limousines, each patiently awaiting its turn to drive up to the palace entrance and discharge its favored passengers, sit the dukes and duchesses, earls and countesses, the former in glittering full dress and wearing their jeweled decorations, the latter resplendent in diamond tiaras, flashing rubies, and emeralds worth a king's ransom. Here and there in the brilliant procession is a car filled with Americans, nervously awaiting their first glimpse of royalty – At Home. In each car there is at least one feminine passenger wearing the magic emblem of the three tiny white ostrich feathers as a tufted coronet to set off her magnificent court gown. It is she who is one of the favored few tonight to tremblingly curtsey before King George and Queen Mary as her name resounds through the mirrored drawing rooms, and hundreds fasten their gazes upon her. For several hours the curtseys continue against a background of soft music, tinkling champagne glasses, and the low murmur of conversation. Finally the long line of debutantes has finished its march past the thrones. The first royal court of the London social season has passed into history. All hurry away to fashionable restaurants, night clubs, and the private mansions of Mayfair to make merry until dawn.*

Then it was all over. The thrill of being presented at Court had come to each. Weeks of preparation for that fleeting moment were ended – countless fittings at the dressmakers, hours of practice in curtseying and walking gracefully across a glistening floor. For the conventions and etiquette of Court must be carefully observed, even though this means hiring an accredited teacher in London's fashionable Mayfair. Queen Mary herself determines some of the more important details of the court gowns which the debutantes shall wear, as well as whether flowers shall be carried. The traditional head-dress of three little ostrich feathers must, of course, be worn. Black evening gowns are generally frowned upon, except in special cases, and extremely low-cut dresses are bound to meet with royal disapproval. Trains this year are to be eighteen inches long, but exceptions are made, as in the case of the strong-willed Countess of Oxford and Asquith, otherwise known as Margot Asquith, who swept in trailing four yards of material behind her.

It must be admitted that Queen Mary has become far more liberal in matters of feminine fashion during recent years. Twenty years ago she made it clear that she did not approve of women riding their horses astride in fashionable Rotten Row. It was found during a check-up that only twenty-two women out of seventy-one rode astride, and King George asked that *none* of them ride astride during the morning hours when little Princess Mary was enjoying her daily canter in the Row. Today you can count on the fingers of one hand the women you will see riding sidesaddle during a trot in that beautiful corner.

---

*Editor's Note. It seems to have been the ambition of every wealthy American mother at that time to have her daughter presented at Court. One hopes the lucky young girls chosen for this honor found the experience suitably glamorous.

My own recollection of this event is of a long, tiring wait in endless Palace ante-rooms before the throne room was reached. By the time I was due to make my curtsey to the Queen, I was suffering from a severe headache caused by the tight headband needed to anchor the traditional three feathers in place on my fashionably "bobbed" coiffure.

Inner Circle at Buckingham Palace
Determined to Break Court Presentation
"Racket"

Impoverished Ladies of Title Who Sell Their Entree
Into Court Circles Are 'Blacklisted' By Lord Chamberlain

Friday, August 5, 1938 – Royal "rackets" have been unknown to Lord Chamberlains and even crowned heads of Europe's past. But the privilege of curtseying before the King and Queen of England is not going to become a "racket" if the inner circle at Buckingham Palace and certain other important personages have anything to say about it.

When Joe Kennedy, America's new and extraordinarily popular ambassador to the Court of St. James's, delivered his inaugural pronouncement to the effect that he was going to put an end to the wholesale presentations of enterprising American debutantes to Britain's sovereigns each spring, there was a long loud wail of frustration from the ambitious mamas of sub-debutante daughters of influential bank presidents of Keokuk Falls, Idaho and back-slapping political leaders of practically every important district in the forty-eight States.

Dreams Shattered

Eager young daughters, some of whom had not enjoyed too great successes in their local society arenas, saw their dreams of triumphs "at Court" during a season abroad ruthlessly shattered by an American ambassador who was as democratic as his shell-rimmed spectacles, and whose wife had no desire to act as social sponsor for several hundred American girls whom she had never even seen. Ambassador Kennedy, backed by the State Department at Washington, ruled that the only American women whom King George and Queen Elizabeth could reasonably be expected to be interested in meeting were the wives and daughters either of diplomatic representatives or of other internationally important personages, or women who were internationally important in their own right.

Aside from certain de luxe tradesmen of Piccadilly and Bond Street, there were few besides the would-be presentees themselves who did not welcome the new ruling in the spirit in which it was made. But hardly had the gasps of Ambassador Kennedy's revolutionary reform died away with the approaching close of the 1938 season at Buckingham Palace than the Lord Chamberlain himself stepped forth to deliver an equally deadly blow at another phase of the whole institution of Court presentations. This was the blunt announcement that "certain peeresses have been notified by the Lord Chamberlain that their presence will not be required at further Court functions this season."

Only Marketable Asset

The move is directed at those impoverished ladies of title who have found it necessary to supplement their sadly reduced incomes by selling to Americans or anybody else their only remaining marketable asset – their entree into Court circles. For fixed fees, ranging from $500 to $5,000, according to the amount of "guidance" required by the neophyte, they have contracted not only to train debutantes and others in the necessary etiquette, but also to arrange for them the coveted privilege of donning court trains and feathers and passing for a brief moment of triumph before the King and Queen.

Heretofore, a casual glimpse at the "Personal" columns of London's leading daily newspapers has been enough to put the aspiring debutante in touch with a peeress to act as her sponsor. Now, all that has been checked. King George himself is said to have expressed himself emphatically on the subject, making it quite clear that down-at-the-heel countesses, duchesses, and the like, were not to be allowed to use their social prestige to financial advantage.

It was not difficult to ascertain which were the offending peeresses. Notices went forth and, as a result, it may safely be said that the secondary or "little season," which takes place in London in October, will be marked by reforms almost as merciless as the one introduced a few months ago by the new American Ambassador.

Thomas Hardy Laid to Rest
Among Britain's Immortals

LONDON, January 16, 1928 – A ghostly conclave of the shadows of Great Britain's immortals seemed to be gathered in a dim corner of Westminster Abbey this afternoon as a procession of the nation's most distinguished figures moved silently down the aisle bearing the ashes of one more of their number – Thomas Hardy, born June 2, 1840, died January 11, 1928.

Thousands of solemn-faced folk gathered mutely outside the ancient grey walls, completely oblivious to the dreary rain and bleak winter day. Inside the cathedral were tense throngs. Suddenly the distant chanting of boys' voices announced the approach of the funeral procession, led by the crimson and gold vested clergy, followed by the richly draped marble casket and the great men who comprised the escort.

Ceremony Is Simple

The latter included Prime Minister Stanley Baldwin, Sir James Barrie, the patriarchal George Bernard Shaw, silver-haired Ramsay MacDonald, distinguished John Galsworthy, benign Rudyard Kipling, with his eyes hidden behind thick glasses, sober-faced Edmund Gosse, as well as A. E. Housman, the distinguished poet. Illustrious representatives from each of the two great universities, followed by personal representatives of the King, the Prince of Wales, and the Duke of York, were also in attendance.

For a few brief moments the casket rested before the altar while the sentences for the dead were read. Then, without eulogies or glowing tributes, the procession was resumed through the transept to Poets' Corner, where, with a few simple words, the casket was lowered beside the tomb of Charles Dickens and a few feet from the resting places of Handel, Sheridan, Thackeray, and Macaulay.

Flowers Are Widow's Tribute

Close by stood a slight black figure, Mrs. Hardy, and the novelist's sister, Miss Kate Hardy. Beside them stood Sir James Barrie, holding a simple cluster of white flowers, which was the widow's mute tribute.

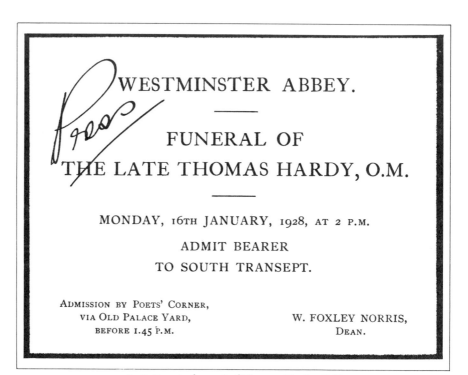

Invitation to funeral of Thomas Hardy, 1928

The great doors of Westminster Abbey were thrown open after the ceremony to admit the multitudes who had been waiting in the rain since morning to file past the few square feet consecrated to the memory of their idol.

Police gently directed the bedraggled, rain-soaked masses as they continued the pathetic procession all afternoon until the doors of the great temple finally were closed in the gathering twilight. The ashes of Thomas Hardy were left alone with the immortals.

Heart Is Buried in Stinsford

Simultaneously another modest little ceremony was held in the church yard at Stinsford, Dorchester, where the heart of the famous writer was buried in the presence of sorrowing villagers.

War With Yanks Is Unthinkable, Britons Told
Chamberlain Tells Plan For New Treaty

LONDON, February 8, 1928 ‒ "I can scarcely speak of arbitration with the United States, either in its narrower or larger sense, without saying once again that whatever our position – and let us make it the best we can for the British government – war with the United States is unthinkable, and the prospect of war with the United States, preparation for war with the United States, never has and never will be the base of our policy in any field," declared Sir Austen Chamberlain, British foreign secretary, this evening in the House of Commons debate on the King's speech.

"I am interested to note the evidence given before a congressional committee by the secretary of the United States Navy," he continued. Throughout the testimony, the secretary repeatedly insisted that in putting forward the program of naval construction which is now being considered, the Navy Department had not had thought of entering any armaments race with any foreign powers.

Denies Infringement of Treaty

He stated that the United States is not engaged in competitive building of warships, and did not intend to do so, and he added that in preparing the program before them the general board considered, primarily, the United States Navy's own needs, which are only indirectly related to the strength of other navies, as well as other construction or replacement programs.

Sir Austen declared he was glad to note Secretary of State Kellogg's frank statement, which he hoped would end once and for all rumors which ought never to have had currency, in view of the fact that it makes clear that there has not been a breach of faith.

"There is no infringement of the letter or spirit of the Washington treaty on the part of his Majesty's Government," continued the foreign secretary, "and I can say for our government, as he has said for his, that our building is not competitive and our program is framed only in view of necessary protection for British interests."

Discussed Pact with U.S.

"That these programs will be modified and that the failure of the Geneva conference has not lessened the desire in this direction, is sufficiently shown by the action we have taken in lessening the announced program for the present two years."

Referring to a renewal of the Anglo-American treaty, Sir Austen recalled the Bryan-Spring-Rice treaty provided that disputes be referred to a commission of conciliation and that a year elapse before resorting to arms. He suggested that the next advance may be made along these lines instead of a strict arbitral agreement.

An opposition spokesman requested details of Sir Austen's treaty intentions as soon as possible, declaring:

"War with any other country is unthinkable, but with the United States at this moment we have a magnificent opportunity of going further, expressing the opinion of the people in both countries."

*   *   *

CHAPTER 11

WEEK-END TRIPS
TO THE COUNTRYSIDE

Introduction

I t is no exaggeration to say that everybody remembers with affection and admiration some teacher or professor from their school or college days.

In the case of P. S. it was Miss Catherine Keck, English teacher at Union High in Grand Rapids. She inspired her more gifted pupils to unusual heights of creative writing, and gave them a love of the English classics that stayed with them all their lives.

Her own special love was Chaucer, and her class was required to memorize *The Canterbury Tales* in the original Middle English. Needless to say, on arriving in London, P. S. could hardly wait for the first opportunity to make his own pilgrimage to Canterbury. Once there, his first thought was to send a postcard to Miss Keck.

Other weekend trips followed by train and bicycle, his enjoyment always heightened by association with the poets and authors who had been brought to life for him by Miss Keck in his high school days.

E.B.S.

* * *

Falstaff Hotel
Canterbury
August 3, 1927

After some fourteen years, I too have made the pilgrimage to Canterbury. It seems incredible, even now, that such wonderful dreams can come true. To be spending the night in this enchanted old Middle Age city made sacred by Chaucer, Becket, Henry IV, and the great archbishops! It's a rare experience, and thank God, I have the capacity for the full enjoyment of it.

Canterbury surpasses my rosiest hopes. Indeed, I hovered up until the last moment between Stratford, Oxford, Cambridge, and Canterbury. My choice was a fortunate one. I left London (Charing Cross) at 10:48 this morning, the sun shining brightly. My traveling companion was a young chap of good appearance, but dressed (dare I say it) in the rather flashy cut suit and brown oxfords of a cheap swell. There was no conversation until we were joined by a rugged old gentleman. He proved to be a retired farmer of seventy, proud of his Kent (the "garden of England"), and pleased to hear of the part Canterbury, Hastings, and Kent have played in my life.

He left us at Ashford, and my remaining companion opened the way to conversation. To my amazement he proved to be a graduate of Cambridge – with a thorough knowledge of France and the Riviera, if you please. We chatted constantly until he reached his home at Wye.

In another few minutes we were in West Canterbury, and I decided to stroll up from the station in search of the Falstaff Inn, which I had noticed on one of the railway carriage pictures.

By rare good luck I found it easily and was soon established in a large double room with charming bay casements hanging over the street. After a quick wash, there was luncheon in a wonderful old oak-paneled dining room, with the great florid old Sir John swinging outside on a board hung from a beautiful iron scroll.

After luncheon, I strolled enchanted through the narrow, winding streets, reminiscent of old Rouen and Beauvais, but somehow different. At a postcard shop, a kindly gentleman reminded me of the great cricket match going on, and we decided it was necessary that I engender some enthusiasm and attend. It was a pleasant walk to the grounds – but imagine going to see a cricket match in Canterbury!

At any rate, I was bored stiff except for the music, supplied by a good band of the King's household guard, and am certain I never want to play cricket. The large audience, for some reason or other, was deathly silent, save for an occasionally brief hand-clapping. What a sport! No thrill, no enthusiasm, no mass psychology! The spectators behave like a tennis crowd at a very one-sided match. Certainly the English are the only people sufficiently patient to endure such a game.

In the middle of the game there was a dash for tea, which seemed to me the most exciting part of the afternoon. I then returned to the center of town, and rambled through the magnificent old cathedral where archbishops have been crowned for centuries.

It was a wonderful treasure-house made easy to enjoy, with its intelligent placards unobtrusively labeling the great shrines. There are some priceless windows and carved stone, but still I missed the Presence of a Roman Catholic cathedral.

From the cathedral, I strolled a few minutes before returning to the Falstaff and bought an intriguing little volume of doggerel called *The Ingoldsby Legends,* which was highly recommended to me by the charming young lady at the bookshop, who declared that it was a typical product of Kent and much beloved here. It looks most entertaining.

Dinner in the oak-paneled dining room, with its leaded casements overlooking the street, and then I sauntered down the street and found my way to the Dane John, a gaily illuminated public park where a large part of the town was assembled to hear a band concert.

I remained until "God Save the King," most movingly played, then wandered up and down a few narrow streets, and then back to the Falstaff. A bit of writing and reading. And so to bed. What would I give to spend a night in Canterbury! Will the ghosts of that immortal procession file past my casement window tonight? It is wonderful when the realization of dreams does not bring disillusionment!

London
August 5, 1927

Yesterday, as though by gracious providential courtesy, broke beautifully clear. I breakfasted regally (as is the English wont) in the oak-paneled dining room where even the abominably slow service can be overlooked, and then strolled over to the cathedral to lounge until 11:30 a. m., the hour scheduled for a guided tour of the city.

Near the cathedral, I was unable to resist buying an inexpensive copy of *The Canterbury Tales* – what is Canterbury without Chaucer at hand? I reported back to the West Gate at 11:30 a. m., and there met the guide, a remarkably intelligent Englishman, an English couple, and the inevitable elderly lady tourist, though this one was really quite charming.

We visited the tower for a wonderful view of the city and then jogged on to make the rounds of old monasteries, hospitals, churches, Roman ruins, and scores of fascinating relics. We wound up at the cathedral, after a most comprehensive tour carefully explained in a way that gave us credit for a little more than fairy tale intelligence.

In the cathedral, we were joined by a howling mob of boy scouts, of such an intellectual curiosity that there was no dodging them – certainly not for our scoutmaster guide. We parted, and I returned to the cloister for a reflective browse over my "Prologue." Somewhere near 2:00 p. m., I sauntered back to High Street for a refreshing pint of ale, of surpassingly mellow cheer, and then took an autobus for the seaside town of Whitstable, an old fishing village some ten miles away. What a view of the sea from the hills!

Whitstable I liked not at all – with the exception of the shrimps, of which I had a huge saucerful with bread and butter, a pot of tea, and a cake, all for slightly more than a shilling. And they weren't "little shrimps" either!

Along the seaside to see the masses holidaying on the stony beach as far as Tankerton, where a regatta was supposedly in progress, though I observed nothing save a sailing boat carrying half a dozen white-trousered gentlemen who occasionally fired a revolver, and a rowing shell carried ashore by a dozen youths who had apparently received an unexpected ducking.

After returning by bus to Canterbury, I once more visited the cathedral and wandered through the grounds and ruins, being particularly interested in the adjoining Kings' School, the oldest boys' school in England. Back to my hotel for the reckoning, tea at a shop nearby, and to London – puzzling all the way over what I should do in the event that war were declared between my country and this. A gloomy conclusion to an otherwise gay and glorious holiday.

Old George Hotel
Salisbury
September 27, 1928

A night's pause at a rare sixteenth century house in ancient Salisbury. It was too enchanting to pass by, and I resolved, upon cycling into the town this morning, that I must pass one of my three precious nights here.

What a jaunt it has been thus far! Off from Bournemouth Wednesday morning, in crackling autumn sunshine – plus fours, a toothbrush in one pocket, safety razor in the other, no hat, and a "push bike." My first stop was old Christchurch, where I had a glimpse of the church and the enchanting little harbor that seems to belong on a calendar, and had a bite of lunch.

North through the Avon Valley to Ringwood, where I happened into the gay Wednesday afternoon market and everything from live ducks to mending cement was being sold furiously. A short pause, then on the the quaint old village of Fordingbridge, famed for its fishing.

What an unforgettable thrill to spin (by one's own power of locomotion) down a country road, over a bridge, and towards the lofty grey spire that looms like a silent sentinel above the little settlement clustered at its feet: that was Fordingbridge! Past quaint signs of chimney sweeps, well-sinkers, etc.!

Tea in the irresistible garden of the Albany Hotel, my table on the bank of the beautiful dreamy Avon (not the Stratford Avon.) Then for a stroll through the village, to dream for a bit in the wistful little grey church. A villager invited me to view the old mill and stream from a point of vantage of his own land and told me proudly that a picture of it which had been painted by Mr. King, now hangs in the Tate Gallery.

Back to the Albany at sundown, and then for a peaceful row under the vaulted stone bridge and up the river a ways before dinner. The usual deathly quiet English hotel dinner, which I no longer resent but rather enjoy. Later, to my surprise my sole remaining fellow diner opened a conversation. He moved to my table during my pot of tea and proposed that we adjourn to the little parlor downstairs, where we sat talking happily over beer and cigarettes before the fire until midnight. Our chat ranged from American slang, to English humor and politics, and back via international understandings and misunderstandings.

It required my hostess to remind us of the hour, and I retired to my comfortable little candlelighted room overlooking the moonlit gardens and river.

* * *

On to Salisbury this morning in the crisp autumn sunshine again, and I soon found the great spire looming before me. I spent the morning in and about the magnificent cathedral which, externally though not internally, must be the grandest I have ever seen! More cycling ten miles north across the Salisbury Plain this afternoon to Stonehenge, that strange relic of a mysterious past. Is it possible that it has been standing since 1700 B.C.! I rode over the brow of a steep hill and saw the great pile on the vast plain beneath me, like building blocks in the middle of a nursery floor. Tea nearby, then on through Amesbury and so back to blue-misted Salisbury in early twilight.

Grosvenor Hotel
Shaftsesbury
September 28, 1928

Awakened to a disconsolate downpour this morning which showed no signs of slackening, even after I had breakfasted and examined the ancient rooms of the Old George (Salisbury) including the room where Samuel Pepys once spent the night!

At 10:30 my restlessness conquered. I strolled round the corner, purchased a mackintosh and cap (18/6 and 1/10), settled my bill at the Old George, and called for my cycle to the apparent concern of the young lady at the desk who warned me it was a long cycle trip to Dorchester.

Through charming little Wilton (of carpet fame) in the rain and on through as much water as I hope ever to see again! Literally drenched to the skin, I reached this ancient little town about 1:00 p.m. and was received with mingled dubiousness and dismay at the Grosvenor when I made my ignominious entry sloshing water in all directions, and, I am sure, resembling a drowning rat more than anything else.

I called for a room with a roaring fire, and then sent the motherly maid-servant scurrying off to dry my shoes, give orders for my bicycle, dig up an easy chair for me, and fetch me tea, bread and butter, and cakes, as well as the morning papers! She performed her several tasks perfectly, and I was soon comfortably established before my fire in a state of nature with my soaked clothes spread out to dry.

After a charmingly quaint and unique afternoon, I finally dressed in my dried clothes and called for my shoes in time for dinner at 7:30 p.m., which tasted not at all badly with a bottle of excellent Beaune.

Later, I strolled around the corner for a touch of the twentieth century movies in ancient Shaftesbury, and was confirmed, as usual, in my contempt for the cinema, though it was mildly entertaining in spots. Tomorrow, God and weather willing, I shall embark on the last lap of my tour, heading for Bournemouth and the sea once more.

Chichester
October 7, 1927

Dear Dick,

Your fine letter reached me just as I was on the point of leaving London for one of these "escapes" that are so necessary to me. The world was becoming just a trifle too serious, and I was fortunately able to throw some things in a bag, jump into plus fours, and slip away to this enchanted little town in the heart of old Sussex near the sea.

Only one person knows where I am, and she has instructions to disturb me with nothing short of a cable or telegram. How seriously (or rather unseriously) I am taking this little five-day retreat, you may guess from the fact that, at the last minute, even my typewriter ("factory" as Peter B. Kyne told me he calls his) was left behind!

You find me then, dreaming by myself in the old walled garden of the bishop's palace just under the shadows of twelfth century Chichester Cathedral.

The place is exquisite today. But the first night, when I rambled through the crumbling cloisters and old gardens in the moonlight, it was almost terrifying in its enchantment. I had expected to be thrill-proof by 1927.

This morning I had a delightful browse in the ancient bell tower of the cathedral. After climbing up the perilous narrow stairway I stood beside the greatest of the bells as it thundered at eleven o'clock with such a roar that I had to stop my ears.

Beside me stood a Britisher whose son was above in the Tower. I mounted to the top for a fine view of the old town, and then descended to the quaint tower room from which the bells are rung.

Here I found a marble plaque commemorating a bell service of three hours and some minutes on December 31, 1894 with the names of the eight ringers and their leader. Over in a deeply recessed window, a case of dusty volumes dealing with bells and bell ringing. Tremendously fascinating. The largest bell, the proud old keeper told me, weighs more than three tons.

Later I visited St. Mary's Hospital, which was a find indeed. The old nunnery and hospice provide eight tiny flats for eight old ladies, one of whom I chatted with in her little sitting room. She was a sweet-faced, grey-haired, cheery little lady who pointed out the electric light as quite a surprise to those who had seen the place in its earlier days, but now the one concession to the times, fully justified from the point of view of safety as regards those "not quite so active" etc., etc.! I thanked her, and returned a moment later to find her sitting serenely by her fire (lighted when she came from the eleven o'clock service) with a reading glass and a book. I left her half a crown "for tea," and her unexpected pleasure was worth it.

This afternoon atop a bus through the paved country lanes, spreading down to Selsey and the sea. I've had nothing to eat since breakfast save a cake of milk chocolate. This precious English tea hour! I'll go in search of it!

Arundel
October 8, 1927

Thirty years!

And my thirtieth birthday among great noble walls in this ancient town. I came on from Chichester at about ten and walked through the little village nestling at the foot of the hill, and up past the castle gates to the quaint little parish church. I liked the beautiful old stone gate with a perfect spider web glistening just at the peak of the center arch.

Across the road to the beautiful new Catholic church built by the Duke of Norfolk – and unable to miss the irony of this forced abdication of the true church from its own ancient walls across the street, making way behind for the "usurper." I liked the few words of explanation to non-Catholics which may be read in the church, which were doubtless written by the Duke himself."

Some Notes on Scotland

August 4, 1928

There is a slickness about the very word "Scotland" that has always appealed to me. It may be the euphony, or it may be the mental associations of the word – maybe both. At any rate, Scotland seems to be nearly as foreign a country, from my English point of view, as is Italy or Spain.

It seemed advisable to break my first journey northward to Scotland for a glimpse of the English Lake Country, so I detoured at Penrith and spent my first night at the charming Keswick Hotel, close to Derwent Water, on whose shores stands a memorial to John Ruskin, who loved the spot. On the other side of the beautiful lake nestles the cottage of Aldous Huxley, proudly pointed out by the skipper of the little motorboat in which I made the rounds of the lake.

An English Lake preface to Scotland may be regarded as a necessary evil, but it is necessary in this case, and it certainly is no evil. Cumberland and the English Lakes are idyllic – not romantic, perhaps, as are those of Scotland; or majestic, as are those of Switzerland – but idyllic!

My second English lake was Ullswater, upon which I embarked in the late afternoon after an unexpected delay at the Ullswater Hotel landing which was far from unpleasant. The lake itself, from the water, was beautiful as evening approached, and we reached Pooley Bridge rather unexpectedly soon. Here we clambered into a waiting charabanc, and it was only by the rarest squeeze that I got into the front seat with my bag. At Penrith, where I was to continue my northward trek, we were stalled on a deep hillside – mild pandemonium – with the result that I was the only passenger left with the driver. (I had been entrusted with the foot brake.) When we parted at the station, there seemed to have been formed a bond between us as the result of having faced together a common danger! At any rate, he appeared greatly pleased with the tanner that I gave him with which to buy a drink.

Straight on to Glasgow! A rather grimy, unattractive city, of which I saw little save the Central Hotel and a luggage shop, where I bought a rather smart-looking bag.

My train arrived in Callander just before tea time, and, after some deliberation, I decided to spend the night and push on to the spectacular Trossachs in the morning. The hotel is practically mine (save, apparently, for a couple of girls who flit restlessly between the fireplace and the gramophone). As for the hotel – yes, it *is* a veritable Dreadnought of cold, forbidding grey stone, that requires little more than a keel to make it a floating fortress.

After tea, I wandered through the hills to Glamhill Falls, a magnificent spectacle of roaring water plunging down through a series of stone gateways to whirling, rock-lined pools, and so under the narrow foot bridge. It was across this bridge, or its ancestor, I believe, that the dashing Sir Walter Scott led his horse, while a breathless group of his friends looked tensely on.

Anyway, it's a thrilling spot despite the flying insects, and I wandered back along the perilously steep bank beneath low-hanging trees until I could view a superb mountain panorama spread out before me. Then, clambering upon a steep hill and so over the brae, I found myself in the midst of a glowing purple patch of heather! Riotous warm purple blossoms with their finely cut leaves, and a huge rock in the center, against which I reclined.

A darting flock of frightened sheep and lambs here and there. Three separate times, as I strode through the heather and gorse, a terrified rabbit scampered off before me through the low brush.

Yes, the Scottish Highlands are as I dreamed them – one more dream realized! Great rolling mountains of bluish-brown and rich purple heather, and the matter-of-fact thistle, disdaining to be touched.

As I watched, the famed Scotch mist fell like a fragile cloak over the mountain tops and lowlands between. A light rain began to fall, supplying an excellent reason for a brisk walk back to the Dreadnought for a hot bath before dressing for dinner.

After the dinner, which was served with great deference and alacrity, coffee and a cigarette before the open fire. Later, a *real* whisky and soda (perhaps I only imagined it to be the best I have ever drunk), then a stroll through the village before turning in.

Down the quiet, grey stone-lined main street, and off on a turning past a little cemetery and across a motionless stream, mirroring the black and grey shadows with a Corotian perfection. An exquisitely tranquil picture, to which a friendly wire-haired terrier added the final touch!

By motorbus around Loch Vennachar next morning, through a driving rain, until the imposing grey stone walls and turrets of the Trossachs Hotel loomed before us. I nervously climbed down from my perch on the bus, seized my heavy bag, paid the driver (who asked me a question or two that was completely incomprehensible), and, feeling decidedly bedraggled, scurried up the steps and into the main entrance of the hotel.

I was put slightly more at ease by noting much less indication of magnificence or stateliness than I had expected. I stammered my requirements to the manager, who appeared in the deserted hallway, and he directed me across to the little office, where an unpretentious young lady promptly signed me up for a room at 8 shillings for the night – much less than I'd expected.

The room was by no means elegant, but it was comfortably furnished, and I lost no time in taking possession, opening my bag, and freshening up a bit for luncheon in the great baronial hall. It is a beautiful old castle, overlooking Loch Achray and with the Trossachs as a background. After lunch, a stroll up through wooded hills to the shores of Loch Katrine, and so on around it for a beautiful series of views of water and mountains. Showers! The heavy rain sent myself and a French *papa, maman, et garçon* scurrying back to the pier for shelter, where I found the autobus from my hotel awaiting the arrival of the steamer. We were whirled back to the Trossachs house for tea – a truly delightful moment for me, since I had the smoking room and a lively open fire to myself. A smiling Scotch lassie helped me kindle it, warning me that I should become accustomed to kindling fires if I remained in Scotland.

I read snugly by the fire (Scottish tales that I had found in the hotel's modest library) until suddenly surprised by a traveling acquaintance with whom I journeyed from London to Penrith. We chatted pleasantly, then I left to dress for dinner – a cheery affair, with coffee beside the fire afterwards. In the evening, letters, and bed.

A delightful ramble through the lower mountains next morning, with the romantic grey stone castle looking imperiously over the lake far, far below. After luncheon, I left, admittedly with a trace of regret, to continue my journey up Loch Katrine, by coach-and-four behind a scarlet-coated driver, to Loch Lomond, and so on up to the Balloch, where a train stood ready to whirl us up along the Clyde and back to Glasgow.

A rather charming young lady from New York was beside me atop the coach-and-four, and we dragged forth a delightfully mutual sense of humor in the rain. I expressed grave apprehension lest one of our countrymen appear in the national dress – just a souvenir of the Highlands – to take back home. I told her I had seen this done in Holland (and to my chagrin), but she expressed the opinion that the Highland costume represented a far more daring stunt, and that she was sure there would be nothing to fear. She proved correct.

We broke our journey for tea at the hotel beside Loch Lomond and then continued. But what a dreadful American woman in that company. An overdressed, coarse-featured woman of about sixty, explaining in a raucous voice the ins and outs of bootlegging to a Scotch gentleman (slightly hard of hearing) and his wife. They appeared rather aghast at being told that it was the police who proved to be the most useful bootleggers. Still later, on the steamer, I heard her offering suggestions for the improvement of service.

I enjoyed Loch Lomond much more than Loch Katrine. It was less cold, and there was no rain save for a slight mist. And it *is* such a beautiful lake, drenched with atmosphere and natural grandeur. The night at Glasgow again, and in the evening to see a mediocre, summer stock company in one of their member's literary attempts called *The Rising Generation*. Quite feeble, but fairly well-acted, and moderately diverting. Next morning, for a jaunt to Ayr, the heart of

Burns' country, and a thoroughly delightful little stream, the Doon, with "Ye Banks and Braes o' Bonnie Doon." A delightful afternoon in the riverside gardens, with their Sunday afternoon crowds listening to a very acceptable orchestra (all ladies) who played familiar music.

To Edinburgh that evening, arriving late at 15 Melville Street, where I was warmly received. Tea and biscuits in my room before retiring. Next morning, a thrilling stroll down Prince's Street, certainly one of the world's outstanding streets, with great Edinburgh Castle towering on the hill above. Inviting shops, pleasant looking people (several with red hair), and all with the delightfully traditional "burr."

An interesting tour of Edinburgh Castle with several of my countrymen, and then wandered into a nearby shop to purchase a beautiful old pistol, said to be some hundred years old! On for the Royal Mile, stopping at St. Giles Cathedral, where I was impressed above all, by that exquisite little modern chapel of the Order of the Thistle – the late Earl Haig's seat, the King's, the Prince of Wales' – sixteen in all. On to Holyrood Castle, including a visit to the imposing private apartments of the King and Queen. What visions! Mary of Scots ... Darnley ... Queen Elizabeth.

A quiet luncheon in a modest lunch room and more strolling before taking a bus ride through the countryside past the birthplace of Robert Louis Stevenson, nestling cozily in the hills. It was here that R. L. S. lived for the first two or three years of his life, before being taken to the farm not far off where he remained until the age of twenty-one, when he went to the South Sea Isles to pass the rest of his wistful life.

*   *   *

Back to 15 Melville Street for a dreary dinner where my table companion was a Frenchman – in Edinburgh to "learn English."

At breakfast I opened a conversation which, apparently, was as welcome to him as it was to me. We discussed, with some liveliness, the relative merits of French and English cooking, Prohibition, etc. The poor chap was dying of boredom and was delighted at luncheon when I gave him my card and London address. I spent my last morning in Scotland shopping, and found a pair of golf hose, a pair of "flashes," and a beautiful Scotch woolen travel rug, which the pleasant buyer who served me declared to be an excellent bargain at 21 shillings.

And so to London on the Mid-Day Scot. En route, an interesting North Englishman sat opposite me at dinner, and we discussed the French and the Germans. "They don't like us!" he told me in a solemn, low voice, referring to the French. I replied that Americans thought they were also unloved by the French, to which he answered that that may be true, but the English are liked still less.

I explained the matter like this: the French are of a temperament that is so

227

foreign to that of the Anglo-Saxon that it is almost impossible to obtain mutual understanding. That, of course, is a platitude. But when will people understand it to the point of accepting it *literally*? It is his property, and there is no reason why it should be explained and apologized for, any more than the Briton or American should apologize for what must be an equally inexplicable temperament to the Latin.

That being the case, and having agreed to accept the Frenchman exactly as he is, it is perhaps profitable, and certainly interesting, to examine some of the aspects of the French temperament that are unique.

It is a case of the more one knows, the more he realizes how little he knows. At any rate, the French are probably the most insular nationality in the world. They have neither affection for, nor even interest in, England, the United States, Germany, or any of the rest. It is not hostility or animosity. It is simply superb indifference. Their interest is in France, whether for better or for worse, and they are generally no more interested in travel beyond their own national boundaries than in what happens beyond them, insofar as it does not directly affect them.

This is undoubtedly responsible, in no small measure, for the familiar whisperings – "The French hate the Americans," "There is a traditional animosity between the French and the Germans," "The French may hate other nations, but they despise the Italians" – to say nothing of my British friend's opinion. It is difficult to penetrate the Englishman's mask, but even after you have penetrated the Frenchman's mask, you have to deal with the most complicated piece of mental, emotional, and spiritual mechanisms I know of.

Certainly I am the world's last person to offer a summary of the Scottish temperament from a week in the Highlands and two days in Edinburgh. Yet, I can say I like them – their generally frank, open faces, sandy hair, and intriguing speech. Surely this is one of the greatest thrills of travel in foreign lands – to discover that places and things are actually as one learned, dreamed, and wanted them to be!

So little disillusion. That, to me, is one of the most astonishing experiences encountered in Europe. To live in a seventeenth century Inn of Chancery at somber Temple Bar in London; to drink beer among duel-scarred students in a café in Aachen; to eat Scotch broth in a turreted grey stone Highland castle in Scotland; to see blood mixed with sand in the bull ring in Madrid; to chat idly in Latin Quarter garrets; to ride a gondola at night on the Grand Canal with soft lights and music coming across the water; to be part of the audience at Sarah Bernhardt's Odéon and Mary Garden's Opéra Comique; to listen to popular songs sung by an Italian soldier in the deserted shadows of the Colosseum!

* * *

EPILOGUE

P.S., Elizabeth Benn, and Sir Ernest Benn, 1935

INTRODUCTION

Paul Shinkman returned to the United States in 1931. During the next three years, he corresponded regularly with Betty Benn, and in the fall of 1934 they became engaged. The wedding took place in July 1935 in the little country church of Tandridge in Surrey, with the reception following at Blunt House. Durand Smith was the best man. The honeymoon, needless to say, was spent in the Latin Quarter of Paris.

Soon after P. S. and E. B. were married, the Benn family brought considerable pressure on their new son-in-law to give up his job in New York with King Features Syndicate, return to Fleet Street, and settle in England. They feared that their daughter Betty would be lost in the wilds "out there" in America! E. B., however, had fallen in love with New York City (as well as with P. S.) on her visit to the States in 1934. She did not want her husband to sever his carefully built ties in the United States.

Until World War II, P. S. did, however, make regular return visits to Europe. He spent the summer of 1938 in Prague, studying the Sudeten-German crisis prior to Hitler's take-over of Czechoslovakia. He returned there in 1948 to witness first-hand how the Czechs had adjusted to Communist domination.

His 1938 lecture, entitled "Twilight in Prague," was delivered to the Town Hall Club in New York shortly after his return to the States. On his return from the same area ten years later, he gave a broadcast entitled "Second Twilight in Prague." Excerpts from these two scripts form a fitting conclusion to his early years as a foreign correspondent in Europe.

E.B.S.
May 1983

*　　*　　*

Twilight in Prague

October 4, 1938

Believe me, it's good to be back in America!

Six short weeks ago, I was all set to take a midnight train from Prague to Berlin. Seventeen strenuous days in the Czech capital had been packed with breathless experiences. In the late afternoon came the word I was waiting for. If I could be at the Kolowrat Palace at 6 o'clock sharp, I might have a private conversation with the Prime Minister, Milan Hodza, himself!

I jumped into a taxi, was whirled across the river and … up the steep Hradcany Hill overlooking the city, down a winding street to an imposing mansion with the ornamented facade, broad entrance, and tall casement windows of the Second French Empire. Two tail-coated secretaries bowed me up the broad, crimson-carpeted staircase into an ante-room, then into a great square drawing room decorated with a magnificent crystal chandelier and rich draperies. A third gentleman stepped courteously forward from the far side of the room. It was Dr. Hozda himself. I glanced twice at the tall, broad-shouldered figure, the thoughtful dark eyes behind scholarly spectacles, and then grasped the strong hand which he had extended in simple, friendly greeting. Little did either of us realize that this was perhaps the last American interview that he was to give as prime minister of his country!

Our discussion began quietly, but soon the former professor of sociology and leader of the agrarian or peasants' party of his country, had warmed to his subject, though his manner was always calm and deliberate. He told me that Czechoslovakia was ready to ensure every means of self-government to the Sudeten-Germans that didn't mean *suicide* for the Republic itself. Autonomy? He reminded me gently but firmly that he had used the phrase "self-government" advisedly. This is an *exact* term, he explained.

Premier Hodza spoke to me of democracy. The Czechs, he said, had always had their own traditions of democratic freedom, even when they were part of a vast empire! This democratic tradition, then, was the blood tie between the young Republic and England and France, its democratic parents to the West, who now have found it necessary to at least partially abandon her.

Premier Hodza pointed with a smile to a doorway leading into an adjoining room. He spoke of the fresh pile of letters that had just arrived from America, and asked me to convey to the senders his heartfelt appreciation of their sympathy and good wishes.

Within thirty days, Milan Hodza himself was compelled to resign as premier of his country! And within two days, I myself was seated fifty yards from Adolf Hitler and Admiral Horthy in Berlin, watching the most staggering military review in modern history!

But I'm getting ahead of my story. Let me take you on a newspaper correspondent's tour through the heart of the Sudeten-German areas on the eve of their projected amputation from Czechoslovakia.

In the quaint Old World *Rathaus*, or town hall, overlooking the central square of Reichenberg, I talked with the acting *Burgermeister* – kindly Anton Richter, worried for the future of his two young children. I talked with other city fathers, some of them industrial leaders of the community. Something must be done, they told me, before it is too late. Prague must give them the same help that it gave the Czechs. Three-quarters of the textile industry of the Sudeten-German lands had fallen into the hands of these same Czechs. Machines had been sold, factories had been closed; and where 60,000 workers had been employed in 1929, there now remained but 15,000!

I also talked with the man who bears the proudest name in all Czechoslovakia, a name that is honored throughout the entire world. He is Jan Masaryk, son of the founder and first president of the Czechoslovak Republic. The younger Masaryk is Czech minister to the Court of St. James's, and it was in the library of his home in London that I talked with him one afternoon just before I plunged into the maelstrom of Central Europe. Tall, broad-shouldered, and athletic-looking, Jan Masaryk took me completely off guard. He began by reminding me that his mother had been American, that he himself had married an American, and that he knew America only as a man could who had done everything in our country from pounding the piano in a cheap cinema to bossing a gang of laborers!

"The problem of Czechoslovakia is the problem of all Europe, if not the entire world," he told me. "Our country is merely one small piece of the great mosaic of international relations which, say what you like, is based upon self-interest. We stand, as a democracy, between the democratic and totalitarian theories of government. My own close ties with America will partially explain why I feel that freedom to express one's own opinions is essential.

But, to return to the Sudeten-Germans themselves: At Haindorf, a band of village players were putting on their conception of Shakespeare's *Twelfth Night,* translated, very freely indeed, into provincial German! The village hall was packed for the occasion, with peasants, tradesmen, young students for the priesthood, and the doting families of the young actors themselves. When the love-smitten Malvolio resolves that he will win his mistress Olivia by adorning himself with a handsome new pair of hose bound with yellow lacings, he suddenly brought the house down by rolling his eyes and commenting solemnly, on the side, that they would of course not be *white* stockings! The short white sox and leather shorts, which are a part of the traditional southern German costume, had just been officially banned in certain parts of Czechoslovakia, as indicating defiance of the government, as indeed they generally did! And so, this rustic Malvolio, with tongue

233

in cheek, solemnly promised that he would not wear *white* sox to court the lovely Olivia!

In a somber little parlor in the Hotel Alcron in Prague, Lord Runciman of England, leader of the Runciman mission, was working to bring about a peaceful settlement of the problem that has gripped the world for months. I sat with Lord Runciman in that room and we discussed the task that he had been prevailed upon to undertake. He told me that it was not an impossible task, and that a peaceful agreement based upon adjustments lay closest to his heart. There was no talk between us of a political readjustment, involving the transfer of national allegiances and the wiping out of international boundaries.

Following my tour of the frontier, I rode back to Prague with a high official of this Sudeten-German party organization. His was a stronger, more determined cry than that I had heard voiced by the simple village folk of the little Sudeten towns. He pointed to the open-faced, young German laborer who sat across from us, intently following our conversation. "That boy," he said, "is a typical example of what is happening here. He has just been told that he is a Sudeten German who, like many others, had to leave his home in Czechoslovakia and cross the border into Germany to find work. Now he has been called back to Czechoslovakia to do his compulsory military service."

Still, the cry for change grew louder as that midnight train carried me from Prague to Berlin. And in the German capital it swelled to deafening proportions on August 25 when, from a seat not far from the *Führer* and his distinguished Hungarian guest Admiral Horthy, I watched for two hours that terrifying cavalcade of war rumble past in review! Sixteen thousand soldiers and the greatest engines of destruction the world has ever seen. All were parading for the benefit of the distinguished visitor, the Regent of Hungary, and for the benefit of the outside world! Something *must* be done about Czechoslovakia, they all said. It was plain what Germany, or, at least, the Reichschancellor and his supporters, thought that "something" should be.

Traveling from Prague to Berlin, we had crossed the border in the middle of the night. Sharing my compartment were a charming little German family, and when the irritating midnight inspections finally were completed, the father, a loyal Nazi, smiled at me wearily and said: "*Such* a bother! Do you have such complications when you travel in your country?" I answered that such travel complications were entirely unknown in America. "Glückliches, glückliches Amerika!" he said. "Lucky, lucky America!"

*　　*　　*

Two Twilights in Prague

September 26, 1948

Four weeks ago last Monday I landed at the Prague Airport. The airport was empty, and the field appeared completely abandoned except for two or three empty planes. We crossed over some war ruins outside the capital. But it had not occurred to me that the airport still would show the effects of war. I soon realized that the deserted, melancholy atmosphere was less the effect of the war than it was the effect of something that happened in Czechoslovakia *since* the war. I was behind the Iron Curtain.

I braced myself for the ordeal of passing through that curtain. Actually, there was no cause for apprehension, at least, outwardly. The long, eagle-eyed inspections of travel documents, personal identification, baggage, and of each traveler's written report of the amount and kind of currency he carried was grueling, but no more so than at every frontier in Europe today. And the Czech officials went about their work courteously, almost as though they were glad to see new faces from the outside world. I knew from experience that the Czech and the Slovak do not easily lose their traditionally pleasant, friendly manner. I was relieved to see that it appeared to be still there – if perhaps, buried a little deeper under totalitarian reserve.

I had my mind made up that I would not let the Communist label prejudice me against what I was to find in the lovely old capital of King Wenceslas after ten tragic years. I knew my old friend Jan Masaryk would not be there. And I knew I should not see the kindly schoolmaster Prime Minister, Dr. Milan Hodza, who had received me for an interview in his official palace ten years ago. But I was not long in discovering that there were other changes. And I did not think that the last war could be held solely responsible for the worried and almost sullen expression of the city and its people.

The handsome Hotel Alcron had become a haunted tomb, and it was impossible to shake off a sense of wistful sadness that seemed to shroud not only the guests, but even those customary purveyors of cheerfulness, the receptionists, head waiters, and doormen. The once-gay dining room of Prague's number one hotel revealed less than half a dozen waiters serving pitifully scant rations to a handful of guests – two thin slices of coarse black bread, an unpalatable square of dubious meat accompanied by a dab of vegetable, stewed fruit, and a cup of undrinkable coffee. The 80 kronen paid for such a meal paralleled the 227 kronen per day asked for my modest room and bath – exorbitant prices for Prague.

I should be the last person in the world to blame the Czechs or their

Communist government for the sad quality and quantity of their food. (I ate as badly on some occasions in England this summer.) And certainly no American can complain of high prices abroad. But there is no question as to where the blame lies for the apathy that has seemed to overwhelm the people themselves in the face of this persistently drab existence. Even in conquered Germany and Austria, and in the rest of Europe, where the fear of war grips the peoples' hearts, there was at least some show of awakening spirit.

During the ten years since I last visited Prague, the ill-fated republic has passed from the shadow of Hitler to the shadow of Stalin, by way of a war that has broken the backs of far stronger nations.

But there is one great difference in the web in which the Czechoslovaks find themselves caught this time. Whereas in 1938 the line between the brazen Nazi sympathizers and the loyal supporters of the Republic was openly defined, today the line between the Moscow Communists and the supporters of Masaryk-Benes democracy is shrouded in treacherous mist. No one can be sure whether his friend or neighbor is with him or against him in the "cold war" that now grips the country.

This shadow warfare has been freely admitted on both sides, despite the fact that the recent elections which put the Communists in power presumably were a free and democratic expression of the popular choice. But these rumblings of a typical police state are only the cruder signs of a crackdown that affects the day-to-day life of the most innocent workman. Almost at the moment that Premier Zapotocky was boasting that the Communists would not only fulfill their Two-Year Plan but would do so earlier than had been expected, the Minister of Industry, Comrade Kliment, was asking people to "voluntarily decide that no free Saturdays should exist in the Five-Year Plan."

"Don't you think it a crime against our building endeavors," he asked, "when we do not work fifty-two Saturdays as well as twenty days annual holidays and twelve days public holidays?"

It remains to be seen how the tired, underfed workers of Czechoslovakia will react to this suggestion that they give up all their holidays and all their Saturdays, with a consequent increase of 30% of their work hours. The Minister of Industry, so far as I have been able to discover, made no mention of corresponding overtime pay. Presumably that detail smacks too much of the capitalistic countries.

Prague is being flooded with Communist literature that bears the datelines of almost every capital in Europe. Newsstands which ten years ago sprouted Nazi newspapers today prominently display special editions of Moscow's official newspaper *Pravda* and Rumania's bimonthly Communist organ, which boasts the resounding title *For a Lasting Peace, For a People's Democracy.*

Last month in Prague I talked with an important official of the Czech government. We sat alone in his private office after he had told his secretary that he was not to be disturbed. I asked him how long he had been in his present government post, hoping to date him with regard to the Communist coup. He seemed to sense my purpose and quickly replied that he had been in the government since the war and therefore was not a Communist appointee. He smiled ruefully when he admitted that he didn't consider newspapermen like myself suited to so-called "official" work or to the rigors of governmental bureaucracy and red tape.

But he had dutifully learned the Communist line. He told me that the great Czech athletic organization known as *Sokol* must be reorganized, not because of the refusal of many of its members to salute Communist President Gottwald at its recent festival but because, after all these years, it has been found to not be sufficiently "democratic." He told me, when I asked about the prime minister's threat to crack down upon unenthusiastic workers, that this was because many of the workers can't seem to get over the habit of sabotage and obstruction at their benches, which they learned to use against the Nazis but for some reason or other are still using against Communists! And he reminded me that any Czech worker is free to change his job, if not his employer. His employer, of course, will continue to be the State, so long as he works for any industry that employs more than fifty people or that is engaged in work considered of vital importance to the government. (Which takes in about everybody except the greeting card writers and the folks who stick the paper rosettes on lamb chops.)

I left my Czech friend with the suggestion that his excellent knowledge of English should entitle him to an assignment in America. He looked thoughtfully at me for a moment and then answered that that was "very possible." Then I asked him if he meant that he might be visiting the United States soon with some sort of mission. He indicated that that was a fair assumption.

I have returned from my first glimpse behind the Iron Curtain with full understanding of that "fair assumption" – an assumption that now has become a conviction. And that conviction, is that America is the most blessed spot on the face of the earth today. I said on my return from Czechoslovakia ten years ago that we were the most fortunate people in the world. I repeat that today with even greater emphasis. We *are* the most fortunate people in the world.

*　　*　　*

AFTERWORD

The history of the subsequent colorful and varied career of P.S. in writing, lecturing, and broadcasting in this country, can be found in the Paul Shinkman collection of manuscripts at the Mass Communications Center of the University of Wisconsin in Madison. It includes his war-time diary, kept when he was editing and analyzing German propaganda broadcasts for the Foreign Broadcast Intelligence Service (part of the Federal Communications Commission), and later covering the White House. These diaries and radio transcripts covered Presidential press conferences, beginning with Franklin Roosevelt (who encouraged newspaper reporters to crowd around his desk, where he charmed them with his jaunty manner) and including Truman, Eisenhower, and Johnson. P.S. also covered Capitol Hill during the time of the McCarthy hearings.

In 1950, P.S. had another brief fling in Europe, staging two spectacular shows sponsored by the State Department at the Funkturm in West Berlin that were designed to counteract Communist propaganda from East Berlin. From 1951 until 1953 he was Press Officer at the American Embassy in occupied Vienna, and also opened two America House libraries in Graz and Klagenfurt in the British zone of Austria.

Back in Washington, he spent the next fifteen years writing syndicated articles for King Features, editing, lecturing, and doing regular radio news commentaries.

To quote from the eulogy given by Algie Wells of the International Atomic Energy Agency in Vienna at P.S.'s memorial service in December 1975:

"Thousands and thousands of people knew the name: Paul Shinkman. Knew his words as they appeared over a span of nearly fifty years in more than one hundred newspapers in North America and Europe: knew the voice from his radio commentaries and lectures. ...

Reporter, diplomat, lecturer, editor – in scope, career enough for several men, and in quality, an excellence all can admire. Paul did not take his importance seriously, however ... "

And therein probably lies the explanation of his reluctance to get his own book between covers.

E.B.S.
May 1983

*   *   *

239